D1548073

Our Moral Fate

Our Moral Fate

Evolution and the Escape from Tribalism

Allen Buchanan

The MIT Press
Cambridge, Massachusetts
London, England

This book was set in Palatino Linotype by Jen Jackowitz. Printed and bound in the United States of America.

Library of Congress Cataloging-in-Publication Data

Names: Buchanan, Allen E., 1948– author.
Title: Our moral fate : evolution and the escape from tribalism / Allen Buchanan, The MIT Press.
Description: Cambridge, Massachusetts : The MIT Press, 2020. | Includes bibliographical references and index.
Identifiers: LCCN 2019025836 | ISBN 9780262043748 (hardcover) | ISBN 9780262357876 (ebook)
Subjects: LCSH: Ethics—History. | Progress—Moral and ethical aspects.
Classification: LCC BJ71 .B83 2020 | DDC 170—dc23
LC record available at https://lccn.loc.gov/2019025836

10   9   8   7   6   5   4   3   2   1

Contents

Preface

Tribalism: that's the term often used to characterize the extreme political polarization manifested every day in the United States and many other countries. In fact, to characterize tribalism as merely political would be an understatement. It is something much more comprehensive, reaching much deeper into our lives, as the phrase "culture wars" suggests. We see tribalism on the Left and tribalism on the Right—but not in the middle, because it's the nature of tribalism to create an unbridgeable, uninhabitable chasm between Us and Them. The tribalistic mentality sees things in black and white, good and evil—as a no-holds-barred, zero-sum conflict between Us and Them, for the highest stakes. Tribalism transforms disagreement into mutual hatred, mild condescension into utter contempt.

Tribalism clumps together very different individuals and issues. It's the ultimate take-it-or-leave-it package deal. *We* are all well-informed and sincerely motivated; *They* are all confused or malicious or both. If you're for gun control, you're also for "socialism" and the mass murder of prebirth human beings. If liberals know you're a gun owner, that's enough; the fact that you understand and applaud that the Second Amendment is compatible with substantial regulation of firearm ownership is never allowed to surface, because you have already been branded as a benighted conservative—one of those individuals who cling desperately to their guns and religion, as President Obama put it. If a conservative hears you say you think abortion should be legal, that's all he'll hear. He won't hear what you say immediately after that: that you think abortion is *not* like trimming a fingernail or removing an appendix and that we should all hope that someday abortions become a thing of the past. That part will be drowned out because the first thing you said was enough to signal that you are one of Them.

When tribalism takes over, it's not the content of speech that matters; it's the signaling function: what is said signals membership in and loyalty to our group and makes it clear beyond a shadow of a doubt that you aren't one of Them. If you think that when people engage in tribalistic discourse, there is a genuine exchange of opposing ideas, you are missing the point: it's all about signaling group identity. Assertions of supposed facts are merely an instrument for doing that.

The secret of tribalism's formidable power lies deep in evolved human psychology: the desperate need to belong, the drive for a group-based identity. If the trend toward tribalism continues, it's not just that civility and respectful discourse won't survive; democracy itself will collapse. Democracy requires respect for those you disagree with and a willingness to listen to them and to compromise, neither of which is compatible with the tribalistic mentality.

Some people think of tribalism as a defection from morality. They think that if people would practice the moral virtues, especially tolerance, just resist the temptation to abandon moral principles, tribalism would abate. Yet if you listen closely to tribalistic talk, it becomes clear that it is moralizing in the extreme. Terms like "hypocritical," "insincere," "treacherous," "unscrupulous," "liars," and "unfair" are hurled back and forth. These are clearly terms of *moral* condemnation. One begins to suspect that tribalism is not a flight from morality but a kind of morality.

Many scientists who study human evolution think an intimate link exists between tribalism and morality. More precisely, they think that human beings are tribalistic so far as their moral nature is concerned, that the evolved moral mind, our basic moral psychology, is tribalistic. If they are right, then the prospects for successfully combating tribalism are slim to none. Science yields a counsel of despair. For if we humans are beings with a morally tribalistic nature, then any escape from tribalism we are able to achieve—any progress toward inclusive morality, morality that is not deeply biased toward one's own group—will be only partial; and it won't be durable, because it goes against the grain of our nature.

Yet moral progress has occurred, and in some of the most significant instances it involves a shift toward inclusion, away from
tribalism. The exemplary public intellectual Steven Pinker has written two fine books to remind us that there has been a great deal of
moral progress. In many societies, the position of women is now
better, chattel slavery has been abolished and serious efforts are
being made to eliminate other forms of involuntary servitude, the
governments of more countries than ever before are constrained by
the rule of law and constitutional principles, homicide rates almost
everywhere have dropped dramatically since the late Middle Ages,
there have been significant strides toward achieving equal civil and
political rights for people of color and national minorities, more
countries recognize the right to freedom of religion than has been
the case throughout most of human history, in many places laws
now curb the worst treatment of nonhuman animals, and so on.

Reflecting on these positive changes, one feels proud and optimistic. Yet if you're like me, you feel a deep, disturbing tension
between Pinker's inspiring message and the belief that humans are
tribalistic, morally speaking. You don't know what to think about
the prospects for moral progress—whether hope or despair is the
proper response to the current situation. And if you look to what science tells us about morality, you're likely to conclude that the great
ape species called *Homo sapiens* is condemned to tribalism—and that
moral progress is therefore likely to be limited and fragile—because
evolutionary science apparently tells us that our moral nature is
tribalistic.

If you think we can't escape tribalism, then you will begin to question an assumption that seems to lie beneath the surface of Pinker's
work and the thoughts of a lot of us who believe that things have gotten better, morally speaking: that there is a march of progress, that
we can count on further improvements—or at least that we don't
have to worry much about losing what we've already gained. Many
people, probably most of the people who believe in moral progress,
take it for granted that the triumph of Enlightenment ideas of human
equality and tolerance, along with the spread of scientific thinking
that dissipates superstition, is permanent and that the only question
is what new progress can we expect. They subscribe to the simplistic
Enlightenment narrative according to which the progress we have

made resulted from developing better scientific and moral reasoning and abandoning the superstitions that prevented our ancestors from seeing straight, morally speaking. They tacitly assume that we won't somehow lose the ability to think clearly and revert to superstitious beliefs and unenlightened behavior.

I am going to deflate that smug self-satisfaction. I'll argue that moral progress is much more complicated and precarious than the simplistic Enlightenment narrative suggests, because of two fundamental facts: first, human moral nature is compatible with a variety of moralities, some progressive, some regressive; second, what sort of morality human moral nature gets expressed in depends on the character of the social environment—and we have absolutely no reason to trust that we will continue to have the sort of environment that is conducive to moral progress. Enlightened ideas of human equality, tolerance, and trust in science emerge and shape social practices only under certain complex social conditions, and attaining and sustaining those conditions is far from a sure thing. There is nothing inevitable about moral progress.

Yet it's crucial to understand that our moral nature isn't tribalistic; it is highly flexible, capable of both tribalism and inclusion. That flexibility makes durable moral progress possible. Some social environments stimulate the tribalistic potential of our moral nature; others stimulate the potential for inclusion. Human beings are capable of producing both sorts of social environments. Furthermore, it's not just a matter of tribalism versus inclusion; variations in social environments produce moralities that contrast in other ways.

The point is that the character of morality isn't fixed; it all depends on the social environment, and social environments change. Whether you are able to be the best sort of person that human beings are capable of being depends not just on your strength of character, the depth of your commitment to being moral, and on whether your parents inculcated moral values in you. It also depends on whether you have the good moral luck to develop as a moral agent in a society that provides the right conditions for realizing your best moral potential.

For the vast majority of us, other people—a tiny minority that wields the most influence and power—shape those conditions; and they are doing so without any attention whatsoever to the effects their actions have on which sort of morality thrives in their society or on what sorts of persons will inhabit it. Our moral fate rests largely in the hands of others who aren't concerned about it. That is deeply disturbing.

Once you understand that the character of a society's pervasive morality and of its moral agents depends on specific circumstances, and also see that control over the nature of those circumstances is unevenly distributed among human beings, you'll have an additional reason to worry about the growing inequality we are witnessing today. Extreme inequality in wealth isn't just a defect from the standpoint of distributive justice or equal opportunity or because it undermines political equality. Those are all serious moral costs of extreme inequality. But another cost has gone unnoticed. Inequality arbitrarily gives some people control over something much more fundamental: what sort of morality will flourish in our society and whether we, as individuals, will be morally progressive beings or morally stunted.

Because humans so far haven't realized how much their moral fate depends on the character of their environment, they haven't tried to shape that environment accordingly. Instead, changes in the social environment have resulted from the morally blind processes of natural and cultural selection and the deliberate actions of individuals and groups who were aiming at other goals, not taking into account the effects their actions might have on the moral possibilities. When changes in the social environment fostered moral progress, it was a matter of sheer luck, not scientifically informed, intentional action.

In spite of these grim tidings, I'm going to offer hope, not despair. That's because I'll show that what sort of morality we have, and what sorts of moral agents we are, is up to us, not a given that we have to accept, but rather something we can learn to shape.

I'll start by arguing that the standard evolutionary story of how our remote ancestors first became moral can't explain some of the most important moral progress that has already occurred. Then I'll show that once we understand *why* it can't, we'll see that the potential for more moral progress is far greater than the "tribal moral nature" idea suggests. That's because the alternative, more accurate scientific moral origins story I will tell makes it clear that human moral nature is highly flexible, that it includes the potential not just for tribalism but also for deeply inclusive moralities.

Think of the moral mind as analogous to the linguistic mind. The linguistic mind is a general set of competencies for learning languages. Which language you learn depends on your environment, whether it is mainly populated by German speakers or Japanese speakers, and so on. Likewise, the moral mind is a general set of competencies for developing a morality, but which morality you develop depends crucially on the social environment you inhabit. What kind of morality you have and what kind of moral agent you become results from the interaction of your moral mind and the particular social environment in which the potential of your moral mind gets realized. Whoever or whatever shapes the social environment shapes you.

If our common evolved moral nature, the moral mind, is highly flexible, then the very idea of moral progress undergoes a sea change. We can know what specific changes in morality are likely to occur to the extent that we can predict how the social environment will change. We will never achieve foolproof predictions of how the social environment will change, because we can't anticipate all the challenges that will cause humans to reshape their social environments to meet them. Yet we can learn to identify some general features of social environments that increase the likelihood that they will be conducive to moral progress. Equipped with that crucial knowledge, we will be able to engage, for the first time in the long history of our species, in *scientifically informed moral institutional design*.

The idea of moral institutional design isn't new—we find it in Plato's *Republic* and in Thomas More's *Utopia*, to take only two instances. But the prospect of *scientifically informed* moral institutional design is new. Economists think about how to design institutions to maximize efficiency; political scientists ponder how to craft them so as to enhance democracy and manage political disagreements in a productive way. The central positive contribution of this book is that we should think hard, using the best available scientific knowledge, about how to design institutions that will contribute to a social environment in which moralities will be progressive and individual human beings will realize their potential as moral beings.

I know that whenever I use the phrase "moral progress," it's bound to raise hackles in some quarters. The term can be a trigger for people who think that the notion of moral progress is a weapon of Western cultural imperialism, or at least that it has been so tainted by colonialism that there should be a ban on uttering it. Or they think that "moral progress" means *universal* moral improvement and worry that such a notion is incompatible with recognizing that more than one valid or reasonable morality may exist. They think the very idea of moral progress is at odds with respect for moral diversity.

The examples of moral progress I discuss are widely accepted as improvements, across a variety of moral perspectives—not just the standpoint of "Western values." So I won't try to *argue*, for example, that chattel slavery is morally abhorrent and that consequently abolishing it was morally progressive. I'm not inclined to spend my time arguing with people who think abolition was a mistake, or with someone who thinks that it's fine and dandy to burn people alive because they have a slightly different understanding of the Trinity from yours, or who believe that setting cats on fire is permissible if you enjoy it, because cats aren't human beings or don't have souls. I'm also not going to waste my time (or yours) in arguing that it is wrong to prevent women from getting an education or holding property or voting or protesting and pressing charges when their husbands beat the hell out of them. It's important to try to help people get those sorts of beliefs out of their heads, but this isn't the place to do so.

I'll focus on two examples of moral progress, what I call the Two Great Expansions of the circle of moral regard. The First Great Expansion is the recognition that all human beings have an equal basic moral status, today usually understood to mean that they all possess certain human rights. The Second Great Expansion is the growing recognition that at least some nonhuman animals have moral standing, that they count morally in their own right (even if they have a lower moral status than humans). I call these "expansions" because they enlarge *the circle of moral regard*. Moralities that encompass them are deeply inclusive, not tribalistic.

The emergence of more inclusive moralities is one important kind of moral progress, but not the only kind. Improvements in understandings of moral responsibility are also important. For example, in many societies, until fairly recently, people were regarded as guilty and were subject to severe punishments simply for having caused the death of another person, even if they did so because of an accident that was utterly beyond their control. (In legal terms, there was no mens rea requirement for the crime of murder.) Also, until recently, notions of collective guilt were pervasive: if someone from your village killed someone from another village, anybody from the victim's village was entitled to kill anyone from your village. Moral progress can also take a different form: we come to realize that behavior previously thought to be morally wrong is permissible. Examples include premarital sex, interracial marriage, masturbation, lending money at interest, and questioning your government when it tells you to kill people from other countries.

There has also been progress of a much more basic sort, progress in how we understand morality itself. Many people have abandoned the idea that morality is just a list of divine commands that we ought to obey out of respect for the being that created us or out of fear of divine punishment. They now believe that morality is essentially about well-being and freedom, and that we ought to do the right thing because it's the right thing, not because we fear punishment or because somebody, divine or human, told us to do it. I will concentrate on one kind of moral progress—the movement toward inclusion and away from tribalism—but what I have to say will have implications for other kinds of progress as well.

What This Book Is About: Rethinking Moral Progress to Learn How to Take Charge of Our Moral Fate

I want to understand how moral progress comes about—especially progress toward greater inclusion and away from tribalism; and I also want to understand the reverse process, how people whose moralities are inclusive can regress to tribalism. But that is not my ultimate purpose: I want to understand moral progress and regression because I'm convinced that doing so will begin to provide the information we need to shape our social environment so that it fosters progress rather than limits or erodes it. In other words, I want to understand how moral progress and regression occur, because doing that is essential for taking charge of our moral fate.

I'm going to try to understand moral change by thinking of morality in evolutionary terms, but I'll argue that flawed evolutionary thinking erects obstacles to an accurate appreciation of the prospects for moral progress and for preventing regression. More specifically, I will criticize two highly un-Darwinian dogmas that some self-proclaimed Darwinians cling to tenaciously, and I'll show that we have to abandon those dogmas if we are to develop a scientific understanding of moral change.

The first un-Darwinian dogma I've already stated: the thesis that the moral nature of human beings is tribalistic. I call this the Tribalism Dogma. The second is that morality is just a collection of solutions to problems of cooperation or that morality is just "a type of cooperation." I call this the Cooperation Dogma.

Evolutionary scientists are not the only ones who cleave to the two dogmas. The notion that human moral nature is tribalistic or parochial, that people's ability to act morally is inevitably sharply limited by their strong identification with and attachment to a group, is widespread. It is reflected in the belief that people are *naturally* partial toward those they regard as their own kind and negatively biased against "strangers" or "foreigners" or the Other. When people take notice of that kind of parochialism or partiality and find it less than wholesome, they often shrug it off as inevitable, saying, "That's just human nature." In doing so, they are tacitly assuming the Tribalism Dogma.

The Cooperation Dogma is not so pervasive outside of evolutionary scientific circles *yet*; but it may well become so if scientific ideas continue to seep out into the general consciousness through the popularity of science blogs and broad-readership books that translate scientific work for the general public. Works on moral psychology with an evolutionary twist are becoming increasingly popular, and as I will show, they tend to assert or assume the Cooperation Dogma.

The problem is that subscribing to the two dogmas precludes the genuinely scientific understanding we need to shape our social environment so that it promotes progress and prevents regression. In fact, the two dogmas make it impossible to understand significant moral change of any kind. That is why I will take considerable care to explain and then criticize them.

Before I get on with that task, I need to answer a basic question: why should anybody who isn't an evolutionary scientist be interested in thinking about morality in evolutionary terms anyway? There are several excellent reasons. For one thing, evolutionary thinking seems to be the only naturalistic (that is, scientific, non-religious, nonsupernatural) way of explaining why humans have robust, complex moralities and chimps and bonobos don't, even though all three of these species are descended from a common primate ancestor a few million years ago.

There's another reason to think that an evolutionary approach to understanding morality will be illuminating: human beings are supremely flexible and successful cooperators. That's what makes us the dominant species on this planet. And it's clear that morality plays a central role in the special kind of cooperation we engage in. Evolutionary scientists want to explain how the distinctively human capacity for complex, flexible cooperation evolved, and doing so requires explaining the evolution of morality. That's because human cooperation, at least when it is successful, is structured by moral rules.

If you're worried about the tribalism we see in the United States and other countries, and if you recognize that tribalism is not a flight from morality but a kind of morality, then it's reasonable to expect that an understanding of the evolution of morality can provide vital information about how to resist the destructive tribalism we see today. In trying to understand tribalism in order to learn how to curb it, we shouldn't rest content with an exchange of subjective opinions; we should try to understand this ominous phenomenon scientifically.

Evolutionary scientists have done a great deal of fascinating work on the origins of human morality. They have explained how our ancestors first developed a distinctively human morality—a morality more robust and complex than that of our nearest primate relatives or any other species. That story *seems* to support the idea that we are morally tribalistic by nature, making it appear to be a well-confirmed scientific hypothesis. Yet the features of the origins stories that appear to support the tribalism thesis create a puzzle: if a sound evolutionary explanation of the origins of human morality shows us to be creatures whose moral nature is tribalistic, how can one square that with the fact that recently some humans' moralities have rather dramatically shifted away from tribalism and toward greater inclusion?

The Two Great Expansions are a reality, and any scientific theory of morality should be able not only to recognize that reality but also to explain it. Yet as I will show, the standard story of the evolutionary origins of human morality makes both expansions mysterious. That should make us suspicious about whether the origins story gets things right and in particular whether it shows that we are creatures with a tribalistic moral nature. Getting the evolutionary story right will be crucial, so bear with me as I introduce some basic evolutionary thinking about the origins of morality.

I have written this book primarily for people who believe there is such a thing as moral progress, or at least are willing to take the idea that there can be moral progress seriously, and for people who care about what sort of morality is dominant in their society and what sort of person they are. Yet I want scientists, as scientists, to read it.

Why should *they* read a book about moral progress (especially one written by a philosopher)? After all, as scientists, they scrupulously avoid the language of moral progress. Their commitment to objective, so-called value-neutral inquiry forbids them to evaluate change as good or bad.

Fair enough. Nevertheless, I hope to stimulate and provoke scientists to ask themselves whether their evolutionary thinking can explain the moral changes that you and I regard as progressive, and also explain how what we regard as regression comes about. Scientists can judge what I have to say on its scientific merits purely as an explanation of how certain large-scale changes come about. They can simply ignore the value-laden modifiers "progressive" and "regressive," which signal a moral stance, and concentrate on my explanation of moral changes. I am addressing scientists because I'm convinced that science should be able to provide us with information that is relevant to determining the fate of moral progress and of ourselves as moral beings.

Acknowledgments

In writing this book, I benefited from the generosity of an exceptionally large number of people. My greatest debts are to Russell Powell, Robert O. Keohane, and Alexander Rosenberg. Powell and I are coauthors of *The Evolution of Moral Progress: A Biocultural Theory*, a work that laid a substantial portion of the intellectual foundations for this book. The current book deploys some central ideas of that earlier volume but breaks new ground in a number of ways. Russell and his mentor Alex Rosenberg introduced me to the best current evolutionary thinking and helped me learn to think like a Darwinian. Alex, whose breadth of knowledge is legendary, has always been ready to help me clarify my thinking and did so on a number of occasions as I struggled with the topic of this book. Bob Keohane, who is widely regarded as the greatest living international relations scholar, has had a tremendous influence on all my thinking, including this book. From my many collaborations with him I've gained a much deeper appreciation and understanding of the role of institutions in human life generally and in moral progress in particular.

I am also deeply indebted to Kristen Andrews, Richmond Campbell, Julian Culp, Jeff Holzgrefe, Mateo Penaherrera-Aguirre, Irina Mikhalevich, Maura Priest, Kyle Stanford, Victor Kumar, Ryan Muldoon, Jonathan Anomaly, and Shaun Nichols for their generosity in helping me improve early versions of the manuscript. They kept my thinking on track and enabled me to avoid some serious errors. I also thank Sandra Arneson, Richard Mamelok, and especially Eric Henney for their helpful comments on how to make the manuscript more accessible and interesting to a nonspecialist audience. Karolina

Wisniewska provided outstanding research assistance, often calling my attention to relevant articles and books of which I was unaware.

I also learned much that was relevant for writing this book from Robert Brandon, with whom I had the privilege of coteaching a course on the evolution of morality at Duke University in 2018. Thanks are also due to the amazingly sharp students in my graduate philosophy seminar on moral change at the University of Arizona in the spring semester of 2019. It's not an accident that this department is rated number one in political philosophy in the world. I feel privileged to be in a department where professors can learn so much not just from each other but also from their students.

I benefited greatly from a workshop on a draft of the manuscript sponsored by the Center for the Philosophy of Freedom at the University of Arizona. David Schmidtz, the Center's founder and director, on that occasion and in every activity he supports, fulfilled his unwavering commitment to fostering a climate that enables vigorous discussion of a wide range of views. People who think the Freedom Center is an ideological instrument know nothing about what actually goes on there.

Much of what is distinctive in this book is grounded in my long-term interest in social moral epistemology—the comparative study of the social conditions that affect the formation, preservation, and diffusion of beliefs that are crucial for living morally. Consequently I am indebted also to Alvin Goldman for his pioneering work in social epistemology and to Miranda Fricker for her work on social moral epistemology.

Finally, much credit is due to my editor, Philip Laughlin. He was expeditious, supportive, and encouraging and strengthened my motivation to make this book the best I am capable of writing.

Introduction: The Darwinians' Un-Darwinian Dogmas, or How Not to Think about Morality

Does the Idea of Human Nature Even Make Sense after Darwin?

We often hear that the Darwinian revolution dethroned the dogma that human nature is fixed, unchanging. Yet a version of the dogma still stubbornly persists, ironically clothed in evolutionary garb, among even some of the best evolutionary scientists. The dogma may be even more widespread among nonscientists. It seems to be a central feature of "folk" anthropology, the way ordinary people think about what kind of creatures we human beings are, the commonsense view of human nature. I'm referring to the belief that human *moral* nature is fixed in this sense: human morality is *essentially* tribalistic, group exclusive, and that's not going to change. In its scientific form, the dogma asserts that human morality is tribalistic because the forces of natural selection in the "Environment of Evolutionary Adaptation" (the EEA for short) in the middle to late Pleistocene era, several hundred thousand years ago, made it that way. The EEA is supposed to be the ancestral environment in which the elements of basic human moral psychology—the moral mind—came together and spread through human populations. The scientific story seems to vindicate the folk anthropology.

To say that human morality is essentially tribalistic (or group exclusive or parochial) means that humans, by virtue of the constitution of the evolved moral mind, acknowledge demanding moral obligations toward members of their own group but don't extend anything approaching the same moral regard to members of other groups, human or nonhuman. Sometimes the Tribalism Dogma is put as follows: part of what is distinctive about human morality, as opposed to the less complex moralities of some other animals, is that humans exhibit altruism toward people who aren't their kin and even toward people who can't be expected ever to reciprocate. (Altruism here means behavior that benefits another but comes at some cost to the benefactor, including a reduction of his reproductive fitness, his success in passing on his own genes to the next generation.) But human altruism, so the story goes, is *parochial*: its scope is limited to those whom we regard as members of our group. That's because it was parochial altruism that natural selection produced in the EEA. The dogma is also sometimes formulated as follows: morally speaking, we are hardwired (or programmed) for tribalism. Notice that tribalism here doesn't just mean that it is our nature to distinguish between Us and Them; it means that we are biologically hardwired or programmed to relegate Them to a markedly inferior moral status or to exclude them from the circle of moral regard altogether.

Some of the best evolutionary scientists who study the emergence of human morality don't explicitly state that human moral nature is tribalistic. Yet, as I'll show, many of them strongly suggest that this is so; and the language they use, as well as the stories they tell of the evolutionary origins of human morality, is liable to encourage other, less careful thinkers to embrace the Tribalism Dogma.

To take one prominent example, consider carefully the following statement by the eminent cultural anthropologist Christopher Boehm in his fascinating and informative book *Moral Origins: The Evolution of Virtue, Altruism, and Shame*:

> I will . . . be reconstructing the behavior of the first fully "modern" humans, as of [not later than] 45,000 years ago, for they are basically the end point of moral evolution in the biological sense. Today, even though we live in cities and write and read books about morality, our actual morals are little more than a continuation of theirs. (Boehm 2012, 17)

In this passage, Boehm slips from saying that the biological evolution of human moral capacities, the emergence of *the moral mind*, was completed no later than 45,000 years ago (and probably much earlier), to saying that *human moralities* aren't much different now from the original human moralities that existed way back then. *He has confused the moral mind with the various moralities in which it gets expressed in different environments.* And Boehm, like most others who apply evolutionary thinking to morality, believes that the moralities that first appeared were tribalistic. Putting the latter belief together with the statement that "our morals" today are little more than a continuation of those early moralities, we are led to the conclusion that we are stuck with tribalism, because tribalism is our moral nature.

I interpret Boehm's term "our morals" to mean the actual moralities that contemporary humans have, not the underlying set of capacities that account for our having moralities, that is, the moral mind. If instead by "our morals" Boehm meant the moral mind rather than contemporary moralities, he chose a remarkably inapt way of communicating an important idea—and he can be faulted for encouraging a profound confusion.

The very title of his book, *Moral Origins*, betrays the same perilous ambiguity: it could refer to the origins of the moral mind or to the origins of the moralities that were its first expressions, or both. My surmise is that Boehm, like many others, hasn't kept that distinction clearly in mind. If you fail to heed the distinction, you won't be interested in providing a scientific explanation of moral progress and regression, because you'll think that moralities haven't changed much—and indeed that they *couldn't* change much. You'll think the evolutionary origins story tells us all we need to know about morality.

Here's another example. Evolutionary psychologist and moral philosopher Joshua Greene, in his book *Moral Tribes*, states that "biologically speaking, humans were designed for cooperation, but only with some people. Our moral brains evolved for cooperation within groups. . . . Our moral brains did not evolve for cooperation between groups" (Greene 2013, 23). Assuming that "our moral brains" means our moral minds considered from a neurological point of view, Greene is saying that the moral mind is tribalistic, that we are tribalistic by virtue of our evolved moral nature. That's why, later in the same book, he says that to overcome tribalism, we must learn to act "unnaturally," that is, contrary to our moral nature. (It's not often one finds a moral philosopher advocating the committing of unnatural acts, at least not publicly.)

We find a third example in the work of the renowned evolutionary psychologist Michael Tomasello. He *completes* his "natural history of human morality" by showing how the transition was made, several hundred thousand years ago, from moral relations of equal respect between pairs of individuals cooperating to hunt large game to a morality encompassing all members *of a cultural group—and no one else*. Tomasello's description of the morality of the cultural group is clearly tribalistic: he says that anyone outside the group is seen as "not really human at all" (Tomasello 2016, 87). He describes the transition to a morality restricted to the cultural group as "the decisive moral step that bequeathed to modern human morality all of its most essential and distinctive elements" (78). Wait just a minute! Really? Do *you* think that people who aren't part of your cultural group aren't really human?

The most charitable interpretation of Tomasello's claim that he has provided a natural history of human morality is that he has told a complete story of how *the moral mind* came to be, in stages. That is quite different from telling a complete story about how the moral mind has been expressed in different moralities over time. Tomasello's book isn't really a natural history of morality; or if it is, it's only the *early* natural history. As a title, *A History of Human Morality Up to But Not Beyond the Hunter-Gatherer Stage* wouldn't be as catchy, but it would be more accurate.

Tomasello is brilliant, so I'm certain that he is well aware that even though the evolution of the moral mind was completed way back then, moralities have changed since the first of them appeared. He can't very well think he is providing a history of all of that, since his story stops so very long ago. Yet if we take him at his word that he has provided a history of the coming together of all of the elements of the moral mind, then we are left to conclude that the moral mind is tribalistic. Why is that so? Because nothing in his natural history explains how humans could ever come to have moralities more inclusive than the tribalistic moralities he ascribes to early human cultural groups. Nothing he says explains how some human beings eventually came to believe that people who aren't part of their cultural group are just as human as they are, possessing the same basic rights. On the contrary, everything Tomasello says points to the conclusion that human moralities will always be as tribalistic as they were when the formation of the moral mind as he describes it was completed.

Evolutionary scientists aren't the only ones who fuel the tribalism dogma by failing to distinguish clearly between the moral mind and the content of the earliest moralities in which it was expressed. Rising star philosopher Sharon Street proclaims that the content of morality—all moralities—or as she puts it "our system of evaluative judgments," is "thoroughly saturated" with its evolutionary origins (Street 2006, 114). She provides no evidence for this strong claim; instead she only recites the standard view that morality arose as an adaptation in the distant past. In fact, her claim is extremely dubious. Given that which particular moralities the moral mind underwrites depends on the nature of the social environments in which the moral mind is expressed, and given that the social environments in which many humans now find themselves are profoundly different from the environment in which moralities first appeared, it would be very strange if the content of current moralities weren't significantly different from the content of the earliest moralities. And as we've seen, the moralities of some people today are indeed remarkably different from the earliest moralities: they are much more inclusive. The key point is that you would expect the content of modern moralities to be quite different if the environments in which they developed lacked the special evolutionary pressures that shaped the content of the earliest moralities. That is precisely the case, as I'll argue later.

I've quoted Boehm, Greene, and Tomasello as individuals whose language endorses the Tribalism Dogma because they are respected, exceptionally influential thinkers in the scientific community. They are also thinkers who write not just for fellow scientists but also for the general public. In doing so, they reinforce and put the stamp of scientific legitimacy on the folk wisdom that, morally speaking, humans are tribalistic by nature. Street writes primarily for a philosophical audience, but the article in which she assumes that the evolutionary forces that created the first moralities have largely fixed the content of all subsequent moralities is widely cited and influential.

The Tribalistic Moral Nature Dogma

Because I appreciate that human moralities do change and see no reason to think they won't continue to change—and because I want to understand how they change—I am keen to remove obstacles to thinking clearly about moral change, including the Tribalism Dogma. I'll begin by driving home the point that the Tribalism Dogma rests on two confusions: a confusion between the moral mind itself, on the one hand, and its expression in particular moralities, on the other; and a confusion between what moralities originally did and what they are capable of now.

The first confusion is the failure to distinguish between two different claims: (1) the distinctively human moral mind, the basic elements of human psychology that constitute our competence for having moralities, first emerged in the Pleistocene, somewhere between 1.8 million and 10,000 years ago, as a result of the particular selective pressures of the environment humans occupied at that time (the EEA), and those same selective pressures also resulted in the moral mind being expressed *at that time in moralities that were tribalistic*; and (2) the particular selective pressures of the environment in which the moral mind emerged produced a *moral mind that is tribalistic*. The first statement is highly plausible and supported by the best evolutionary thinking about human evolution. The second statement turns out to be false. Later, I'll adduce all the evidence for its falsity.

For now, I want to make clear that the truth of the first statement does nothing whatsoever to support the second statement. You can consistently accept the first statement and reject the second. In fact, once you understand how flexible the moral mind is, you will see why the second statement is false.

If anything deserves the title of human moral nature, it is the moral mind, the basic set of cognitive and emotional competencies that enable humans to have distinctively human moralities. That's because the moral mind, as evolutionary scientists understand it, is something that is fixed (at least for the foreseeable future), a product of natural selection that came to exist as much as several hundred thousand years ago and hasn't changed much, if at all, since then. A thing's nature is supposed to be a fixed set of traits that all things of that kind have and that is invariant across different environments.

The idea is that the moral mind is basically the same for all normal human beings. Human moralities—as particular bundles of rules, values, and emotional responses—obviously vary among human beings and apparently have done so as long as humans have been moral creatures. The crucial thing is to distinguish carefully between the moral mind, which turns out to be a highly flexible set of moral competencies, and the various particular moralities that the exercise of those competencies produces in response to different environments.

Recall the analogy with language. All cognitively normal human beings have the same linguistic mind—a set of competencies for learning languages—but which language any individual learns depends on which language-learning environment she is exposed to. If you grow up around Urdu speakers, you'll learn Urdu; around French speakers, you'll learn French. Similarly, it is highly likely that all human beings (sociopaths aside) have the same moral mind, the same fundamental moral psychology, including the competencies for developing moral responses (approval, indignation, shame, etc.), internalizing moral rules, and having a conscience. Evolutionary thinkers tell a credible story about how and why the moral mind came to be: it emerged on the biological foundation that we shared with our earlier ancestors, including the predecessors of modern chimps and bonobos, because it contributed to human reproductive fitness in the harsh circumstances of the EEA.

It's also highly likely that when the first human moral minds came on the scene, the environment in which they existed (the EEA) featured selective pressures that resulted in the competencies that constituted the moral mind usually being expressed in moralities of a particular kind, namely, tribalistic moralities. However, this doesn't mean that humans are fated to have only tribalistic moralities; it doesn't mean that the moral mind itself is tribalistic. And if the moral mind isn't tribalistic but instead is highly flexible and capable of underwriting quite different kinds of moralities, some tribalistic, some not tribalistic, depending on the environment, then that makes a big difference. It means that the space of possible human moralities—the full range of forms that human moralities can take—may be very large indeed. And the possibilities for moral progress may be correspondingly great.

The Highly Flexible Moral Mind

To make this basic point clearer, think of it this way: the moral mind consists of some *very general competencies* for producing a wide range of behaviors, attitudes, and emotions and accordingly is *highly variable in its outputs*. The results that the exercise of these competencies produce can vary widely, depending on the character of *the inputs*, the stimuli that activate the competencies. Different environments feature different inputs, with the result that the outputs of the exercise of the general competencies that constitute the moral mind vary accordingly. Some environments will tend to result in the moral mind being expressed in one kind of morality; other environments can lead to it being expressed quite differently.

Niche Constructors Par Excellence

Here's the kicker: *the environment in which the human moral mind was forged by the pressures of natural selection (the EEA) was profoundly different from the environment in which many human beings now find themselves.* "Find themselves" is inapt; better to say that the culturally constructed niches that humans have now created for themselves differ radically from the environment in which the human moral mind was first expressed in tribalistic moralities.

This is an important point, because it reveals the second idea that is key for avoiding the Tribalism Dogma and for understanding how moral change occurs and how environments shape our moral possibilities. The first crucial idea was the flexibility of the human moral mind, which includes its ability to generate different moralities in different environments. The second is that human beings are "niche constructors" par excellence: they continually tailor their environments to suit themselves and thus (unwittingly) expose themselves to new selective pressures and in some cases buffer themselves from the influence of selective pressures that had played a fundamental role in shaping them in the past (Sterelny 2012, 145).

When we combine the idea of the flexibility of the human moral mind with the idea that humans are niche constructors par excellence, we can see why it is highly unlikely that human beings are morally tribalistic by nature—*even if it is true that most human moralities, throughout most of history, have been tribalistic*. The flexibility of the human moral mind allows for the same basic, universal, and unchanging features of human moral psychology to produce different outputs, moralities with different contents, some more tribalistic, some more inclusive, depending on the character of the niches that humans construct for themselves, because those niches feature different inputs for the functioning of the moral mind. If, for most of human history, the environments in which the moral mind operated favored tribalistic moralities, then human history would *look like* the story of a being who is tribalistic by nature. The preponderance of tribalistic moralities doesn't show that the moral mind is tribalistic; it only shows that most of the environments in which humans have lived have stimulated the moral mind to express itself in that sort of morality.

Thus the answer to the question "Is human moral nature tribalistic or inclusive?" is "It's neither, though it is capable of producing both tribalistic and inclusive moralities." There's a much more general, far more important point here: because humans continuously shape and reshape their social environments without end, we should expect the highly flexible moral mind to keep generating new types of moralities and new types of moral agents. If we can learn how that works, we can take charge of our moral fate.

The Constancy of Basic Human Psychology

Why would one think that the moral mind is fixed, unchanging? The point is not that it will never change—presumably it will, unless humans go extinct, because all existing species are subject to evolutionary forces, even in their most basic features. The idea, rather, is that it is highly unlikely that the moral mind has changed significantly, if at all, since it first emerged among our remote ancestors and also unlikely that it will change anytime soon. The human moral mind is the product of natural selection on genes, and large changes through that kind of selection almost certainly could not have occurred in such a short period of time.

A bit of confirming evidence is that the remaining hunter-gatherer groups that most closely resemble the humans among whom the moral mind first emerged seem to have the same moral minds that you and I have and that all human beings appear to have had throughout history. What I'm suggesting is that you can remain true to Darwin and still talk about human moral nature, if you're careful to restrict that term to the moral mind and are equally careful to distinguish the moral mind from its various expressions in different moralities.

Here's a qualification that's needed to avoid a misunderstanding: to say that the moral mind was produced by selection on genes doesn't preclude culture playing a role in its emergence. Many evolutionary scientists now think that human culture has exerted a strong influence on which genes get passed on to the next generation and hence on the biological traits of human beings. Culture does exert a selective force on genes, but whereas culture itself can change very rapidly, genetic change occurs much more slowly. That's why we can treat the moral mind as fixed (for the foreseeable future), even while admitting that culture played a role in its formation. With that qualification in mind, let me repeat the central idea on which I'll build a theory of moral change: *our biological evolution produced the moral mind, but how the competencies that constitute the moral mind get expressed has increasingly become a matter of how cumulative culture, through niche construction, shapes the environments in which the moral mind operates.*

Flexibility Everywhere

Earlier I drew a parallel between the human linguistic mind, the universal competence for learning languages that all cognitively normal humans have, and the moral mind. Here's another analogy. An intriguing species of water flea exhibits a kind of flexibility that evolutionary biologists call *adaptive plasticity*. If the baby water flea is developing into an adult in water that includes the chemical signatures of creatures that prey on water fleas, it develops a helmet and spines to defend itself against predators. If the water around it doesn't include the chemical signatures of predators, the water flea doesn't develop these protective devices. That's a nifty trick, because producing spines and a helmet is costly, in terms of energy, and conserving energy is essential for an organism's ability to survive and reproduce. The water flea only expends the energy needed to produce spines and a helmet when it needs to. So it may well be that this plasticity is an adaptation: a trait that came to exist in a species because it contributed to reproductive fitness. There are many cases, across many species, of adaptive plasticity. Plasticity is conducive to fitness if there is sufficient variation in the environment.

Suppose you were a biologist studying water fleas, and you happened to have only observed water fleas in aquatic environments in which there were critters that preyed on them. Because the only water fleas you ever observed all had spines and helmets, you might (wrongly) conclude that it was in the nature of water fleas to have spines and helmets, when in fact it's in the nature of these creatures to either develop spines and helmets or not, depending on the environment.

I'm suggesting that something like this is going on in the case of evolutionary thinking about human evolved morality. If you're resolutely focused on that peculiar early environment in which the moral mind first emerged, you may also be fixated on the particular kind of moralities that were the first expressions of the competencies that constitute the moral mind. And that fixation may lead you to slip from talking about the former to (unwittingly) talking about the latter. I think this is what has happened: because evolutionary thinkers have concentrated pretty much exclusively on trying to use evolutionary principles to explain the *origins* of human morality, *not its subsequent development*, they've focused only on the expression of the moral mind in that particular environment. Note again the ambiguity: "the origins of human morality" or "moral origins" could refer to the origins of the human moral mind, the thing that makes human moralities possible; or it could refer to the origins of the first human moralities. The bottom line is that the original human moralities were most likely tribalistic, but that doesn't mean the moral mind is tribalistic.

The Cooperation Dogma

The tendency to confuse "the human moral mind came to be and hasn't changed since it first appeared" with "human moralities are essentially as they were when the moral mind first appeared" is reinforced by a second dogma: the belief that morality is just "a type of cooperation" or "a collection of solutions to cooperation problems." If you believe that, you'll also believe that understanding how moralities facilitate cooperation will tell you everything there is to know about morality.

Unfortunately, the Cooperation Dogma seems to be widespread. Here are three examples of prominent evolutionary thinkers explicitly embracing it. Michael Tomasello states that "morality is a type of cooperation," thereby implying that every feature of morality can be explained by showing how it facilitates cooperation. What he should have said—and what I think he meant to say—is that morality *began* as a type of cooperation or as something that facilitated cooperation and continues to play a major role in cooperation, and that the moral mind evolved to facilitate cooperation. That's compatible with recognizing that the moral mind can do lots of other things.

In fact, though he says that morality is a type of cooperation, in one passage he acknowledges that morality extends beyond that: he acknowledges that people recognize obligations to individuals who can't cooperate because they are disabled, but with this important qualification: if they are members of the same cultural group (Tomasello 2016, 116). That qualification turns out to be important. Later, I'll show that Tomasello's supposedly complete story of the stages of development that resulted in "modern human morality" can't account for extending moral regard beyond one's cultural group. That leaves out both of the Great Expansions.

Consider also the subtitle of a recent article in the journal *Current Anthropology*: "Is It Good to Cooperate? Testing the Theory of

Morality as Cooperation" (2019). The subtitle is remarkably inaccurate because the article does nothing to test the assumption that morality is all about cooperation or is just a type of cooperation. The article characterizes the theory of "morality as cooperation" as the view that "morality *consists* [my emphasis] of a collection of biological and cultural solutions to the problems of cooperation recurrent in human social life" (48). Then, rather than testing *that* theory, which would require seeing whether some human moralities include features that aren't solutions to cooperation problems, the article simply provides evidence that a wide range of moralities from around the world solve cooperation problems in similar ways! Those results are fully compatible with recognizing that morality, for some people, has features that can't be explained by showing that they contribute to cooperation. Showing that several things share features that contribute to X doesn't show that contributing to X is all those things do.

Joshua Greene, whom we encountered earlier as a tribalism dogmatist, provides another clear example of the Cooperation Dogma. In his book *Moral Tribes*, he confidently states that "morality is a device for enabling cooperation" (Greene 2013, 28).

Greene and Tomasello are major figures, and *Current Anthropology* is a respected peer-reviewed journal. So these examples don't represent fringe views in the scientific community; on the contrary, they are mainstream and extremely influential. And they are shaping (or rather misshaping) the understanding of morality of ordinary people who pay attention to science.

I cheerfully acknowledge that moralities *originally* were all about cooperation, and that moralities *remain essential* for successful cooperation today and always will be. I also heartily endorse the hypothesis that the basic features of human moral psychology, the moral mind, came about through natural selection because they contributed to cooperation and thereby to reproductive fitness. Nevertheless, I will argue that some moralities are more than a collection of solutions to cooperation problems. If they weren't, the Two Great Expansions could never even have begun. To summarize: the Cooperation Dogma rests on a confusion between *what morality originally did* and *what it is now*, and that confusion reinforces the Tribalism Dogma.

Suppose that human morality first came on the scene because it facilitated cooperation by resolving conflicts; encouraging individuals not to be free riders on the cooperative scheme in their group; enabling the group to develop effective ways to deter free riding and to punish it when deterrence failed; and by supplying rules requiring reciprocity in aiding one another, rules for fairly dividing the spoils of the hunt, rules to regulate potentially disruptive sexual behavior, to curb violent behavior among members of the group, to suppress efforts by some individuals to dominate the rest, and so on. The idea is that by doing all these things, morality contributed to successful cooperation—cooperation much more effective, complex, and flexible than that achieved by other animals—and that this distinctive kind of cooperation in turn contributed to human reproductive fitness. That's a highly plausible story.

Here's another plausible story: the human shoulder joint, with its extraordinary rotational flexibility, evolved from a less flexible ancestral primate joint because it facilitated the throwing of projectiles, a skill that contributed to reproductive fitness when early humans began hunting large game. But this doesn't mean that the shoulder joint is just a type of projectile thrower. It can do lots of other things. And knowing that it can throw projectiles doesn't tell you everything you might want to know about the capabilities of the human shoulder joint. Similarly, from the fact that human morality emerged because it facilitated cooperation, it doesn't follow that morality is just "a type of cooperation" or just "a collection of solutions to cooperation problems." Nature abounds with cases where something evolved because it performed some particular function that was conducive to reproductive fitness but then came to do other jobs as well. The Cooperation Dogma rests on a simple mistake: confusing the original function that morality performed with a full characterization of what morality is and can be.

How the Cooperation Dogma Reinforces the Tribalism Dogma

How is all of this relevant to the Tribalism Dogma? The point is simply this: the story that evolutionary thinkers tell about how morality came to be because it facilitated cooperation is a story about cooperation *within* groups—the small, widely scattered groups of humans that existed in the EEA. If you assume that morality is "a type of cooperation" (not just something that facilitates cooperation, which is compatible with it doing other things, too), and if you think that cooperation is always cooperation in some group, then you'll be on your way to thinking that morality is group exclusive, that is, tribalistic. Altruism will be parochial, sympathy will be parochial, moral regard will be parochial—all limited to members of one's group, the people one cooperates with.

If you also think, as many evolutionary scientists do, that violent competition occurred among human groups in the EEA, then you'll be even more inclined to think that morality, as something that is fully constituted by its function in facilitating cooperation, is essentially tribalistic. Why? Because violent competition for resources among groups in the EEA would have selected for moralities that featured fear, distrust, and preemptive aggression toward out-group members—in a word, tribalistic moralities. That's the kind of morality that would have enabled groups to survive and reproduce in an environment of ruthless intergroup competition.

The big point here is that in the EEA humans supposedly hadn't yet developed social practices and institutions that allowed for peaceful, mutually beneficial cooperation between groups, so the relationship between groups was zero-sum: success for one group meant failure for another. The problem is that even if that story is correct, it only shows that the moralities that took shape *in that environment* were tribalistic, not that the moral mind is tribalistic.

Suppose that when the moral mind first emerged, its only expression was in moralities that were nothing more than devices for facilitating cooperation, and that those first moralities limited moral regard to fellow cooperators, who, in that environment, happened to be a small number of people composing one's hunter-gatherer band. Suppose also that human moralities first functioned not just to facilitate cooperation within the group, but also to allow the group to compete successfully with other groups. If all these things were true, then one would expect that moralities *at that time, in that environment*, would be tribalistic.

Yet this conclusion leaves open two possibilities: first, in significantly different environments, the moral mind would have been expressed in quite different types of moralities; and second, in some environments, the moral mind might get expressed in moralities that were not "all about cooperation." Those options are open, if the moral mind is sufficiently flexible and if the nature of the environment plays a big role in what sort of moralities the moral mind underwrites. If you take those two options seriously, you'll be much more open to the possibilities of moral change than you would be if you stuck to the two dogmas.

The most destructive thing about the two dogmas is that they divert attention from the momentous fact that what sort of moralities we have, as well as what sort of moral agents we are, is being shaped — unwittingly and with no concern for the moral consequences — by the ongoing process of niche construction. In constructing niches, we are constructing our moral selves, but so far we've been doing so without forethought or understanding. It's time to change that. It's time to make our moral fate a matter of choice, not chance. This is the central message of this book.

I will argue that even though human morality (including here both the moral mind and various particular moralities in which it gets expressed) facilitates cooperation, and even though moralities first emerged because they facilitated cooperation, some moralities are not now just a type of cooperation: that's particularly true of inclusive moralities, those that have embraced the Two Great Expansions.

Evidence for the Flexibility of the Human Moral Mind

Why do I keep saying the human moral mind — the basic set of competencies that make having moralities (plural) possible — is flexible? Why think that the same basic moral psychology can yield different moralities, some tribalistic, some inclusive, and can even result in morality encompassing more than its original function, namely, facilitating cooperation. Before answering that question, we need to get a better fix on what the moral mind is, at least in broad strokes.

The moral mind is a suite of cognitive and emotional capacities that build on the psychological architecture of our primate predecessors but exceed it in significant ways — ways that create possibilities for novel and distinctively human forms of cooperation that are structured by internalized moral rules. I think that most moral psychologists today would agree that the moral mind includes at least the following features:

1. The capacity to experience the moral emotions of guilt, shame, pride, indignation, and disgust.
2. The ability to distinguish between what someone (including oneself) *prefers or desires* to do or what will serve her best interests or the interests of the people she is most closely attached to, on the one hand, and what she *ought* to do, on the other. Sometimes this is called the ability to internalize moral rules in such a way as to regard them as "objective."
3. A "theory of mind" or "mind-reading" ability that allows one to make reliable judgments about what others are thinking and feeling on the basis of their behavior and to take their perspective (which includes empathizing with them).
4. The capacity to form shared intentions that enable joint, coordinated activities—the ability to think "we are going to do this together" and to make a commitment to realizing such joint intentions.
5. The capacity for extra-kin altruism, that is, for incurring net costs to benefit people to whom one is not related.
6. The ability to determine who is a reliable potential partner in cooperation and who is not, along with the ability to signal convincingly to others that one is a reliable partner. (To the extent that cooperation is based on moral rules, this will mean the ability to detect who is moral and to signal to others that you are moral.)
7. The tendency to sympathize when one witnesses the suffering of other humans or at least a tendency to react aversively to that suffering (this may be in part the basis for 5).
8. A motivationally potent sense of moral identity, the deep commitment to acting so that one can convince oneself and others that one is moral and hence a reliable partner in cooperation and a person worthy of respect and trust.
9. The ability to apply moral rules to new situations, which includes the ability to engage in reasoning, that is, to perform inferential cognitive operations, regarding moral matters. This reasoning includes at least moral consistency reasoning, inferential thinking that resolves conflicts between particular moral responses and firmly

held moral principles or that resolves conflicts among moral principles (Campbell and Kumar 2012, 302).

My hypothesis is that a being that didn't have these capacities couldn't have the robust sort of morality that normal human beings have and that makes them supercooperators. All these capacities appear to be at work in distinctively human moralities, no matter how much they vary in other respects.

Richard Joyce, a pioneering and exceptionally original philosopher of the evolution of morality, rightly emphasizes items 1 and 2, noting that any view that omits them and focuses only on the capacity to exhibit sympathy-based altruism toward nonkin is not really an account of distinctively human morality (Joyce 2000, 93–95, 137–138). Later I'll emphasize the connection between 1 and 2, on the one hand, and 8, on the other, and explain the pivotal role of this connection in moral progress.

All these competencies are quite general: depending on the environmental inputs, the outputs they generate can include a wide variety of moralities. For example, depending on what culture you grow up in, you may find gay sex disgusting or not. Similarly, if your moral community has extremely egalitarian rules concerning the fair division of resources, your threshold for experiencing indignation when someone takes more than others may be very low. Likewise, which rules you regard as objective, as binding regardless of your preferences (rather than as mere prudential rules of thumb), will depend on how your society teaches you to distinguish right from wrong. In one society, what is shrugged off as a mere breach of etiquette may count as a serious moral wrong in another.

Cumulative Culture

Whether it's included as an element of the moral mind or as a vital adjunct to it, *the capacity for cumulative culture* is also crucial to humans' ability to develop moralities and also helps explain why they haven't developed just one morality. Researchers disagree about what culture is and how we should use the term "cumulative culture" in the context of evolutionary thinking. Yet there's considerable agreement that cumulative culture involves the transmission, accumulation, combination, and recombination of information, techniques, social practices, and technologies across generations. Some other animal species apparently have culture, but the evidence suggests that they don't have cumulative culture.

There is also some agreement about the character of some of the social learning mechanisms that enable cumulative culture. These include various cognitive learning "biases"—predispositions to learn from individuals that fit certain categories, such as being prestigious, or being like oneself, or being successful. Another mechanism of social learning is "conformity bias," the tendency to learn to do what most people around you are doing.

The development of a culture as a continuing accumulation and recombination of resources exhibits "path dependency." Cultural innovations are often (some would say "always") a response to new challenges. A society that starts off in one environment, at one point in time, will face a distinctive set of challenges even though, as a human society, it will also share some challenges that all human societies face. Where a society starts off matters, because the options it takes early in its development can have disproportionate consequences for where can go in the future. That's what path dependency means.

Here's a simple example to illustrate path dependency. When you first start building a house, you have more options for what sort of house you can end up with than when you've already laid the foundations, built the walls, and erected the roof.

Given the path dependency of cultures—and given that there is more than one effective way to solve the problems of cooperation that the moral mind was created to solve—one would expect diversity in human moralities. The extraordinary human capacity for cumulative culture and the path dependency of cultures, when combined with the flexibility of the moral mind, results in diverse human moralities.

Why the Moral Mind Is Flexible

Now that we know the main features of the moral mind and the importance of its connection with the human capacity for cumulative culture and the ongoing niche construction that cumulative culture facilitates, we can return to the question of why one should expect the moral mind to be quite flexible. There are two reasons.

The first is that psychologists, neuroscientists, and cognitive psychologists are converging on the conclusion that the human mind is highly flexible. Even though it features some degree of modularization (specialized functional subsystems physically expressed in certain regions of the brain), it also includes highly flexible, general capacities.

From an evolutionary standpoint, one would expect that humans evolved to have highly flexible minds, because that would help account for our peculiar success as a species. We occupy almost every region of our planet and, unlike our nearest *Homo* relatives (Neanderthals, Denisovans, etc.), have not only survived drastic climate shifts and other potentially lethal environmental changes but also increased our numbers quite dramatically.

It's improbable that the rest of the human mind is highly flexible but the moral mind isn't, for two reasons. First, it's really just a convenience to speak of the moral mind as if it were something separate from the rest of our cognitive-emotional-motivational apparatus. Moral reasoning may well be largely just an application of more general reasoning capacities to moral matters. And reasoning facilitates great flexibility in responses to social and environmental challenges.

When I refer to the moral mind, I'm *not* assuming that it is a separate functional module, localized in some particular region of the brain. (When I use the analogy of the linguistic mind, I'm not assuming that it's a separate, neurologically localized mental module, either.) It may turn out that what I'm calling the moral mind is just a matter of our ability to apply some more general capacities for feelings, motivations, and thinking to the aspects of our lives that we put under the heading "moral." The only point of talking about the moral mind and analogizing it to the linguistic mind is to emphasize that there's a difference between the capacity to have a morality and the particular morality you have. That simple distinction turns out to be much more momentous than it first appears to be.

Second, even if the moral mind were separate from other aspects of our mental equipment, it is our moral competencies, especially so far as they facilitate cooperation, that have played an especially large role in our being so adaptively successful across a wide range of environments. If our success is due to our being highly flexible cooperators (unlike social insects, we constantly develop new forms of cooperation), and if our highly flexible cooperation is due in large part to our being moral creatures, then it seems reasonable to conclude that the moral mind is highly flexible.

Still another reason for thinking the moral mind is highly flexible is the sheer diversity of human moralities (despite the fact that all normal human brains and the basic cognitive and emotional capacities they enable are pretty much the same). Building on an arresting passage from Boehm's book, *Moral Origins*, here's a small sample of variations in human moralities. In some societies, sex between men and boys is considered immoral, but in others adolescent boys are initiated into manhood by performing fellatio on older men or being subjected to anal intercourse by them. In some societies, the dominant morality denies the very possibility of a husband raping his wife, because it is assumed to be right and proper for a husband to have intercourse with his wife whether she consents or not—in fact, the very idea of a woman consenting to intercourse is not even in the domain of moral thinking. In other societies, spousal rape not only makes sense but is condemned as immoral. Some people now think that they should do their utmost to extend the lives of their parents, even when this means refusing to help them engage in physician-assisted suicide, while in some hunter-gatherer societies, it is thought right and even obligatory for children to cause the deaths of their aged parents. (In the case of the Inuit, this is done by leaving the aged parents on an ice floe to die of hypothermia; in the case of a hunter-gatherer society living in a radically different, tropical environment, children strangle their aged parents [Boehm 2102, 186].) Different moralities also draw the circle of moral regard differently: in some the circle is very small, restricted to the tribe or ethnic group or nation; in others the circle is enlarged to include humanity.

To the extent that, inter alia, moralities function to facilitate cooperation, you would expect to find some commonalities across moralities, and you do: norms of reciprocity, including rules about keeping promises, prohibitions against killing members of one's own group, rules constraining sexual behavior, rules specifying how to divide valuable resources among members of the group, and so on. But these similarities are compatible with lots of variations, both in particular moral rules and in how different moral rules are weighted relative to one another when they conflict. It's not just that the same human moral mind gets expressed in a plurality of moralities that are different from each other and in some cases flatly contradictory; in addition, that diversity includes differences along a spectrum from full-throttle tribalism to much more inclusive moralities, moralities that extend the circle of regard far beyond any particular group.

I think it's true that most human moralities *so far* have been situated toward the tribalistic end of the spectrum. That wouldn't be surprising if, for most of human history on most parts of our planet, the human social environment encouraged moralities to take a tribalistic shape. Yet recently, some human beings have come to have moralities that are more inclusive. That makes good sense if you appreciate something I'll elaborate on as we proceed: *some modern environments are radically different from the EEA, in ways that are conducive to moralities that are more inclusive than those that typically developed in the EEA.*

Why are some modern environments friendly to inclusive moralities? Because substantial numbers of humans have achieved what the eminent cognitive scientist Nicholas Baumard, in a recent BBC commentary, called "surplus evolutionary success." I prefer the term "surplus reproductive success" because it's a bit more precise. Baumard observes that once humans solved the basic problems of survival and reproduction, their brains were free to develop in new ways, including the creation of science.

I want to make a similar point about morality. Quite recently humans have succeeded in constructing niches in which they do so very well in achieving sustainable reproduction that they can afford to have moralities that would have been reproductive suicide in early environments. Achieving surplus reproductive success doesn't mean that we're no longer subject to evolutionary forces. It just means that we can do many more things and explore many more ways of living, because the options are not as tightly constrained by fitness as they previously were. Under conditions of surplus reproductive success, humans have more ways to change that are either fitness neutral—that neither increase nor decrease our ability to pass on our genes—or that don't decrease our fitness to the point where those changes aren't sustainable and don't spread. We achieved surplus reproductive success through niche construction.

Here's the crucial point: *surplus reproductive success enables the Great Uncoupling—the loosening of the previously tight connection between what moralities are like and their ability to promote reproductive fitness* (Buchanan and Powell 2018, 391). Once the Great Uncoupling occurs, the space of possible moralities enlarges enormously. Moralities can become relatively "fitness independent." They can also become more than bundles of solutions to cooperation problems; and they need not be tribalistic.

Evidence against the Tribalism Dogma: The Two Great Expansions

The evidence clearly suggests that human beings don't have a tribalistic moral nature, if that means they are fated to have only tribalistic moralities. The most dramatic examples of this evidence I know of are the Two Great Expansions. Nowadays, the dominant form the First Great Expansion takes is the idea of human rights: that all human beings are entitled to be treated in certain ways simply because they are humans, that is, by virtue of their humanity, not because they belong to our nation or our "race" or ethnic or cultural or religious group, and independently of their gender or sexual orientation.

Notice that the very idea of human rights reflects a separation between morality and cooperation: every human being is said to have certain rights simply by virtue of being human, not by virtue of being an actual or potential partner in cooperation. That should make one suspicious of the idea that morality is just all about cooperation.

The First Great Expansion involves a change in *beliefs*—some people's beliefs about who has equal basic moral status—but it is much more than that. The idea of human rights is now *embodied* in international law and in the domestic law of many countries, and considerable costs are incurred in trying to make that law effective. Contemporary international relations scholars have documented that human rights discourse and law actually have some significant effects on the behavior of some states, even leading them to recognize limits on their own sovereignty (Sikkink 2012, 17–19; Simmons 2009, 3). For example, member states' compliance with judgments by the European Court of Human Rights is impressively high, even though there is no police force or army to enforce them. So the First Great Expansion is not merely an aspiration, though it is far from universal and only partly realized.

There's a second respect in which the moralities of some humans have become much more inclusive than the tribalistic moralities that most probably were the first expression of the moral mind: a greater proportion of humanity than at any earlier point in human history now acknowledges that at least some nonhuman animals have moral standing—that they count morally in their own right— even if they have an inferior moral status to human beings. Again, this Second Great Expansion is not merely a behaviorally inert belief, a moral aspiration without consequences for how people live. The laws of many countries now prohibit previously ubiquitous practices inflicting suffering on animals, and considerable social resources are devoted to achieving compliance with that body of law. In most of the countries in which extensive medical research is being conducted, scientists are required to expend much time and resources in minimizing the suffering and death of animals used in experiments, even in research aimed at alleviating the most lethal human diseases. The Two Great Expansions aren't just aspirational, then; they are a reality that science should be able to explain. And the scientific explanation of these remarkable changes should at least be compatible with, if not illuminated by, a proper understanding of how humans evolved to become moral creatures.

Evaluating the Supposed Evidence for the Tribalistic Moral Nature Thesis

Most of our experience of human moralities and most of what we know about them from studying the past may *appear* to confirm the dogma that humans have a tribalistic moral nature for the simple reason that the Two Great Expansions are quite recent and haven't penetrated all human moralities. In other words, when it comes to evidence for the hypothesis that human moral nature is tribalistic, history so far may well be what researchers call a biased (or unrepresentative) sample! If most of the human moralities we know about have exhibited the psychological equivalents of the water flea's defensive spines and helmets, then it's not surprising that many people jump to the conclusion that tribalistic moralities are just human nature at work. My favorite example of biased-sample thinking is the guy who was convinced that the female orgasm is a myth because he'd had sex with several women, and none of them had one.

Attempts to Soften the Tribalism Dogma

Given that, for significant numbers of humans, the First and Second Great Expansions have occurred, people who subscribe to the dogma that human beings have a tribalistic moral nature have two main options. Either they can give up the dogma entirely and admit that they simply didn't appreciate the flexibility of the moral mind because they confused the moral mind with the kind of moralities it was first expressed in; or they can soften the dogma by acknowledging that culture has stretched the tribalistic evolutionary leash in some cases, but assert that its doing so was a matter of going against our evolutionary grain, and that consequently any shift toward inclusion is bound to be anemic and unstable.

Obviously, I think the first response is the best: the belief that we are beings with a tribalistic moral nature should just be abandoned. To those who take the second option, my reply is simple: given that human moralities exhibit great diversity and that some people's moralities are not tribalistic, why should we say that our moral nature is tribalistic? It won't do for the die-hard defender of the dogma to cite evidence of the pervasiveness of tribalistic moral attitudes and beliefs, whether the evidence is historical or based on experiments, even if it is cross-cultural, because any such evidence is compatible with the hypothesis that our moral nature (the moral mind) is neither tribalistic nor inclusive, but rather so flexible as to be capable of being expressed in either tribalistic or inclusive moralities, depending on the environment.

In other words, to take historical or experimental evidence of tribalistic moral attitudes or behavior as conclusive confirmation of the thesis that humans have a tribalistic moral nature is to ignore the biased-sample problem I noted earlier. If the human-constructed niches in which the moral mind can get expressed in inclusive moralities are rare and recent, then concluding that human moral nature is tribalistic because most human moralities have been like that would be no more cogent than concluding that water flea nature includes protective spines and helmets because most of the water fleas you happened to have observed has those features.

The tribalism dogmatist has recourse to one last desperate fallback position: he can admit that human moral nature sometimes permits nontribalistic moralities, but insist that tribalism nevertheless is part of the moral mind itself, and that it is therefore still accurate to say that humans have a tribalistic moral nature. For the reasons given in the preceding paragraph, I don't think that we should say that tribalism is an element of our basic moral psychology, part of the moral mind itself—unless we quickly add that the moral mind also includes the capacity for inclusion. But if one grants that the moral mind is tribalistic in that weak sense—that tribalism is only one aspect of a moral nature that also encompasses inclusion, the result is a Pyrrhic victory.

Why? Because the thesis that humans have a tribalistic moral nature loses its punch if one admits that humans can act contrary to that aspect of their nature because of another aspect of their nature, namely, their capacity for inclusive morality. Admitting that our moral nature is dualistic saps the force of the assertion that we have a tribalistic moral nature.

Suppose that the last-ditch tribal dogmatist rejects the idea that our moral nature is dualistic and in response to the obvious fact that some moralities are now inclusive says that inclusion nonetheless goes against our nature. That is, suppose he still asserts that our moral nature is tribalistic, period, not tribalistic and inclusive. Allowing for our moral nature to be overridden—saying, in effect, that we can act "unnaturally"—dilutes the notion of the nature of a thing. And that greatly reduces the interest and importance of the grand thesis that we are beings with a tribalistic moral nature. It also renders that thesis incapable of yielding any significant predictions about the scope of potential moral change or the space of possible moralities.

What I have to say in this book will still be important even if you dispense with talk of human moral nature altogether and fall back to a weaker, much less sexy thesis: namely, that human beings, by virtue of their evolutionary history, are *predisposed* to behave in a morally tribalistic way. To say that they are predisposed to tribalism means that exhibiting tribalistic moralities is the default position for humans, the way they tend to act, even if that tendency is sometimes not realized because of cultural influences. It's the default position, because the disposition to tribalism is an especially powerful aspect of our moral psychology.

If you hold that much weaker thesis, you can read me this way: I will show that in spite of this supposed predisposition, some humans have developed inclusive moralities, moralities that are not merely aspirational but socially and politically potent; *and* I will explain *how* they did that. In other words, I'll explain how they moved from situations in which that supposed predisposition largely determined the character of human moralities to situations in which that predisposition was inhibited or overridden or neutralized to such an extent that they developed inclusive moralities. In explaining this shift, I will show that the supposed predisposition to tribalism is not nearly as severe a constraint on the possibilities for moral change as one might think. I'll show that inclusive moralities are likely to persist, if the environments that are friendly to them are sustained. Inclusive moralities are fragile, in the sense that the capacity for tribalism never disappears; but that doesn't mean that inclusive moralities are inherently unstable and doomed to decay.

Finally, let me emphasize that there is a way of interpreting the experimental and historical evidence of tribalistic moral attitudes and behaviors that is compatible with rejecting the Tribalism Dogma, even in its weaker forms. Such evidence can be explained *without* concluding that humans have an especially powerful, deeply rooted, biologically based predisposition to tribalism if we make the following reasonable assumptions: (1) the moral mind is highly flexible; (2) most humans have lived in environments in which that flexibility issued in tribalistic moralities; (3) culture has developed in ways that sustain tribalistic moralities, even when they no longer promote reproductive fitness and are no longer necessary for successful cooperation; and (4) some people have an interest in maintaining (or resurrecting) tribalistic tendencies and they have the ability to do so effectively.

Each of these assumptions is highly credible. Let's focus on the third and fourth, since they're new to our discussion. The evidence suggests that cultural practices that evolved to perform certain functions in a particular environment can continue for long periods of time even when the environment changes in ways that result in those practices no longer performing those functions. One example is the well-documented higher prevalence of violent responses to perceived insults characteristic of men who grow up in the American South rather than in other parts of the United States. A common evolutionary explanation of this heightened propensity toward reactive violence is that it is, in effect, a cultural hangover. Historically this propensity may have served to enhance reproductive fitness in the herding culture of people from the border region between England and Scotland who later predominantly settled the American South. Over time, this behavior has been sustained through the cultural transmission of ideas of male honor in new environments in which it no longer enhances reproductive fitness (Nisbett and Cohen 1996, 4). Similarly, cultural practices that resulted in the moral mind being expressed in tribalistic moralities may have been adaptive in earlier environments, but may have been sustained in quite different environments either because they performed other functions or simply because in later environments they weren't so costly in reproductive terms as to have been winnowed out by selection. (Here we need to avoid a mistake I'll explain more fully later: the error of hyperfunctionalism, the assumption that everything that exists is now performing some function that promotes fitness.)

The central point here is that if a society develops effective mechanisms for transmitting cultural values across generations, those values may persist so long as they don't reduce reproductive fitness to the point of nonviability or cause other serious damage. Call this cultural inertia. It may account for some of the behaviors that people too quickly assume demonstrate that human moral psychology includes an extremely strong predisposition to tribalism.

Elements of culture, including tribalistic attitudes and social practices, that first arose because they performed one function, namely, enabling cooperation that contributed to reproductive fitness, can come to have other functions and be sustained for other reasons. (Remember the shoulder joint.) One reason that we see a good deal of tribalism is that it is in the interest of some people to encourage it! We all know that it's common for leaders or would-be leaders to stoke tribalistic moral responses when doing so increases their power. For example, they can gain power by persuading people that some other group poses a grave threat and by presenting themselves as the savior who will avert the threat.

If, owing to cultural inertia, current moralities still contain significant tribalistic residues even in environments where more inclusive moralities have begun to take root, and if some people nourish these residues to advance their own interest or promote some cause they're committed to, then we will see tribalistic attitudes and behaviors. When this happens, the correct explanation will *not* be that such attitudes and behaviors are the inevitable expression of a tribalistic nature or even of a predisposition that will usually be dominant no matter what the environment is like.

There are several reasons, then, for not taking the pervasiveness of tribalistic moral beliefs and behavior either today or in the past as conclusive evidence for even the weaker thesis that human beings have a deep-seated, especially strong predisposition to tribalism—a predisposition that is so robust as to greatly limit the space of possible moralities. We need to take seriously the possibility that even if tribalistic moralities have been and still are pervasive among human beings, this may be largely a matter of environment and culture rather than biology.

The Cognitive Pathology of the Cooperation Dogma

Evolutionary thinkers have done an impressive job of explaining the origins of human morality; yet as I've already shown, by using the ambiguous terms "human morality" and "moral origins," they often haven't been as clear as they should be about the distinction between the emergence of the moral mind and the first moralities in which it was expressed. However, there may be another, less innocuous reason for most evolutionary scientists' lack of attention to the development of inclusive moralities: they've made the mistake of slipping from "morality first evolved because it facilitated cooperation" to "morality is just a type of cooperation" (that is, facilitating cooperation isn't just *a* function of morality; it's a function that fully *constitutes* morality).

If you make that slip, you'll be likely to overlook the First and Second Great Expansions. Why? Because both of these expansions of the circle of moral regard are based on the idea that whether a being counts, morally speaking, does *not* depend on whether it is even a potential partner in cooperation. If you believe that morality is only something that facilitates cooperation, you'll only focus on understanding the parts of morality that do that. That limited perspective will make you overlook the Two Great Expansions, and that in turn will blind you to the possibilities for moral progress.

The vast majority of the nonhuman animals that many people now believe have at least some minimal moral standing don't have the ability either to enter into cooperation with us or to obstruct our cooperation with each other. So the Second Great Expansion can't be explained if we limit ourselves to the idea that morality is just a type of cooperation or something that is fully constituted by the function of facilitating cooperation. The First Great Expansion, most clearly when its central idea is articulated in the concept of human rights, also makes moral regard independent of cooperation in this sense: every human is said to have certain rights simply by virtue of being human, independently of whether she can participate in cooperation of any sort. Perhaps evolutionary scientists have concentrated so intently on the first order of business, explaining the origins of human morality, that they haven't thought much about how morality, for some humans, has changed since it originated.

Explaining Descent with Modification, Not Just Origins

Understanding the origins of human moralities is important; but so is understanding how moralities evolve. Remember: you have to understand how moralities evolve if you want to understand moral progress and how to sustain it against the threat of regression—and if you want to understand the conditions that shape you as a moral agent.

The most general definition of evolution is "descent with modification." There is clear evidence that there has been descent from the first human moralities, with modification. Even if the very first moralities were highly similar, different moral communities have followed different paths as time went on, and each community's morality has changed over time, in response to new challenges. So why shouldn't evolutionary scientists try to explain moral change—especially change that is large scale and widely regarded as progressive?

If you focus only on how moralities facilitate cooperation, it may not even occur to you to try to explain how the Two Great Expansions could have transpired. In addition, if you mistake the fact that the first moralities were tribalistic for evidence that we are morally tribalistic by nature, then you will likely feel even less obliged to explain the Two Great Expansions. Even if you acknowledge their existence, you'll blithely brush them off as an unstable aberration or, as one of my primatologist friends said, an "epiphenomenon" (which is a fancy way of dismissing something as inconsequential and derivative of the stuff that really matters, not worthy of the attention of genuine scientists).

Explaining Progress Is the Key to Understanding and Stopping Regression

Those of us who believe that greater inclusion in the form of the Two Great Expansions is moral progress regard the prospect of a return to tribalism with alarm.

An especially nasty and destructive variety of tribalism is on the rise in the United States and in many other countries. This is an exceedingly dangerous development, one that imperils the hard-won progress toward deeply inclusive morality that humans have only very recently achieved. Many people think, quite reasonably, that this tribalism also poses a dire threat to democracy, because it undermines the mutual respect and genuine, sincere communication among citizens that democracy requires. Maybe if we figure out how the shift toward inclusion came about, we can learn how to halt or even reverse the deeply disturbing shift back toward tribalism.

Tribalism is not a finished product of evolution (nothing is, unless it's a trait of an organism that has gone extinct). It's still evolving. Whereas tribalistic morality among our remote ancestors involved distrust, hostility, and even preemptive aggression against people who were members of other societies, tribalism has come to take on an additional form, namely, *intra*societal tribalism: within our own society, we divide people into Us versus Them and in the most extreme cases exhibit the same negative attitudes toward Them that our ancestors exhibited toward actual foreigners.

What we need is a theory of moral progress that rests on a deeper, more general explanation of how moral change comes about, including changes that are progressive and those that are regressive. But first we need to explain how some human beings could have developed moralities that are much more inclusive than the moralities humans exhibited when they first became moral in a distinctively human way. Understanding that dramatic change will give us clues about moral change more generally.

My goal isn't to provide a complete solution to the puzzle of how beings with initially tribalistic moralities could come to have moralities that include the Two Great Expansions, but rather to make a good enough start to do two things. First, to develop a more general theory of moral change that will provide information about how to foster progress and prevent regression—that's my urgent practical aim. Second, I want to convince the best scientists, including especially evolutionary psychologists and evolutionary anthropologists, to direct their skills and energy toward solving this intriguing puzzle and in the process of doing so develop and extend the account

I'm offering of how moral change occurs. We need that knowledge if we are ever to learn how to take charge of our moral fate.

As scientists, they will scrupulously avoid talking about "progress" or "regression" because these are evaluative terms, and a scientist's job is to explain, not to evaluate. Nonetheless the Two Great Expansions, the reversion to tribalism, and more generally the phenomenon of large-scale moral change are worthy of their attention, if only because they are such fundamental changes. No evolutionary approach to morality that restricts itself to characterizing the moral mind and the features of the first moralities it spawned is truly an evolutionary account of morality, because moralities are dynamic, continuously evolving.

Strategy

My strategy is to use a detailed examination of how the Two Great Expansions occurred to gain general insights into how all forms of moral change occur, and then to use those insights to make the case for taking charge of our moral fate by constructing a theory of moral institutional design. This book can be read, then, in two quite different ways. First, if that's what interests you, you can focus on the general theory I offer to explain how large-scale changes in human moralities occur. Constructing such a theory is of the greatest practical urgency, because once you see that what kind of morality will be predominant in your society, as well as what kind of person you are likely to be, depends on specific features of the social environment, then you can't escape the conclusion that we had better find out which environments are conducive to social and individual moral progress and figure out how to produce and preserve them.

Second, if you're only interested in understanding how some members of our particular great ape species only recently developed more inclusive moralities, and in particular want to know how the Two Great Expansions came about, then you can concentrate on that part of the investigation. So even if you aren't interested in finding out what a general theory of large-scale moral change might look like or in learning the most general facts about how social environments shape our moral possibilities, you may find the particular project of explaining the shift toward inclusion that the Two Great Expansions represent interesting in its own right. You surely will, if you think those shifts toward inclusion are something humanity should be proud of—and if you're worried about their being undermined by new forms of tribalism.

Finally, I want to emphasize that when I speak of large-scale changes in human morality, I don't mean the morality of all humans; and I am not assuming that the diversity of human moralities is going to diminish, with everybody converging on a shared inclusive morality. My explanatory framework recognizes the diversity of human moralities and provides no resources for predicting any such a convergence.

1

Large-Scale Moral Change: The Shift toward Inclusive Moralities

The Late Arrival of the Concept of a Human Being

The Native American group whom most people know as Comanches called themselves "Numunuu," which is usually translated as "the human beings." (The name "Comanche" is derived from a Ute word meaning "those who fight us all the time.") In the not-so-distant past, many peoples called themselves—and only themselves—the human beings. The names that people who called themselves the human beings had for people of other groups were often rather unflattering. They frequently translate as "the enemy" or "the ones we always fight," or denote dangerous or unclean animals or inferiors of one kind or another or focus on some alleged feature of the Other, often a rather unattractive one.

If the name they gave themselves is an indication, the Numunuu confused being Numunuu with being human. They apparently didn't understand that non-Numunuu were human beings. And if they didn't understand that, then they didn't really understand who they themselves were, namely, only one group of humans among many, just one part of humanity.

Whether we should take the Numunuu's name for themselves as a clear indication of their concepts is open to dispute, but there's a big point to be made here. To put it bluntly: people who think that they are the only human beings don't really know what a human being is, and they don't appreciate the moral significance of just being human.

If that's the way the Numunuu thought, they weren't unusual. For most of human history—until quite recently, in fact—most human beings lacked the moral concept of a human being, whether their names for themselves and for others reflected that fact or not. They didn't have the idea that everyone, whether one of their own people or a member of other racial or ethnic groups, has an *equal basic moral status*, that all are equally entitled to moral consideration and respect, simply because they are human. Instead their concept of basic moral equality was tied to group membership. In contemporary terms, they didn't have the idea that we all have human rights, that we are all morally entitled to be treated in certain ways, just by virtue of our humanity.

Even today, when people who believe we are all equal in some fundamental moral sense find themselves in dire circumstances—or when propagandists convince them that they are—they may either abandon that belief or fail to behave as if they took it seriously. They "dehumanize" the Other and act accordingly. During the genocide in Rwanda in 1994, Hutus routinely referred to the Tutsis they butchered as "cockroaches." Hitler called the Jews a bacillus infecting the body of Europe. Racists refer to Africans as monkeys or baboons. President Trump speaks of the "infestation" of illegal immigrants crossing the US border with Mexico, conjuring images of nasty and potentially dangerous insects or rodents. In October 2018 a participant in the Fox network television program *Fox and Friends* said that Central American people headed for the United States carried smallpox, overlooking that this disease was officially declared eradicated worldwide in 1980 (with the last recorded lone case occurring in Somalia in 1977). Representing somebody only as the carrier of a deadly disease characterizes them solely as a threat, undermining the belief that what really matters is that they are a human being, just like us.

Tribalism dehumanizes in another way. The tribalism at work in American society today often doesn't directly or at least explicitly attribute less-than-human status to compatriots on the other side of the ideological divide. It pays lip service to their being equal citizens and may begrudgingly acknowledge that they have human rights. Nevertheless, the ideologies that drive this new form of tribalism do in a sense dehumanize: they present the Other as *beings with whom one can't reason, either because they are irremediably confused about the nature of society and what is valuable or because they are insincere (or both).*

If you think genuine human beings are amenable to reason, are reason-*able* creatures—and believe that's part of what distinguishes them from other animals—then you won't regard people you believe to be incorrigibly unreasonable as fully human. For example, when college students shout down speakers on their campus and refuse to let them speak because they've already branded them as racists and hence disgusting and not entitled to be heard, the students are in effect categorizing the speakers as creatures one needn't feel obligated to listen to and engage in reasoned disagreement with.

It's one thing to argue that hate speech is not protected by a proper understanding of freedom of expression; it's quite another to sidestep the question of whether what someone is saying really *is* hate speech by attaching the label "racist" to the speaker (especially if this is done on the basis of a dubiously expansive or inchoate notion of what racism is). When you're in the grip of tribalism, merely labeling someone as a racist (or a socialist) is enough to justify dismissing what that person says or not listening to it, much less trying to evaluate its truth or falsity. And that's especially dubious if you've never thought much about how to define racism (or socialism) in the first place.

Please note that I'm *not* assuming or in any way implying that the Numunuu or other people who lacked the moral concept of a human being were immoral. It's more accurate to say that they had a truncated, incomplete morality. They acknowledged moral duties toward members of their own group, often very demanding ones. Yet they regarded other human beings as beyond the moral pale or at least as having a much lower moral status. They were moral beings, but their morality was incomplete because they lacked the moral concept of a human being.

From the moral standpoint that I (and I expect you) occupy, this incompleteness wasn't a minor defect. A lot can go wrong in how you treat other members of our species if you don't recognize them as fellow human beings in the moral sense. You may think it is perfectly acceptable to throw them off the land they've always occupied, kill them, enslave them, cause them pain for your own amusement, hunt them for sport, or even butcher and eat them. Humans have done all these things to one another. In fact, until recently in the long history of our species, these kinds of behavior were quite common, including cannibalism. (Given that the Paleo diet probably included substantial portions of human flesh, just how committed to it are you?) So there's another way to put the point that some humans have made moral progress in the direction of greater inclusion: by becoming more inclusive, some moralities have become more moral. If regression occurs, moralities become less moral.

To fend off the inevitable charge of Eurocentrism or colonialism or ethnocentricity (or whatever your favorite bad sort of "-ism" happens to be), let me make one thing clear. To say that many humans (perhaps most humans who ever lived) have had an incomplete morality because they lacked the moral concept of a human being is *not* to say that if your morality includes that concept, it's complete or without defect. Although a morality that isn't deeply inclusive is incomplete and seriously defective, it may have a lot else going for it. I'm only focusing on one important element of morality that I (and I imagine you also) think is especially important.

The Two Great Expansions of the Circle of Moral Regard

Something has profoundly changed; a remarkable transformation has occurred. Nowadays, the idea of a common humanity, of an equal basic moral status shared by all human beings, is pretty widespread: we speak of human dignity, not just the dignity of this or that group. We talk about human rights, not just the rights of Frenchmen or Americans or Hutus or Tutsis and so on. Because it is so momentous, this shift from morality as a purely parochial, exclusive, tribalistic affair to one that is deeply inclusive merits a suitably dramatic name: the First Great Expansion. It's an expansion because it amounts to an enlargement of one's conception of who is a member of the primary moral community, the set of beings who have first-class moral status.

Most people today who acknowledge the fundamental moral equality of human beings came to have that moral orientation in the same way they received other items of cultural inheritance: they learned it through imitation of, and inculcation by, their parents and peers. Most of us didn't think it through on our own, at least not explicitly. Consequently we're not likely to notice this transformation. We take it for granted.

It's worth pausing and reflecting on just how momentous the First Great Expansion is. It makes a great difference whether you believe that all human beings are equal in some fundamental sense or whether you think—as most people did throughout most of history—that there is a natural order of superiority and inferiority. There's a funny thing about moral progress: once it has occurred, it's largely invisible and hence unappreciated. Steven Pinker's work is extremely valuable because he makes what had been invisible visible. That's the first step toward appreciation—and gratitude. I will argue that there is a second step that's just as important: understanding how much luck was involved in human beings' getting to the point where they could make that sort of progress—and how fragile that accomplishment is.

The First Great Expansion involves a radical reconfiguration of our attitudes toward human beings, all human beings. The basic idea is that all are equal at the most fundamental moral level, meaning that all are entitled to be treated in certain ways simply by virtue of their humanity, quite apart from which human group they belong to, whether they can interact with us in mutually beneficial ways, and whether they have done something to earn their being treated in those ways. A few centuries ago, the idea of the equal basic moral status of all human beings took the form of the doctrine of natural rights; today we speak of human rights. The world looks different for those who have embraced the First Great Expansion: when they identify a creature as a human being, they understand that it is their humanity that matters, at least so far as the most basic rights are concerned. Differences among human beings (race, gender, class, nationality, ethnicity, etc.) are ruled out as irrelevant.

A Second Great Expansion has also occurred: the growing recognition that not just all human beings count morally, but that at least some nonhuman animals do, too (even if they don't have the high moral status that we humans do). Extreme cruelty—gratuitous infliction of pain that was often a source of pleasure for humans, not just an unfortunate side effect of food production—has been common throughout most of human history. As the eminent historian Norman Davies documents, in Europe in the Middle Ages cat burnings were considered a wholesome form of public entertainment (Davies 1996, 543). During the same period, a popular "sport" involved nailing a cat to a post and having young men compete in how many head-buttings it took to them to kill it. Treating nonhuman animals in such ways is now considered by many people—many more than ever before in human history—to be grossly immoral. That's a large-scale change in the moralities of some humans. It amounts to the recognition that at least some nonhuman animals are not mere things—objects that we can use for our own purposes, without moral constraints of any kind. For those who have embraced the Second Great Expansion, the world looks radically different: the line between mere things and beings that count morally in their own right has shifted dramatically.

The First Great Expansion enlarges the pool of humans considered to be first-class members of the moral community. The second enlarges the class of beings that count morally at all.

The Second Great Expansion, like the first, is incomplete. I'd say it's barely begun. Even today a town in Indonesia holds an annual "barbecue" festival where kittens are bludgeoned to death, roasted with blowtorches, and then eaten. Cockfighting and dog fighting—both of which result in the death of the "contestants"—still occur in the United States, though both "sports" are now illegal there and in many other countries. Furthermore, even though some corporations have yielded to pressure and made their methods of killing food animals and the conditions under which they are raised less brutal, the total *quantity* of suffering that humans inflict on animals is probably much greater today than ever before, because of the sheer scale of factory farming.

This book addresses not only why the Two Great Expansions have occurred for some of humans, but also why they haven't become universal. It also explains why, where they have occurred, they have been late arrivals—and why they are fragile, alarmingly subject to regression.

Admitting that the Two Great Expansions aren't universal and are only imperfectly acted on even where they have occurred isn't the same as saying they are insignificant, much less that they are merely different ways of thinking, rather than huge behavioral shifts. Many human beings, as individuals and through collective action in their political life, *live* both the idea that every human has an equal basic moral status and the idea that at least some nonhuman animals count morally in their own right.

So far, the most fully articulated and institutionally embodied expression of the First Great Expansion is the culture of human rights. It shapes the legal systems, including the constitutions, of many countries around the world, and scholars have documented that the culture of human rights is now a significant force in international relations, even though sheer power still often determines important outcomes in many instances. Massively expensive efforts by international organizations and global nongovernmental organizations are undertaken in the name of human rights, and sometimes they actually have significant effects, so one can't dismiss human rights as being merely aspirational (Sikkink 2012, 17; Simmons 2009, 3). As impressive as the cultural and institutional impact of the modern idea of human rights is, however, it's important to remember that it is only one way, not the only way, in which the idea of basic moral equality has been worked out or can be worked out. As I'll explain later, people still disagree about what exactly counts as equal basic status and about what properties of a being make it appropriate to ascribe equal basic moral status to it. Nonetheless, the First Great Expansion is a fact, and it's a case of large-scale moral change.

Similarly, the Second Great Expansion, sometimes called animal liberation, is also more than just a change in language or thinking. Many countries, at all levels of government, now have laws that curb some of the practices that cause extreme suffering in animals, and governments often expend a great deal of money and other resources to try to enforce those laws. Just ask any scientist who works with laboratory animals how much more complicated and costly her work is than it was a generation ago. Scientists in most countries that are at the forefront of medical research must take great care in how they treat lab animals, even those used in experiments designed to discover cures for diseases that inflict great suffering and early death on human beings. Powerful corporations, including McDonald's and Walmart, have found it necessary to change the way they operate in response to pressures from individuals and organizations that are convinced that cows, chickens, and pigs are not mere things.

The Big Puzzle

How did these two seismic shifts in moral orientation come about? What makes the question so interesting is that behind it lies what I'll call the Big Puzzle: given what evolutionary theorists tell us about how human morality originated in the remote past, how could it have become deeply inclusive? *How could creatures like us, organisms who evolved in the way we did, ever come to embrace the Two Great Expansions?*

That puzzle appears large because, according to a standard evolutionary explanation of how human morality came to be, one would expect it to be purely parochial, exclusive, tribalistic, not at all inclusive. One would expect all humans to lack the moral concept of a human being and all that goes with it, and expect that no one would ever have come to believe that nonhuman animals count morally in their own right. It would seem even more preposterous that humans would ever come to limit the pursuit of their most vital self-interest for the sake of nonhuman animals used in vital medical research. Evolutionary accounts of human "moral origins" (with some difficulty) explain altruism toward nonkin humans; but they seem to be at a complete loss when it comes to explaining altruism toward nonhuman animals.

Later I'll have much more to say about what exactly the standard evolutionary view of the origins of morality is, but for now a short summary will suffice. According to the standard view, morality is an adaptation (in the proper, Darwinian sense): something that first arose and then spread because it contributed to reproductive fitness. How did it contribute to our reproductive fitness? By facilitating cooperation *within* human groups—including cooperation that allowed a group to compete successfully with other groups.

Morality as an Adaptation

In the standard evolutionary account, human morality came to be because it performed certain functions—managing conflicts, coordinating behavior, reducing free riding, dealing with the problem of how to share scarce resources, regulating sexual behavior—that facilitated successful cooperation *within the group*. And by facilitating successful cooperation, morality enabled humans to pass on their genes to the next generations, as well as to reproduce their cultural practices and traditions. In brief, morality, when it first appeared among our remote ancestors, was all about cooperation, cooperation that contributed to reproductive fitness.

The striking thing about this evolutionary understanding of morality is that it leaves members of other groups, as well as non-human animals, out of the moral picture. Given the standard evolutionary account of the origins of human morality, you wouldn't expect human beings to be capable of inclusive morality, of believing and acting as if they believed that the moral community includes all humans and at least some animals, not just members of their own group, and that all humans have the same high basic moral status.

A Nonsolution to the Big Puzzle

Let me forestall a quick solution to the Big Puzzle that you might be tempted to offer—a solution that, if correct, would warrant tossing this book aside right now. You might think that the view that morality is all about cooperation is correct and that it can explain how the circle of moral regard gets expanded, namely, by expanding cooperation to include more participants. In other words, you might think that we now recognize the basic moral equality of all other human beings because, through cultural innovations over the centuries, we have expanded the circle of cooperation. After all, it's frequently said that we are all linked together now in a global economy. If morality is just an evolved device for facilitating cooperation, then as more people are included in cooperation, then the moral circle will expand to include them.

That explanation doesn't work. Most obviously, it doesn't explain the Second Great Expansion, the fact that many people now recognize that some nonhuman animals have moral standing—that they count morally in their own right—even though they aren't and never will be participants in our cooperative schemes. The idea that morality is all about relations among cooperators might explain why, if you happen to be a shepherd, you might think you ought to treat your sheepdog reasonably well; but it can't explain why you think you shouldn't consume factory-raised poultry. In fact, it can't even explain why you would believe you shouldn't burn cats—who are notoriously noncooperative—if doing so gives you pleasure. It also can't explain why human beings to whom we are not bound by sympathy based on kinship or close association, and who are so severely disabled that they can't participate in our cooperative schemes, are nevertheless now widely regarded as having the same basic human rights as those who can participate in cooperation and those we happen to be attached to.

In addition, the fact that human cooperative networks are now global does nothing to explain why some (though not enough) of the world's most fortunate people try to alleviate the deprivations of distant strangers with whom they will never interact at all, much less cooperate. Nor can it explain why anyone would come to believe that they should try to include those people in the cooperative schemes they participate in when they don't really need to, rather than excluding them from cooperative arrangements altogether or dictating terms of "cooperation" that deny them anything approaching basic equal moral status. In chapter 3, I'll have a lot more to say about why the expansion of cooperation doesn't explain the enlargement of moral regard represented by the Two Great Expansions.

The Puzzle Deepens

It's not just that evolutionary thinkers, by focusing on the origins of morality, haven't tried to solve the Big Puzzle (or even acknowledged that it needs to be solved). In addition, some of the best work by evolutionary developmental psychologists, including Tomasello and the creative students he has nurtured, actually makes the Big Puzzle bigger. That work emphasizes that very young children tend to learn whom to cooperate with—and to do so in a way that demonstrates moral values like fairness—by noticing certain resemblances between themselves and others. Even children as young as four months interact morally and cooperatively with individuals who are like themselves in terms of ethnicity, language, and dress, but not with people who don't resemble them in these ways (Tomasello 2016, 94).

These criteria for partner choice make sense, because whether someone is like you in those ways may be a fairly accurate predictor of whether they will be enough like you in their beliefs and values to make mutually beneficial cooperation with them work. Also, the more someone is like you, the more experience you will have had with people like them, and the more likely it is that you'll be able to predict whether they are genuine cooperators or free riders, whether they'll abide by simple rules of reciprocity.

Yet it's clear that the resemblances that Tomasello's cadre and other theorists of moral learning have identified do *not* provide a reliable guide when it comes to knowing whether someone who is quite different from you could be a valuable cooperative partner. More importantly, the fact that humans rely on those resemblances to determine who would make a reliable partner in cooperation does nothing to explain why a lot of people nowadays would ever have come to believe that other individuals are worthy of basic moral respect *regardless of whether we do or ever will cooperate with them.*

On the contrary, relying on those sorts of resemblances can lead us to conclude that the Other is not worthy of respect. That's how racist cues (like skin tone and hair texture) work to promote tribalistic morality, rather than overcome it. So this kind of valuable scientific work on how children become moral cooperators doesn't solve the Big Puzzle; *it deepens the puzzlement.* That fact should make one wonder whether there is something very wrong about trying to understand the Two Great Expansions as progress in *cooperation.* More fundamentally, it should make one wonder whether morality is really just about what makes cooperation work, whether it is really nothing more than a device for successful cooperation. Maybe morality now, for some people, is more than that, even if that's all it was originally.

Morality Is More Than What It Originally Was

Many traits, across the whole range of organisms, came about because they helped the organism do something that promoted its reproductive fitness. However, these traits can also produce other results, including reductions in fitness. The philosopher Stephen Stich gives a striking example: the frog's lightning-fast, elongated tongue may have evolved to enable it to catch insects and to gobble up their small round eggs, because that enhanced its reproductive fitness. But some frogs have been observed to flick out their tongues to grab and swallow BBs (small round lead pellets fired from air guns and shotguns)—and that's not good for them.

Evolutionary science offers lots of other examples of items that evolved to do one thing but are capable of doing a lot more. These include human genitalia, which evolved to enable reproduction but are now employed for a wide range of activities that have nothing to do with generating new human beings (including, in the case of some edgy conceptual artists, using them to paint pictures). Similarly, the cognitive architecture of the human brain evolved to be what it is because it enhanced our reproductive fitness by helping us solve problems in the ancestral environment that we needed to solve to survive; but now it can be used to construct astrophysical theories, write symphonies, and play video games.

If you confuse the statement that the moral mind came about because it facilitated cooperation (and thereby enhanced reproductive fitness) with the statement that everything of importance about human morality can be explained by showing that it facilitates cooperation, you'll be making a huge mistake. More specifically, you won't be able to explain the Two Great Expansions by trying to show that people whose moralities include those enlargements of the circle of moral regard have an advantage in cooperation. If you make the mistake of thinking that, because the basic elements of human moral psychology are an adaptation for cooperation, everything about human morality can be explained by showing how it contributes to cooperation, then you'll be blind to the possibility that some features of the moralities of some human beings require a different kind of explanation. You won't be in a good position to explain significant moral change that isn't just a change in the solutions that morality offers for cooperation problems. And you won't be alive to the urgent question of whether your society is moving forward or backward, morally speaking, when it comes to inclusion versus exclusion.

Here's another reason to be careful not to slide from "moralities came to be because they facilitated cooperation" to "morality is a type of cooperation" or "morality is all about cooperation." Some moralities, including ancient Stoic morality and most forms of Buddhism, encompass ideals of individual excellence that have nothing to do with cooperation. In fact, some moralities actually advocate withdrawing entirely from cooperation, presenting the life of the meditative hermit as the ideal of moral excellence. If the die-hard cooperation dogmatist replies "Oh well, but those aren't really moralities," he'll have to justify that claim without indulging in definitional tricks and circular reasoning. It won't do to say that genuine moralities are all about cooperation, and that hence Stoicism and the like aren't moralities, because that just assumes precisely what is at issue.

Cautious Darwinianism

My goal is to take human biological evolution seriously, without being a biological determinist. To do so, I'll have to give both culture and biology their due in the story of how some moralities became more inclusive. My explanatory framework for large-scale moral change will assign a significant role to biological evolution—but only up to a certain point, the point at which the moral mind emerges. After that, understanding the interplay between the evolved flexibility of the moral mind and cumulative culture becomes the main resource for explaining large-scale moral change.

The trick is to show how "descent with modification" has occurred in human moralities despite the fact that the basic features of human moral psychology that together constitute the moral mind have probably not changed much, if at all. Let me rephrase: the trick is to show how the features of the moral mind, *combined with our capacity for niche construction*, explain *why* human moralities change, and more specifically why certain large-scale changes have occurred. The specific explanatory task, which I'll use to make some more general points about how to explain moral change in a wider range of cases, is to provide an account of how the same moral mind that produced tribalistic moralities under the selective pressures of the earliest environments has only very recently been expressed in more inclusive moralities.

An Overview of the Investigation

This chapter has added detail to my initial description of the Two Great Expansions and shown why appreciating these amazing transformations—and, more generally, understanding moral change—requires getting the evolutionary science about "moral origins" right. In chapter 2, I set out, in the needed detail, the standard attempt to understand human morality in evolutionary terms, listing the main features of what evolutionary thinkers call the Environment of Evolutionary Adaptation (EEA), the set of ancient conditions that created the pressures of natural selection that forged both the moral mind and the first distinctively human moralities.

Notice that I just said "that forged distinctively human moralities" (plural), not "that forged a distinctively human morality" (singular). Most evolutionary scientists and nonscientists who take evolutionary theory seriously refer to the origins of human morality, not moralities in which it was expressed. That's not good, for two reasons. First, it's pretty likely that a distinctively human kind of morality didn't develop in just one early human group and then spread to all others. On the contrary, that new kind of morality probably originated in a plurality of human groups. And we have every reason to believe that these original moralities were not identical; they surely varied, depending on features of the local environment in which they developed. That's one reason to talk about the origin of human moralities, rather than human morality.

Even if you assume that there was one original human morality, a second reason still applies: if you refer to human moralities,
you'll avoid the ambiguity of the term "morality," which can refer
either to the moral mind or to some morality or moralities in which
the moral mind is expressed. In other words, using the phrase "the
origins of human morality" or "moral origins" encourages the confusion I've shown must be avoided: the confusion between the character of the moral mind and the character of the moralities it initially
underwrote.

Chapter 2 explains exactly how the standard evolutionary
"moral origins" story set out in chapter 1 generates the Big Puzzle, the apparent inconsistency between our supposedly tribalistic
moral nature and the Two Great Expansions. Chapter 3 canvasses
some contemporary attempts to explain moral change in the direction of inclusion and shows why they don't succeed. Chapter 4 goes
back to square one, providing a revisionist account of the origins
of human moralities in the EEA, the environment in which distinctively human moralities supposedly first appeared.

This revisionist account doesn't so much solve the Big Puzzle as
begin to dissolve it. I argue that it is likely that there wasn't just one
EEA; there were variations in the early ancestral environment, and
these variations fostered a special kind of flexibility: the ability to
respond to strangers in tribalistic ways when that kind of response
was required for reproductive fitness, but in inclusive ways when
being inclusive was conducive to fitness.

The key to understanding how the character of morality can vary
depending on features of the environment is to appreciate the connections between (1) the distinctively human capacity for cumulative
culture and three other important human traits: (2) the impressive
flexibility of moral sentiments, beliefs, and behaviors in response to
environmental changes that the moral mind allows, in particular the
ability to extend sympathy to "strangers" and at least some nonhuman animals; (3) the capacity for niche construction (the ability to
create new environments in which we are subject to new pressures
for natural selection and in which different potential moralities can
be realized); and (4) moral identity (the powerful motivation to convince others and ourselves that you take moral norms seriously,

which you have to do if you're to be regarded as a reliable partner in cooperation). Working together, these four features explain how human beings became supercooperators—a species whose capacity for cooperation is much more robust and flexible than that of any other species.

Chapter 5 explains these four features, describes how they work together, and begins the task of developing an explanatory framework for large-scale moral change, something that is essential if we are to understand how moral progress can come about and how it can be protected from regression. Focusing on the relationship between the flexibility of human moral responses and the cumulative cultural capacity for niche construction, I show how humans first made the transition from exclusive, purely tribalistic moralities to *shallowly inclusive moralities*, moralities that facilitate cooperation with people of different ethnic or cultural groups and extend to them the *limited* sort of moral regard that such cooperation requires.

Shallowly inclusive moralities fall short of the *deep inclusion* manifested in the Two Great Expansions, but they take a necessary step in that direction. The basic idea of chapter 5 is that, through cumulative cultural innovations, human beings constructed new niches in which they could *afford* to develop more inclusive moral beliefs, concepts, rules, and attitudes—environments in which extending limited moral regard to strangers no longer risked reproductive suicide. I also show how having a shallowly inclusive morality actually is highly beneficial, in both social and reproductive terms, again in certain environments. The fundamental message here is that a human being who is capable of both exclusive morality and shallowly inclusive morality is more adaptable than one who can only respond morally in an exclusive, thoroughly tribalistic way.

Chapter 6 fills out the solution to the Big Puzzle by developing in more detail what cognitive capacities, motivations, and social conditions are required for people to incorporate the Two Great Expansions into their moral orientation, to go beyond shallowly inclusive to deeply inclusive moralities. Here I focus a good deal of attention on two remarkable human traits that most likely were necessary for the radical moral reorientation that the Two Great Expansions represent: the capacity for critical, open-ended moral reasoning and the powerful motivating force of moral identity. Critical, open-ended moral reasoning is crucially important for moral change because it enables us to challenge the moral status quo. Moral identity is crucial because it can give us the courage to exercise our capacity for critical, open-ended moral reasoning and act on the results.

In this sixth chapter, I also explore the question of whether we can provide an evolutionary explanation of the existence of the capacity for critical, open-ended moral reasoning and, more important, whether there is an evolutionary explanation of its coming to be exercised by some human beings in a way that leads to a profound rethinking of which beings have moral standing and which have the highest, equal moral status. In addition, I explain why anybody would be *motivated* to exercise the capacity for critical, open-ended moral reasoning in a way that leads toward the Two Great Expansions. The answer to this question is that the source of the needed moral motivation is moral identity: the robust motivation to be, and to be regarded by others as, moral.

There's a rather broad consensus among evolutionary scientists that the powerful motivation to sustain moral identity evolved because it was vital for the kind of cooperation that only humans engage in—and for the reproductive success of individual humans, whose survival depended on their being regarded by their fellows as desirable and reliable partners in cooperation. Under the right conditions—in the new niches that humans constructed using their capacity for cumulative culture—the motivational power of moral identity could and did lead some human beings toward the Two Great Expansions.

Chapter 7 examines regression to tribalistic, exclusive moralities. Given the increases in racism and xenophobia revealed by recent elections and public political discourse in the United States and much of Europe, this is a topic of more than theoretical interest. I argue that the key idea to understanding regression to tribalism is this: if people actually find themselves in conditions that are like the elements of the EEA that were hostile to inclusive morality—*or if they become convinced that they are in those conditions even when they aren't*—they tend to revert to tribalistic moral thinking and behavior.

Chapter 8 shows how tribalistic moral thinking and behavior have evolved since their earliest manifestations: how creatures who previously often excluded from full moral status only actual strangers—members of other societies—have come to practice elaborate forms of "intrasocietal tribalism," relegating other groups *within their own society* to an inferior status. This happened in slave societies and caste systems, but it also in the United States and other liberal constitutional democracies like Canada, Sweden, and Denmark during the era of eugenics, when certain members of society were ruthlessly segregated and subjected to forcible sterilization because they were thought to harbor defective genes that were responsible for all major social problems. Another, more recent American example of intrasocietal tribalism is the hysteria during the early 1990s over the threat posed by an allegedly distinct class of urban African American men dubbed "super predators"—a term that evokes primal EEA-like fears if there ever was one. Today's deep division of American society between "liberals" and "conservatives" is also a form of intrasocietal tribalism.

Chapter 8's account of the evolution of modes of intrasocietal tribalism relies on the same evolutionary story that chapters 1 and 2 told to explain why our remote ancestors often exhibited exclusive moral attitudes toward members of other societies. But it adds something new and important: it shows how *ideology*, a more recent cultural phenomenon, though one that is grounded in our original evolved moral nature, makes this new kind of tribalism work—and why it is so hard to stop it. In chapter 9, the book's final chapter, I sum up the main conclusions of my investigation, including several quite general insights about the possibilities for large-scale moral change that the detailed examination of the Two Great Expansions has yielded. Here I also offer guidance for how to resist tribalistic regression, focusing on the key role of institutions in determining whether the social environment is friendly to inclusion or to tribalism. Most importantly, I make the case for taking seriously the fact that how the human environment is shaped—and by whom—determines what sort of morality will be dominant in a society and whether individuals will be progressive moral agents or stunted specimens of what they could have been.

If I'm right that, given the flexibility of the moral mind and the cumulative cultural capacity for niche construction, the space of possible human moralities is quite large, there is good news and bad news. The good news is that we are not morally tribalistic by nature: whether tribalistic moralities dominate depends on what sort of niches we create for ourselves. The possibilities not just for moral change but for moral progress may be so great that we can't even imagine them.

The bad news is that it's misleading to say that *we* construct the niches whose character determines the possibilities for human morality. The process of niche construction is far from democratic. The sobering fact is that some people—a very small proportion of the human population—exert disproportionate influence over the character of the niches that humans now occupy, because power is distributed extremely unevenly among human beings. The powerful few wield disproportionate influence over what sorts of moralities are likely to be dominant and over what sorts of moral agents we are likely to be. The problem of domination that the earliest human societies had to solve was simple: how could the group control bullies who were physically aggressive toward other members of the group and hogged resources? In modern societies, the problem of curbing domination is more complex because new, more complex forms of domination have evolved through cultural processes. (In fact, one could interpret human history as a coevolutionary arms race between modes of domination and modes of counterdomination, an idea that's the object of my current research.) One crucial aspect of the modern problem of how to suppress domination has gone unnoticed: how can we develop institutions that prevent some people from shaping the moral environment in ways that prevent us from being as good as our moral minds make us capable of being?

It's a pretty safe bet that most of the people who wield the most power over niche construction aren't guided by any thoughts about how the niches they construct will influence the character of human moralities. On the contrary, their aims and motivations for wielding that power are typically shortsighted, often self-interested, and utterly uninformed by any scientific understanding of how the moral mind expresses itself differently in different environments.

While some hierarchy, some inequality in power—if it is multiple, and the various hierarchies are independent of one another—may actually be necessary for moral progress, as I'll argue later, hierarchy also carries a great risk. If hierarchies enable some people to shape the moral environment in ways that make it hostile to inclusion or other forms of moral improvement, then inequality will hinder moral progress and create a risk of regression.

If my explanation of large-scale moral change turns out to be valid, it won't be correct to say, as many people do, that culture enables humans to "stretch the evolutionary leash" of a fundamentally tribalistic human moral psychology. Instead, the right conclusion will be that our flexible moral mind, when combined with our capacity for cumulative culture and the ongoing niche construction that it facilitates, enables us to be *both* tribalistic and exclusive, depending on the human-made niches we occupy. In other words, some human beings have developed inclusive moralities, not *in spite of* our evolved moral psychology, but *because of it*—in particular, because of its flexibility in the face of different environments. If one wants to speak of human moral nature, one should say that it is dualistic, encompassing the potential for both inclusive and exclusive moralities.

This book, then, is a detective story. Like any good detective story, it starts with a mystery to solve, the Big Puzzle: how could creatures whose first moralities were tribalistic come to have deeply inclusive moralities? As in any good detective story, the route to solving the mystery will include false leads, dead ends, and flashes of insight that occur only when we question the assumptions that originally framed our understanding of the mystery itself. Solving (or dissolving) the mystery will take a great deal of effort on my part and considerable patience on yours, but it will be worthwhile, because solving it is vitally important—assuming that we care about what it means to be human, about what it is to be moral, and about what the prospects for human moralities are.

Anyone who is curious about what human beings are and how they got that way should find my detective story interesting—if I can tell it in a sufficiently engaging way and convince you that my beginning of a solution makes sense. This is a detective story about you and me, not just about some abstraction called *Homo sapiens*. Morality is not something that is out there and with which we engage while remaining the same. It isn't an alien force that constrains us from without; it lies at the core of our being. Our morality in large part determines who we are. And—though unwittingly and utterly without design—we have determined what our moralities, and hence ourselves, are like, by determining what sort of social environment we live in.

As the detective story unfolds, it will become clearer just what I mean by "tribalistic moralities." But to avoid a misunderstanding that could abort the investigation before it even gets started, let me say right now what I *don't* mean by that phrase. I *don't* mean just any morality that includes a prominent role for group-based identity. For reasons that I'll explain later, I think that humans generally have a strong desire, indeed a need, for identity, for a sense of who they are, and that an important element of identity, for practically everyone, is a perception of oneself as belonging to a group (usually more than one). The question I focus on in this book is not "how could we have evolved to attach so much importance to the group-membership aspect of our identity?" though I think that question is profoundly interesting. Instead, I home in on a particular kind of group-membership identity, one that involves a serious kind of moral exclusion of the Other.

Many, perhaps all, kinds of group-membership-based identities not only involve a distinction between Us and Others but also tend to regard Us as superior in some respect. That's not what I mean by "tribalistic moralities." The kind of group-membership identity I target goes beyond that. It represents the Other in such negative terms that it becomes an obstacle to achieving the First Great Expansion.

What Tribalism Is and Isn't

A pair of concrete examples will clarify what I mean and don't mean by "tribalistic moralities." If you think that in general the francophone Swiss are more cultured or nicer than Swiss people whose primary language is German, that doesn't mean you have a "tribalistic morality" (though it probably does mean you're a francophone Swiss). Thinking that foreigners suspected of terrorism may justifiably be tortured because they aren't Americans and hence aren't morally entitled to the legal protections of the US Constitution does show that your morality is tribalistic. That kind of thinking means that you have not yet made the First Great Expansion, or you've regressed from it, because it implicitly denies that foreigners suspected of terrorism have fundamental human rights and assumes that the only question is whether they have the particular legal rights that are specified in the Constitution. People who think like that just don't get the idea of *human* rights, or their moral reasoning in this case displays a pretty gross inconsistency. Perhaps their fear in the wake of 9/11 or other terrorist attacks has disabled their ability to apply the idea of human rights consistently in the case at hand.

As I noted in the preface, there are somewhat less extreme forms of tribalism than those that deny that members of some other groups have even the most basic human rights (including the right not to be tortured). But the most extreme and milder forms of tribalism share certain common features: the tendency to clump individuals and issues, the tendency to think in grossly simplified, black-and-white terms, and the assumption that we are in a winner-take-all struggle for the highest stakes in which compromise is not an option because of the degenerate character of our opponents and the momentous moral disagreements that divide us from them.

Given our evolved nature, I don't think it's feasible or desirable to disregard group-membership identity or to try to prevent it from playing a significant role in morality. Yet I think that reducing the power of the particular kind of group-membership identity that I call "tribalistic morality" is an extremely important undertaking, and achieving this goal is an especially significant kind of moral progress.

Before we plunge into the investigation, a disclaimer and a plea for tolerance are in order. The disclaimer is that I am not providing a thoroughly scientific theory. Much of what I'll say in developing a solution to the Big Puzzle will be speculative. That's not surprising, given that scientific thinking about the evolution of morality is new and quite undeveloped—and that it hasn't yet extended to grappling with the Big Puzzle, because it has been restricted to the origins of moralities, not their ongoing evolution. So my attempt to solve that mystery won't be "hard" science by a long shot.

Nevertheless, it is worth emphasizing that in the early stages of any line of research there is a legitimate role for speculation—a larger role than when considerable progress has been made. Speculation in the early stages is acceptable and even necessary, but only if it is responsible. That means two things: first, it must be consistent with the best existing theories that are relevant to its subject matter; and second, it must be liable, eventually, to being disconfirmed or confirmed by solid empirical research. I believe my thinking satisfies those criteria. If I'm right, then my speculations merit your tolerance.

2

The Big Puzzle: How Could a Tribalistic Great Ape Species Ever Develop Inclusive Moralities?

Origins Stories Old and New

According to Navajo tradition, their own tribe and all others were late arrivals in the complicated process of creation, which involved at least four distinct worlds, one appearing after the other. According to the creation story contemporary Christian fundamentalists endorse, God didn't begin with human beings, either. Yet even when creation stories don't say that things started with human beings, they typically reserve a special place for them, at least for those human beings who are thought to be ancestors of the particular group whose creation story it is. Traditional creation stories that give a special place to the first appearance of human beings typically highlight how they differ from other creatures.

Evolutionary creation stories are no different: they present the first appearance of human beings as a late development in the history of life on planet Earth, and they attempt to explain how we differ from other creatures that were forged by evolutionary forces and with whom we share a common ancestor. Evolutionary scientists think that a big part of what is distinctive about humans is that they have a robust, complex morality. So it's no surprise that their creation story includes an account of how our particular branch of the primate tree became the peculiarly moral creatures we are.

Why the Origins of Human Moralities Matter

What if you aren't an evolutionary scientist; why should *you* take seriously the idea that morality is the kind of thing that is apt for evolutionary explanation? I've already given one reason: if you want to understand tribalism to combat it effectively, and if you recognize that tribalism is a kind of morality, then you should want to find out what science has to say about human morality, and that will include exploring what evolutionary scientists who study "moral origins" can tell us.

There are several other good reasons. First, the tiny minority of sociopaths aside, morality is ubiquitous among human beings and as far as we know always has been; but no other creatures on our planet, including our nearest primate relatives, have anything approaching a morality that is as complex and powerful as ours. So we need an explanation of why, even though we share a common ancestor with chimps and bonobos, we came to have the sort of moralities we have and they lack. Unless you believe in a special creation by some supernatural being or in some other creation story that denies that common primate ancestry, the explanation of the difference would have to be an evolutionary explanation: as Darwin puts it, a story of "descent [from a common ancestor] with modification" (Darwin 2003, 335).

Second, as I've already noted, what distinguishes human beings from all other living creatures is that we are *supercooperators* and, unlike social insects, highly flexible cooperators who are constantly and rapidly developing new, more complex forms of cooperation. In his intriguing and instructive book *The Secret of Our Success: How Culture Is Driving Human Evolution, Domesticating Our Species, and Making Us Smarter*, the star cultural evolutionary theorist Joseph Henrich emphasizes that we have outcompeted all other species because we are supercooperators (Henrich 2015, 11). The fact that we alone are supercooperators cries out for an explanation.

Henrich emphasizes that we are highly flexible cooperators because we have *cumulative culture*—which I defined earlier as the ability to pass on information, ideas, skills, techniques, and technologies across the generations and to continue to combine and recombine them and build on them in new ways. So far as we know, no other animals have cumulative culture.

Our being flexible supercooperators depends crucially on one central aspect of our cumulative culture: morality. To be supercooperators, we have to be able to regulate our interactions with one another according to moral rules, to have moral motivations (sympathy, a sense of fairness, and indignation or disgust when people violate moral rules), and we have to be able to apply moral rules to new situations, which requires moral judgment and moral reasoning. In their brilliant book *A Cooperative Species*, cultural evolutionary theorists Samuel Bowles and Herbert Gintis show that, without morality of that rich sort, we couldn't coordinate with one another in the flexible, highly complicated ways that make us supercooperators (Bowles and Gintis 2013, 3–4).

A moment's reflection makes it clear that virtually all human cooperation—unless it's based solely on some people forcibly dominating others, an extremely anemic sort of "cooperation," if you can call it that—requires all or at least most participants in cooperation to act morally to some extent. Successful cooperation requires that cooperators restrain the pursuit of their own self-interest, do their allotted share of the needed work rather than shirking, defer immediate gratification for the sake of achieving common goals that take time to achieve, and be willing to bear some costs in helping ensure that the rules are followed, where this can include punishing violators.

Successful cooperation of the sort that humans engage in requires *reliable partner choice*, the ability to decide whom to cooperate with. Individuals must be able both to discern who is a reliable potential partner in cooperation and to signal to others that they are themselves reliable partners. Across a wide range of environments, both of these skills are conducive to an individual's reproductive fitness: if you are good at choosing reliable partners in cooperation, then you will thrive or at least survive; if you are not, you'll be exploited by free riders or fail to achieve the goals of cooperation because your partner isn't up to making his contribution to cooperation. If you're good at signaling to others that you are a reliable partner, you'll be included in their cooperative endeavors and reap a share of the benefits; if you fail to convince others you are reliable, you'll be shunned, excluded from cooperation and the benefits it yields.

Evolutionary thinkers have recently argued—persuasively, in my opinion—that much of our basic moral psychology came to be because of its contribution to solving the problems of reliable partner choice, reliable partner signaling, and partner control (to make sure our partners don't lapse into free riding or try to dominate us, taking more than their share of what we produce together). Choosing reliable partners requires ascertaining whether they are committed to following moral rules, and signaling that you are a reliable partner requires convincing others that you do so. That means convincing them that you're moral.

Being Supercooperators Makes Us Distinctive; Moralities Make Us Supercooperators

So if you want to understand why humans are supercooperators, so good at cooperation that they have come to dominate the planet, you need to understand why humans came to have the rich sort of moralities that they alone possess. And to do that, you need to understand why and how such moralities came into existence among us and not among other creatures, including those with whom we share a common, fairly recent primate ancestor. In other words, you need an *evolutionary* explanation of the origins of human moralities. And if you also think, quite reasonably, that the evolutionary origins of things have some implications for what moralities are like, then you'll also assume that studying the evolutionary beginnings of morality can tell us something important about moralities as they exist today and even about what they might become in the future (Joyce 2006, 222–230).

We have another reason to try to discover the evolutionary origins of human moralities: the moral mind appears to be an *adaptation* (or a collection of adaptations). An adaptation is a trait that arose because it solved some problem and thereby enhanced reproductive fitness. The main way to explain something in evolutionary terms is to show that it is an adaptation. To understand what the problems were that led to the emergence of the moral mind and how human moralities solved them, we need to identify the key features of the ancient environment that created the problems that moralities helped solve. Evolutionary theorists call that the Environment of Evolutionary Adaptation, or EEA for short.

Before considering what the EEA was supposedly like, I want to emphasize a simple point: to say that something is an adaptation is to make a purely retrospective statement about it. A trait is an adaptation if and only if it *came to exist* in a species because it contributed to reproductive fitness, that is, its existence contributed to genes being passed on to the next generation (Lewontin 1978, 213, 215). Traits contribute to reproductive fitness by performing certain functions—by doing things that need to be done if the organism in question is to survive long enough to reproduce and pass on its genes.

Note that the statement "X is an adaptation" (though it's framed in the indicative mode) is purely backward looking, a fact about the history of some species. The fact that a trait came to exist because at some point it performed a function that contributed to reproductive fitness has no implications whatsoever about whether that trait is *now* performing that function or any function that contributes to reproductive fitness. To the contrary, that trait, even though it "is" an adaptation, may *now* be reducing reproductive fitness. That would be the case, for example, if the environment in which the trait first arose was quite different from the one in which the species now finds itself.

All of this may sound like nit-picking, but it is vitally important for understanding evolution, including the evolution of human moralities. Why? Because even if moralities are adaptations—more specifically, even if they originally came to exist because they performed the function of facilitating cooperation in early human groups in ways that contributed to reproductive fitness—this is perfectly compatible with moralities no longer being limited to that function. What is more, the idea that moralities first came to exist because they contributed to reproductive fitness by facilitating cooperation in early human groups is also perfectly compatible with some features of current moralities actually reducing reproductive fitness or being "fitness neutral"—neither increasing nor decreasing fitness. Why? Because once humans have created environments in which they have solved the basic problems of survival—once they achieve surplus reproductive fitness—they can afford to act in ways that aren't maximally conducive to reproductive fitness. More specifically, they can afford to develop moralities that are more than just cooperation facilitators.

Avoiding Mistakes about What "Morality Is an Adaptation" Means

My main point in clarifying the notion of an adaptation is to avoid two serious mistakes: first, failing to see that to say that something is an adaptation is a strictly backward-looking statement, an assertion about why it came to be at some point in the past, not a statement about what it's doing now; second, wrongly assuming that if something now performs a function, then knowing how it performs that function suffices to explain everything about it. The first error is pretty obvious: it's just a matter of being fooled by the indicative mode of the phrase "is an adaptation." The second is subtle. We make it when we fail to see that things can come to exist for all sorts of reasons, and that even in the cases where they first appeared because they performed a particular function, they can later come to perform other functions or to have effects that aren't best described as performing functions at all.

Avoiding the second error is especially important for what I'm trying to do in this book. I want to argue that even if moralities first came to exist among humans because they performed the function of facilitating cooperation, and even if moralities still perform that function, understanding how they perform that function will not suffice for fully understanding human moralities—in particular, for understanding certain crucial aspects of some moralities as they are now, including their incorporation of the Two Great Expansions.

The Mistake of Hyperfunctionalism

One more error that people who try to think in evolutionary terms sometimes make is to commit the sin of hyperfunctionalism. This amounts to assuming not only that everything in nature has a function but also that the only adequate explanation of anything in nature is one that identifies the thing as having a function. The evolutionary version of hyperfunctionalism is to think that everything has a function that contributes to reproductive fitness, and that the best—indeed, the only satisfying—explanation of anything is to show that it has a function that contributes to reproductive fitness.

Although nowadays it's usually dressed up in evolutionary togs, hyperfunctionalist thinking predates the Darwinian revolution. In fact, it is a kind of archaic teleological thinking to which humans seem naturally disposed, even though it should and can be resisted. It may well be a kind of anthropomorphic projection onto nature. As human beings, we like to think of ourselves as purposeful, as doing things for reasons, to accomplish certain ends. Explanations in terms of purposes are sometimes (though not always) pretty reasonable when it comes to human behavior. But our thinking goes awry if we see purposes everywhere and think that if something exists, it must have some purpose.

A paradigm case of the overuse of purposive explanations that has done enormous damage in human history and still does so in some cultures is the belief in sorcery. Until fairly recently in the long history of our species, most people were disposed to regard any serious mishap that befell them as a malicious action performed by some other human (or spirit or god) who was out to get them. If your crops died or your cow ran dry or you cut yourself with an ax, it must be because someone put a spell on you, magically manipulating you or some items in your environment. You and I take for granted that bad stuff happens for all sorts of reasons, but that's because we have the idea of impersonal causes operating without purpose or intention. That idea hasn't been pervasive until recently and it still isn't universal.

The tendency to see purposes everywhere takes on a new form when, under the influence of evolutionary discourse, people substitute "function" for "purpose," see everything in terms of supposed functions, and assume that the only good explanation of anything is to show that it performs some function. Such thinking leads them not only to assume that every trait is an adaptation—something that came to be because it performed some function (and thereby contributed to reproductive fitness)—but also to assume that everything important about the thing now must be explainable in terms of its performing some function.

That's a big mistake, first of all, because not everything is an adaptation (Brandon 1990, 9). Some things result from essentially random processes, including "genetic drift," and others are not adaptations but rather by-products of adaptations—traits that just happen to coexist with adaptations because of contingent causal relations that exist in the process of an organism's development.

Here's an example of a by-product that I think you'll remember. Apparently there has been natural selection for aggressiveness in female spotted hyenas, because more aggressive females secure more food for their pups and therefore pass on more of their genes. In other words, aggression appears to be an adaptation; it came to exist among female spotted hyenas because at some point in the past one or more females had genetic mutations (just as a matter of chance) that under the selective pressures of that environment led to higher levels of testosterone, which in turn led to greater aggression, which in turn enhanced their reproductive fitness. (Like humans and other mammals, male and female hyenas both have "female" and "male" hormones, including testosterone.)

Now it just so happens that a side effect (a causal by-product) of high testosterone levels in female spotted hyenas is hypertrophy of the clitoris—a clitoris that is at least as large as the male hyena's penis. (My students' reaction to that fact is a term they typically overuse but that may be spot-on in this case: "awesome!") If you assume that the huge clitoris exists because it must have contributed to reproductive fitness at some point back in the spotted hyena lineage or is doing so now, you are barking up the wrong tree (so to speak). You're committing the sin of hyperfunctionalism.

Sometimes the hyperfunctionalist mistake I've just identified gets combined with the second mistake I noted earlier: not only thinking that something must have come to be because it performed a certain function but also assuming that that function is still so important that, to explain what the thing is now like, all you have to do is characterize that function. In the case of morality, this would amount to thinking that if it came to be because it performed the function of facilitating cooperation and still performs that function, then everything important about morality can be explained in terms of showing how it performs that function.

Unfortunately, I think that some people who try to apply evolutionary thinking to human morality are hyperfunctionalists and make some or all of these mistakes. If I'm right, that's ironic, because it means that though they are trying to be modern and scientific and evolutionarily sophisticated, they are really thinking like prescientific folks who saw purposes everywhere, in effect anthropomorphizing the whole of reality.

The Environment of Evolutionary Adaptation (EEA)

So much for my attempt to get some basic evolutionary concepts straight and preview why doing that will turn out to be important as my thinking unfolds in this book. Now let's get back to the task at hand: understanding what the EEA, the environment in which human moralities first arose, was supposed to be like and why understanding what it was like appears to lead to the conclusion that we are morally tribalistic beings.

The EEA is defined as the set of conditions in which the basic features of human cognition and motivation, including those that make moralities possible, first emerged in our species. This crucially formative period is thought to have occurred somewhere between 1.8 million and 10,000 years ago. (Ten thousand years ago is the cutoff point because that's roughly when the Neolithic Revolution began, the transition from hunting and gathering to agriculture and the domestication of animals. When that shift occurred, human life became profoundly different.)

The main features of the EEA that are supposed to be most important for the formation of the moral mind are the following: (1) There weren't many humans, and they lived in small, widely scattered groups. (2) When they encountered individuals from other groups, they were in a desperate competition for survival resources. (3) Because these groups were widely scattered, they had different immune histories, which meant that if you encountered people from another group, you might become infected with lethal pathogens (like the native peoples of the so-called New World when they came into contact with Europeans). (4) Individuals from other groups not only presented a risk of biological parasites but also could be social parasites, free riders on your group's cooperative practices, because they hadn't internalized your group's rules and weren't bound to you by the ties of loyalty that your group's traditions and practices fostered. Or, at the very least, strangers could disrupt your group's cooperation because they simply didn't get how you do things. (5) There was little or nothing in the way of social practices or institutions to enable peaceful, mutually beneficial cooperation among different groups (no markets, no governments that united different groups under common laws, etc.). (6) Because human groups were widely scattered and had their own histories, they had different languages, different styles of bodily adornment, clothing, hairstyles, and so on, and different ways of doing the basic things that all human societies have to do to survive. Later I'll explain that these differences aren't just natural contingencies; some of them are contrived because they performed the vital function of enabling people to distinguish quickly and reliably whether someone was one of Us or not.

Some evolutionary thinkers believe that a turning point in this process of developing robust moralities as facilitators of cooperation may have occurred between 400,000 and 450,000 years ago. Around that time, the climate in which humans existed changed significantly, with the result that much of the vegetation and small game they had depended on became scarce. Some early humans adapted, first by cooperatively scavenging game killed by large predators (using simple stone tools to crack open the carcasses' large bones and skulls to extract high-calorie, protein-rich marrow and brains), and then by learning to cooperate to prey on larger, more dangerous game. To do the latter, humans needed to develop complex social coordination that enabled them to work together to find, chase down, and kill game through teamwork. The teamwork required not only ramped-up cognitive skills, including planning, forming "we" intentions rather than just individual intentions, and creating a division of labor (for example, between the individuals who funneled game into narrow gorges and those who killed them there), but also the development of rules for dividing the spoils of a successful hunt (Bowles and Gintis 2013, 2; Tomasello 2016). Moreover, the harsher new environment meant that collisions among groups became more deadly as they competed more desperately for scarcer resources (Boehm 2000, 41; 2012, 136; Lambert 1997, 77–110).

Groups that didn't develop in these ways were unable to cope with the demands of the new environment. Groups that did were able to reproduce not just biologically but also culturally, passing on the moralities they created, with later generations solidifying and elaborating them. You and I are moral beings because we are descendants of people in the groups that survived because they developed moralities.

The Evolutionary Roots of Tribalism: Cooperation among Us, for Competition with Them

Whether the crucial change occurred in just that way at just that time may not be essential to the evolutionary explanation of the origins of human moralities. Some scientists doubt that around 400,000 years ago was a tipping point. They think it occurred considerably later, after humans had become such successful cooperators that their numbers increased, leading to more collisions among groups and more conflicts and consequently in strong selection pressures for the development of moralities that facilitated successful intergroup competition. In spite of these differences, scientists largely agree on the broader outlines of the standard evolutionary account: human moralities developed because they facilitated *cooperation within the group, including cooperation that allowed the group to compete successfully with other groups when necessary*—to avoid the threats that encounters with other groups entailed and to secure control over survival resources (Bowles 2009, 1293–1295; 2008a, 326–327; 2008b, 1605; Bowles and Gintis 2013, 2–4; Choi and Bowles 2007, 638; Joyce 2006, 21; Keeley 1996, 15, 31, 117; Richerson and Boyd 2005, 244; Sober and Wilson 1999, 79, 84). It's worth noting here that we needn't take the extreme view that moralities emerged only because they facilitated competition among groups. It's more likely that they came to be because they facilitated cooperation within the group that had nothing to do with intergroup competition *and* also because they enabled successful competition with other groups.

According to this evolutionary origins story, the basic elements of human moral psychology, like other features that were selected for in the EEA, such as the fine motor control of hand muscles that allowed toolmaking and the rotational flexibility of our shoulder joints that allowed our ancestors to bring down game with projectiles, persist to this day.

The scientific study of moralities in different societies around the world reveals great diversity, but some commonalities: every society (that lasts for any length of time) features certain general types of moral rules and practices. There are rules against killing your fellows, against taking what isn't yours, rules that require you to reciprocate when others help you at some cost to themselves, rules that specify how scarce and valuable resources are to be divided among members of the group, rules that serve to curb the tendency of stronger individuals to dominate others, rules designed to discourage free riding, and rules that not only permit but require punishments for infractions of rules (Boehm 2000, 141; Bowles and Gintis 2013, 20).

An evolutionary approach to understanding human moralities can help explain both what is common across different moralities and what is different. Remember: evolution, in the most basic sense of the concept, is descent with modification. Even if all early human groups had to solve certain problems to cooperate successfully and even if, to do so, they needed the same core moral rules, the character of the problems they faced may have varied somewhat, creating selection for different rules or different priorities among the rules.

Perhaps more important, even when groups faced the same problems, different groups found different ways of solving them equally well, or well enough, from the standpoint of reproductive fitness. Think, for example, of rules that are strictly conventional coordination devices, like the rules of the road. What's important, in any given locale, is whether we all know to drive on one side of the road; but whether it's the left or the right doesn't matter. If the problems that early human groups faced varied across different environments, and if they developed different conventional ways to solve some of them, then different groups would go down different paths in developing moralities.

Risks Humans Faced in the EEA and How They Shaped the First Moralities

As you can see from the list of EEA features, encounters with other groups posed several kinds of risks, and all were potentially lethal in that harsh environment: the risk of biological and social parasitism, the risk that the other group would expropriate your group's survival resources (chase you off your foraging grounds; steal your women, thus reducing the human resources you needed to survive; or eat you). In addition, there was the risk that if you allowed strangers into your group, their "foreign" values or ways of doing things would disrupt your cooperation and thus reduce your reproductive fitness. If they weren't simply clueless, unwitting disruptors, foreigners might be free riders, reaping the fruits of your cooperative efforts but not doing their bit.

For early human groups—hovering on the margins of subsistence—free riding was always a huge problem. Letting in foreigners only exacerbated it. Groups that developed moralities that successfully countered these threats survived and reproduced; those that didn't disappeared.

The Asymmetry of Risks and Benefits of Interacting with the Other in the EEA

So far I've identified the risks that human groups supposedly faced in the EEA if they encountered members of other groups. What about the benefits? Remember that in the EEA (according to the standard account) human cultures had not yet developed social practices and institutions for peaceful, mutually beneficial cooperation among groups. For this reason, a dramatic asymmetry existed between the risks and benefits of encountering members of other groups. The risks were great; the benefits were minimal or nonexistent. Under these conditions, risk-management strategies would have evolved and, along with them, a corresponding set of psychological and moral responses to strangers that allowed the strategies to work: fear, distrust, hostility, and preemptive aggression toward strangers (Haselton and Nettle 2006, 53).

Prehistoric Risk-Management Techniques

To implement effective risk-management strategies you would first have to be able to identify individuals, to distinguish between Us and Them. If you encountered another creature of human form on the savanna, you needed to be able to know at a glance whether he was one of Us or one of Them, because, due to the asymmetry of risks and benefits, correct identification would be a matter of life and death. Natural selection fostered cultural practices that allowed quick and easy identification, and this explains why item (6) above was a salient feature of the EEA: differences in appearance were necessary for distinguishing Us from Them.

Humans evolved not just to be able to detect such differences but also to *invent* them. Different groups developed different visible traits, everything from distinctive forms of greeting, to nose, lip, and ear piercing, to tattoos, and different modes of dress and hairstyles. Such differences were presumably adaptations: they came about because they facilitated recognizing whether someone was one of Us or one of Them, and doing that was necessary for reproductive fitness. But here's the bad news: although the easily detectable differences (such as skin color or hair texture or bodily adornment) may have been fairly reliable proxies for identifying Us versus Them in that early environment, they don't provide reliable guides to what is morally important, namely, our shared humanity in the moral sense.

We all know that humans have a history of mistaking superficial differences for morally important ones. In apartheid South Africa, a quick test the authorities used to determine whether someone was "white" or "nonwhite" was to insert a comb into the person's hair and see if it remained upright. If the comb stayed upright, the conclusion the authorities drew wasn't that you had hair with exceptional body and didn't need a volumizing shampoo; it was that you didn't have certain basic rights. The explicit conclusion was that you didn't deserve to be treated the way white people were. The implicit justification for not treating you like white people was that by being nonwhite you were inferior, perhaps not even fully human.

If the foregoing characterization of the EEA is correct, and if moralities were adaptations to cope with the problems that the environment posed, then one would expect moralities *in that environment* to be tribalistic—exclusionary and xenophobic. Human moralities in the EEA would feature highly developed and demanding requirements so far as interactions among members of a cooperating group were concerned, but "foreigners"—out-group members—would be fair game, morally speaking, and literally as well.

Furthermore, if moralities in that environment were nothing more than adaptations that enhanced the reproductive success of the group by facilitating cooperation among its members, then one wouldn't expect even the most moral people to regard nonhuman animals as worthy of moral consideration. Because early human groups had to work hard to subsist, and because their subsistence depended largely on exploiting animals to the fullest, one wouldn't expect their moralities to regard the well-being of animals as having any independent moral value, apart from how well it serves human interests. Vegans or even vegetarians wouldn't have flourished in the EEA; groups that ruthlessly exploited animals for protein and fat would have outcompeted them.

So if the standard description of the EEA is accurate, early humans would be blind both to the moral equality of all human beings and to the moral standing of nonhuman animals. The Two Great Expansions would be absent. In that environment, natural selection would have produced tribalistic moralities.

Imagining What the Environment of Evolutionary Adaptation Was Like: Hobbes's State of Nature and *The Walking Dead*

If you want to get a firmer grip on what the EEA was supposedly like and the kind of moralities it supposedly fostered, I suggest you either read the seventeenth-century philosopher Thomas Hobbes's description of "the state of nature" or view a couple of episodes of the popular television series *The Walking Dead*. These two major cultural phenomena have a lot more in common than meets the eye.

For Hobbes, the "state of nature" was the hypothesized original condition of humankind before states were created to enforce law and order and enable human beings to cooperate peacefully with one another (Hobbes 1982). Hobbes's state of nature, like the

EEA, lacks institutions and practices for peaceful, mutually beneficial cooperation. The only big difference between Hobbes's state of nature and the EEA is that in the EEA there is at least peaceful cooperation within groups (though not among them). In contrast, Hobbes thought that in the state of nature individuals were on their own, facing a continuous war "of each against all."

In that respect, the standard description of the EEA is more realistic than Hobbes's characterization of the state of nature, because we have every reason to believe that as long as there have been humans, they have lived in cooperative groups, even if the groups were originally only as large as nuclear families. So if ruthless competition characterized the state of nature, it was mainly competition between groups.

In spite of this difference, what evolutionary theorists say about asymmetrical risk management in the EEA is precisely what Hobbes says about the state of nature: the best survival strategy is distrust and preemptive aggression toward the Other. Hobbes realizes that though that strategy is rational for each, it is disastrous for all. He concludes that so long as people remain in that EEA-like condition, there is no hope for them. Life, he famously says, will be "nasty, brutish, and short."

The only solution, according to Hobbes, is to create a "sovereign"—an individual or group of individuals who have the overwhelming might needed to impose rules of peaceful interaction so that humans can develop social practices and institutions that enable them to engage in genuine cooperation according to moral principles rather than continuing forever in a competition for dominance. But Hobbes doesn't really solve the problem of how to escape the state of nature; he limits himself to a proposal for peaceful, moral cooperation at the level of what we call the nation-state. He thinks of international relations as a state of nature, a realm of perpetual insecurity, a moral dead zone.

If seventeenth-century political theory isn't your thing, consider another way to appreciate the EEA as evolutionary moral origins stories typically depict it and the sort of moralities it would have fostered: have a look at *The Walking Dead*. Here's the nub of the plot, for those who can't tolerate the gore. An infection of unknown origin has converted most human beings into mindless, human-flesh-eating zombies. As a result, the surviving humans exist in small, scattered groups, in an environment in which all the infrastructure of civilization has broken down. Because there are no longer any social practices or institutions that allow peaceful cooperation among groups, and because there is intense competition among groups for the meager means of survival (mainly what can be scavenged from the ruins of civilization), trust has broken down, and the rational strategy seems to be to regard every stranger as a lethal threat. The groups that survive develop robust, demanding moral bonds among their own members but tend to regard members of other groups as predators or prey. In other words, the zombie apocalypse has re-created the EEA (or the group-conflict version of Hobbes's state of nature, if you prefer).

The world of *The Walking Dead* is the EEA, but with a crucial difference: unlike our remote ancestors, the survivors in this series remember what it was like to live in a world that was friendly to inclusive moralities. Hobbes's state of nature is supposed to be what things were like *before* civilization; the world of *The Walking Dead* is the way they would be *after* civilization has been destroyed.

It's not the zombies that make *The Walking Dead* morally interesting. (They're a pretty dull lot, mindlessly wandering around looking for people to munch on, and they don't seem to have any interesting relationships among themselves other than a tendency to travel in herds.) The zombies are just a mechanism for *re*introducing the EEA and depicting how contemporary humans might cope with it. So people who think that the only value of *The Walking Dead* is that it provides valuable instruction on a multitude of ingenious ways to dispatch zombies (on the off chance you'll ever need to do that) are missing the point. It's a marvelous primer on political theory and on evolutionary anthropology.

The genuine drama of the series is that it portrays with great pathos how hard it is for even the best-intentioned people to preserve an inclusive morality in circumstances that are profoundly hostile to it. In other words, what makes the series so interesting is that it grapples with the very problem that I take up in chapters 7 and 8: how we can stave off regression to tribalism (or, if that isn't possible, recover from regression once it has occurred).

Evoconservatism: Pessimistic Lessons from the Origins Story

Some people who think that the correct account of the evolutionary origins of morality implies that human moral nature is tribalistic go on to draw pessimistic conclusions about the possibilities for moral progress (Buchanan and Powell 2018, 116). I call these folks "evoconservatives." They think that because evolutionary thinking teaches us that our evolved moral nature is tribalistic, it follows that deeply inclusive morality is a pipe dream, a mere aspiration that we can never really *live*. Or they think that there are severe limits to how inclusive humans can be and that we've probably already reached them. Evoconservatism has practical consequences. It breeds pessimism about moral progress, and that can sap the motivation to try to make things better.

Because they think that inclusiveness goes against the grain of our evolved moral nature, evoconservatives also conclude that whatever meager gains in inclusivity humans may have managed to achieve are extremely fragile, not likely to endure. For example, in *The Limits of International Law*, Jack Goldsmith and Eric Posner go so far as to predict that our tribal moral nature dooms the project of creating genuinely cosmopolitan international institutions (Goldsmith and Posner 2005, 8–17). They don't explain how, if we are so tribalistic, humans could have developed moral bonds with tens of millions of fellow nationals they will never see or interact with—and be willing even to die for them in wars and other national emergencies. Nor do they explain why, if the circle of moral regard can expand that far, it can go no farther.

Evoconservatism is a pretty depressing view. So before we make the move from "morality was tribalistic in the EEA" to "morality is and always will be tribalistic," we should think carefully about whether the inference is valid. At lot is at stake here; more specifically, the fate of human moralities is at stake.

It should be clear why the inference the evoconservatives draw is invalid and hence why it shouldn't prompt pessimism. The slide from "was in the EEA" to "is and always will be" fails to distinguish between the moral mind and its earliest expression in particular moralities—and it overlooks just how different the EEA was from the niches that multitudes of humans now occupy.

The Way Forward

Avoiding the failure to distinguish between the moral mind and the different ways its capacities can get expressed in different environments won't by itself explain how morality got more inclusive, but it demystifies the process considerably. In chapter 4, I further the demystification by offering a revisionist prehistory: I paint a more subtle picture of the origins of human moralities by offering a more nuanced view of what the EEA was like. That will enable me to draw a clear contrast between the highly plausible claim that the central features of the moral mind were fixed in the EEA and the highly dubious claim that the moral mind is so rigid that we should expect all moralities to be as tribalistic as those in the EEA supposedly were. But before that, in chapter 3, I'll work through some unsuccessful attempts to reconcile the fact that human moralities are a product of evolution with the fact that, for some of us, morality is now not so tribalistic—I'll scrutinize some notable attempts to explain the Two Great Expansions. Showing why they lead to dead ends will, I hope, convince you that, like good detectives, we need to retrace the steps of our investigation and question our starting assumption—in this case, the way we've been thinking about the ancestral environment in which distinctively human moralities first appeared.

3

Failed Attempts to Solve the Big Puzzle: Cooperation Is Not Enough

When I began this detective story, I lamented that in spite of all their other contributions, scientists haven't paid enough attention to using evolutionary principles to explain how moralities have changed over time—and in particular that they haven't provided or even tried to provide evolutionary explanations, whether biological or cultural, of the Two Great Expansions. And so they haven't tried to determine how evolutionary thinking can illuminate the possibilities for moral progress. Now I want to examine attempts to solve the Big Puzzle by people from another discipline, philosophy.

Philosophical Thinking about the Big Puzzle

A few contemporary philosophers have been impressed with how the circle of moral regard has expanded, *and* tried to explain it with an eye toward what evolutionary scientists say about the origins of human moralities. In this chapter, I focus on those thinkers, in particular Philip Kitcher, Peter Railton, and Peter Singer. I think they've all made valuable contributions to understanding human moralities. Yet I think that none of them has succeeded in explaining how the Two Great Expansions can be squared with the standard view about the evolutionary origins of moralities. In fact, they don't explain the Two Great Expansions, even if we set aside the question of how they could have come about, given the standard evolutionary origin story. My purpose here isn't criticism for its own sake. Understanding where these attempts to explain the Two Great Expansions go wrong will put us in a position to get the explanation right.

Solutions That Focus on How Morality Facilitates Cooperation

I'll start with Kitcher's and Railton's views, because they have a lot in common. I will argue that neither of these formidable thinkers can explain either of the Two Great Expansions because they make the same mistake: they try to explain how the circle of moral regard expands by showing how human cooperation changes. Kitcher (2011, 131–138) seems to commit the error I flagged in the introduction: thinking that we can explain expanding the circle of moral regard as resulting from expanding our cooperation to include more people. Railton (1986, 200) has a squeaky-wheel explanation for how some important forms of moral regard get extended to people who previously were disregarded. He thinks that under certain conditions, when a society neglects the important interests of a significant portion of its population, those people may mobilize and disrupt the cooperative scheme, leading to a new form of cooperation in which they are treated more equally.

What these two accounts have in common is that they are still shackled to the Cooperation Dogma, the assumption that we can explain human moralities and whatever changes have occurred in them by focusing exclusively on how moralities facilitate cooperation. As we'll see, sticking with that assumption renders both accounts incapable of explaining either of the Two Great Expansions.

Kitcher's Understanding of What Morality Is (and All It Is)

Kitcher's rich and ambitious book, *The Ethical Project*, makes it clear that he believes that expanding the circle of moral regard is a good thing, in fact perhaps the most important kind of moral progress. And he wants to explain it in evolutionary terms. He starts out as evolutionary scientists do, expounding on how our remote ancestors became moral beings because changing in that way enabled them to cooperate successfully, where success means reproductive success. To his credit, he doesn't think of human morality as a fait accompli, something that was completed at some time back in the middle to late Pleistocene. He thinks it is a work in progress, a *project* that humans are still engaged in (hence the title of his book).

Kitcher thinks that moralities first appeared as adaptations that helped early human societies solve or avoid "altruism failures"—selfish behaviors that disrupted cooperation. Even if natural selection produced humans who were *somewhat* altruistic (at least toward their kin and perhaps other members of their group as well), altruism was limited or, what amounts to the same thing, humans didn't evolve to automatically always succeed in inhibiting the pursuit of their own interests when doing so was necessary to benefit others. So Kitcher thinks there were "altruism failures," resulting in conflicts, free riding, and other behavior that impaired cooperation and thus reduced reproductive fitness. Groups that developed moralities—rules, social practices, and moral responses that coped well with "altruism failures"—survived and reproduced; those that didn't went under. So eventually all human groups had moralities.

Kitcher doesn't explore the possibility that morality nowadays does more than cope with "altruism failures." In other words, Kitcher is a clear example of thinking of morality in purely functional terms, of assuming that morality is *constituted* by the function it originally evolved to perform, namely, facilitating cooperation and thereby contributing to reproductive fitness. Thinking that way ignores the possibility that morality nowadays, for some people at least, has features that are not functional in any sense that connects with evolutionary thinking. That's a mistake, as my example of the human shoulder joint makes clear. If you think that morality (nowadays) is nothing more than a device for facilitating cooperation, then you have only one option for trying to explain moral progress in the dimension of inclusion: you'll have to say that the circle of moral regard expanded because the circle of cooperation expanded.

That strategy doesn't work. It can't explain why people would extend moral regard to humans they will never cooperate with (either because those individuals are so disabled that they can't cooperate or because one simply won't ever *need* or even *want* to cooperate with them, either to maximize our reproductive fitness or for any other purpose). So it can't even begin to explain the First Great Expansion.

Nor can it explain the fact that nowadays many people think that even in the case of humans we do or may cooperate with, their capacity to cooperate is not the *only* basis of our moral regard for them, that instead they have a high moral status just because they are human beings. (Remember, the idea of human rights is that of rights you have by virtue of your humanity, not your ability to participate in cooperation.) Even more obviously, no cooperation-facilitator view of morality can explain why we should give a damn, morally speaking, about nonhuman animals that we'll never cooperate with.

Another problem arises for any view that characterizes morality as being constituted by the function of facilitating cooperation (in Kitcher's case, by overcoming altruism failures): it can't explain why for some people morality includes *intrapersonal* ideals of excellence, commitments to living in certain ways that have nothing to do with cooperation or with any interpersonal relations at all. I have in mind something I mentioned earlier: some central features of the account of virtues in Stoic philosophy and the core of Buddhist thought, and many other examples as well, including Christian and Hindu ascetic ideals. These moralities provide prescriptions for how a person's soul or psyche should be ordered that are independent of placing a value on any social effects such an ordering might have. In fact, some of them have advocated separation from society, dropping out from all cooperative schemes. An evolutionary understanding of morality that that cleaves to the dogma that morality is all about cooperation can't explain the existence of these sorts of moralities.

Expanding the Circle of Cooperation Doesn't Produce the Two Great Expansions

The idea that the circle of regard has expanded because the circle of cooperation has expanded can't even begin to explain the Second Great Expansion. The vast majority of nonhuman animals simply aren't capable of being included in any form of cooperation that humans engage in. Yet many of us think that—and act as if—those animals have moral standing.

Most of the animals that people now think should be treated less cruelly than they traditionally have been just don't have what it takes, cognitively or motivationally, to cooperate with us in any meaningful sense. They can neither benefit us by cooperating with us nor disrupt the cooperation we engage in. When we recognize animals as having any moral standing at all, we are operating with an understanding of the basis of moral standing that is nonstrategic, not cooperation based.

Even in the cases where it makes sense to say that humans and animals are cooperating (as in the interactions between sheepdogs and shepherds or bomb-sniffing dogs and their handlers), the power asymmetry is so great that the nature of the cooperation doesn't require the human side of the partnership to treat the animal side as equals or even to treat them in ways that avoid gratuitous suffering on their part. Sadly, anthropologists have documented that even people who depend on dogs for their survival, including Inuits who rely heavily on their sled dogs, routinely treat them in extremely cruel ways, inflicting pain on them, not because the pain is necessary to motivate the animals to perform the tasks assigned to them, but apparently just because they find it fun (Edgerton 1992, 20). And even if people treat animals on whom they depend with some minimal constraint, if they do so only for instrumental reasons, that is, because such behavior is necessary to reap benefits from those animals, this is not the same as recognizing that animals are worthy of moral consideration in their own right.

Successfully cooperating with humans or nonhuman animals doesn't require treating them with proper moral regard; it doesn't even require *thinking* that you ought to treat them well just because of what they are like, independently of whether treating them well advances your own interests. But remember, the big idea that the Two Great Expansions have in common is the idea that some beings are worthy of moral regard in their own right, simply because of what they are like, independently of whether treating them well advances our interests, through cooperation or in any other way.

What is more, in many cases of human–nonhuman animal relationships, it's wrong to speak of "interaction" at all, much less interaction that could meaningfully be called "cooperation." Instead, humans act, and animals are merely acted on. Where one party is an agent and the other only a patient, no cooperation occurs.

So it simply isn't true that for many people the circle of moral regard has expanded to encompass nonhuman animals because human beings have made a corresponding expansion of their cooperative schemes to include them. Most of the animals we treat badly and should treat better are not even potential cooperators, much less actual cooperators, with us. The idea that the circle of moral regard expands because the circle of cooperation expands is a nonstarter if your goal is to explain the Second Great Expansion.

How do people, like Kitcher, who hold that morality is constituted by its function of facilitating cooperation, try to explain the First Great Expansion? They suggest that as global institutions, communication, and travel technologies have linked all humans together, it is becoming vital for successful cooperation that all or at least most of us show some basic regard for all humans. Because human cooperation has gone global, they think, it is now prudentially rational for practically everyone, including the world's richest and most powerful people, to ensure that there is at least significant movement in the direction of greater equality. People who paint this rosy picture don't usually go so far as to proclaim that modern global cooperation requires acknowledging *equal* basic moral status for all. If they did, their claim would be highly implausible. But they do at least suggest that as global cooperation develops, there will be significant pressure to move in the direction of according equal basic moral status to everyone. I wish that were true, but I don't think it is.

Global Cooperation without Equal Regard

Why am I skeptical that further globalization will expand the circle of moral regard sufficiently to move us toward the First Great Expansion? Because it's unlikely that the most powerful people in our world, the people who largely control the structure of global cooperative networks, will suffer, in terms of reproductive fitness or in any way that matters to them, unless they do a lot to reduce the enormous inequalities that now exist. In fact, those people seem to be able to reap plenty of benefits from global cooperation by treating some people—millions of them—as if they don't count at all, or at best as if they count a whole lot less than they themselves do. Sustaining the cooperative schemes from which the best-off benefit doesn't require moving toward deep inclusion; it doesn't necessitate the First Great Expansion or even make it probable.

So I don't think the expansion of the circle of cooperation explains the expansion of the circle of moral regard, even in the case of humans, leaving aside the case of nonhuman animals. It certainly can't do so for the case of humans who are unable to participate in global cooperative networks either because of debilitating diseases like malaria or because of severe mental retardation or psychological disorders or lack of literacy or numeracy.

It also can't explain something more fundamental: if every human has equal basic moral status, then we ought to try to construct our cooperative schemes so as to ensure that more people *can* participate. In other words, people who say the circle of moral regard expands because the circle of cooperation expands, put the cart before the horse: they think that the expansion of the cooperative scheme to include more people drives the extension of basic equal moral status, when in fact, from the point of view of an inclusive morality of the sort they say they embrace, recognition of the basic equal moral status of all people should drive the expansion of our cooperative schemes to include as many of them as we reasonably can. If you don't see that, you're missing a major message of the disability rights movement: the idea that society ought to make its cooperative schemes more inclusive. For those who have acknowledged the First Great Expansion, the point isn't that if you can cooperate with us, you have equal basic moral status; it's that because you have equal basic moral status, we should try to ensure that you are able to participate in cooperation with us.

The depressing fact of the matter is that a handful of the most powerful nations, led (at least so far) by the United States, has created a global economy that, viewed purely as a smooth-running cooperative scheme, is quite impressive but at the same time highly inegalitarian, profoundly hierarchical. Moreover, inequality seems to be increasing, not decreasing, as the global economy expands, even though absolute poverty is declining. And presumably at least some of those growing inequalities, if they become great enough, are incompatible with genuinely acknowledging in practice the idea that all human beings have the same basic equal moral status.

The big problem for any attempt to explain the expansion of the circle of moral regard as resulting from expansions in cooperation is that even though cooperation has expanded to include most of the world's population in one way or another (at least if you have a thin enough notion of "cooperation"), it isn't true that this expanded cooperation doesn't run smoothly unless everybody is treated as having equal basic moral status. In fact, the existing global cooperative scheme's running smoothly doesn't even seem to require that most people *think* that everyone deserves to be treated as having equal basic moral status. And it certainly doesn't require that the best-off take seriously in their actual behavior the idea of realizing human rights for all.

I'll offer one more obvious and compelling reason to reject the thesis that the circle of regard expands because the circle of cooperation expands, even if we restrict this claim to the First Great Expansion and don't worry about its painfully obvious failure to explain the Second. The circle of cooperation has expanded many times in human history. Two examples come to mind: the Roman Empire, at its peak of power and influence, created a sophisticated cooperative network that encompassed around 70 million people and all the lands bordering the Mediterranean; and in the two decades preceding World War I, what many historians call the first truly global economy appeared. Yet in neither case do we see a clear expansion of the circle of moral regard, at least not anything approaching the First Great Expansion. In fact, both of these dramatic expansions of the circle of cooperation were marked by extreme inequalities: pervasive slavery in the former and Western colonial domination in the latter. Historically, then, we can observe no clear correlation between the expansion of cooperation and the First Great Expansion.

So expanding the circle of cooperators can't by itself explain expanding the circle of moral regard in anything like the strongly egalitarian way the First Great Expansion requires. At most, pointing to the fact that the circle of cooperation has gone global could help explain why human morality would have developed a moral psychology that allows humans to have *shallowly inclusive moralities*, to accord the limited sort of recognition that is required for effective cooperation among strangers with whom it is advantageous for them to cooperate—something akin to the sort of limited moral recognition that was required for long-distance trade or military alliances in the distant past or perhaps a bit more than that, but surely far less than full recognition of basic equal moral status. At present, the prediction that the further development of global cooperation will decrease inequalities in wealth and political power, much less contribute to the realization of the First Great Expansion, is not supported by evidence about how the global economy works. It might happen, but it might not.

The Deeper Flaw in the Functionalist Understanding of Morality

That's not really the point, however. The point is that even if such a hopeful prediction comes true, it wouldn't explain the First Great Expansion, much less the Second. However much global cooperation expands, it won't include every human being who is worthy of equal basic respect, because there will always be some humans who aren't able to participate in the global economy or indeed in any form of interaction that could be called "cooperation" in anything like the sense in which evolutionary theorists use that term. Nor will it ever include most nonhuman animals.

The mistaken idea that morality is constituted by its original function of facilitating cooperation gives rise to a correspondingly limited understanding of how human beings regard moral status and moral standing: namely, that they restrict them to those beings who are or can be cooperators (or who can disrupt cooperation).

Fortunately, many people nowadays don't have that limited view of what confers moral status and standing. The fact that they don't will remain utterly mysterious so long as one operates with the limited view of morality, namely, that it is just a device whose function is to facilitate cooperation.

The Squeaky-Wheel Model of Moral Progress

Let's consider another way that people who assume that everything interesting about morality can be explained by understanding how it facilitates cooperation try to explain moral progress in the direction of inclusion. They appeal to a kind of friction or squeaky-wheel theory of progressive change.

The renowned philosopher Peter Railton offers a prime example. He thinks that when the social practices and governmental structures of a society give short shrift to the important interests of some substantial portion of its members, the oppressed sometimes shake things up—disrupt cooperation—and that this process can lead to a new equilibrium, a new state of affairs where the interests that were previously disregarded are at least to some extent realized. Because Railton believes that a morally good society is one in which everyone's interests are taken seriously, he believes that establishing a new equilibrium that serves previously disregarded interests is an instance of moral progress. But there's a catch: he frankly admits that this kind of progressive change will only occur if the people whose interests were previously disregarded *are able to mobilize effectively enough to disrupt the existing cooperative arrangements* (Railton 1986, 200).

When the Wheel Can't Squeak Loudly Enough

The oppressed aren't always able to disrupt the status quo. A large body of literature in political science explains why the oppressed are often not able to solve collective-action problems needed for effective mobilization and consequently can't exert sufficient pressure on the best-off to shake things up and make society work better for them.

The squeaky-wheel or friction model is plausible as a theory for some cases of successful social revolution. It's a far cry, however, from explaining the Two Great Expansions. It clearly tells us nothing about how the Second Great Expansion could ever occur. Barring some enormous evolutionary leap (something like the deeply flawed scenario of *Planet of the Apes*), the animals that humans have usually treated so badly aren't likely to mobilize and disrupt our cooperative schemes. (As much as I'd like to, I can't imagine chickens going on strike in a factory farm, much less a horde of angry pigs storming Hormel's corporate headquarters; can you?)

A Deeper Flaw of Squeaky-Wheel Views

Certain historical cases do fit the squeaky-wheel model—wars of liberation from colonialism come immediately to mind. That is, in some instances, oppressed people have been able to mobilize effectively enough to create a disruption that leads to a new equilibrium where their interests are taken more seriously and to that extent have moved their society in the direction of equality.

Yet it's simply not true that the origination or the spread of the idea of the basic equal moral status of all human beings has always, or even most of the time, been the *result* of the oppressed being able to shake things up sufficiently to disrupt social cooperation. The 800,000 people who were liberated when slavery was abolished in the British Empire in 1834 didn't accomplish that feat by disrupting Britain's economy. Emancipation did disrupt the British economy, but emancipation didn't occur because the slaves disrupted the economy, which would have had to be the case for the squeaky-wheel model to apply. (In later chapters, I'll have a lot to say about the abolition of Atlantic slavery and how it illustrates my theory of the interaction between the moral mind and certain recently constructed human niches.)

The squeaky-wheel theory can explain why power elites should be willing to grant concessions that reduce inequalities *to those who are capable of disrupting cooperation from which the elites benefit*—but *only* to those people. It can't explain why the elites or anybody else would or should care about the moral status of beings, whether human or nonhuman, who aren't capable of disrupting cooperation.

It's also quite clear that sometimes those who achieve progressive moral change do *not* do so by disrupting cooperation. For example, I believe it is evident that the successes of the animal liberation movement have been due more to persuasion (through appeals both to reason and to emotion) than to the limited and probably counterproductive disruptive actions of organizations like PETA.

In fairness to Railton, I should note that at one point he states that progress in the direction of inclusion can occur when those who *represent* the interests of the oppressed (but aren't themselves oppressed) disrupt cooperation. This is a purely ad hoc move, however, because he does nothing to explain why they would be motivated to do so and how such motivation is compatible with the standard evolutionary moral origins story. This move doesn't explain how thinking of morality simply as something that facilitates cooperation can accommodate the First or Second Great Expansions.

Two Different Understandings of the Basis of Moral Regard: Strategic and Nonstrategic

Views that understand morality solely in terms of how it facilitates cooperation have something in common: they conceive of actual human morality as a way of thinking and acting that confers moral status on beings strictly on the basis of their *strategic capacities*—more precisely, their ability either to contribute to or to disrupt cooperation. As long as you continue to think of morality in that way, as something that is at bottom purely strategic, you will never be able to explain the Two Great Expansions. And if the Two Great Expansions are an important aspect of human morality, then as long as you proceed under that limitation, your understanding of morality will be seriously incomplete.

The Two Great Expansions constitute a radical shift in understanding what the basis of moral standing and equal high moral status is. Instead of grounding moral regard for an individual, whether human or animal, in that being's strategic capacities, that is, his ability to contribute to or disrupt cooperation with us, people who have embraced the Two Great Expansions implicitly ground moral regard in a different way. When moral standing or high moral status are conferred on a strategic basis, they are conferred only as the product of a kind of implicit bargain: I will show moral regard for you if you will show moral regard for me.

When the Two Great Expansions occur, people abandon the purely strategic point of view. Instead of assuming that a being's strategic capacity is what counts, people focus on other characteristics that they believe to be morally significant. For Kantians, the relevant nonstrategic characteristic is the capacity for practical reason or, as contemporary Kantians usually put it, responsiveness to reasons, the capacity to engage with others in the practice of giving reasons for how we ought to act. For Utilitarians, the relevant nonstrategic characteristic is sentience, the ability to experience pleasure and pain.

Sentience and the capacity for practical reason are nonstrategic characteristics, in Utilitarian and Kantian moral theories respectively, in the sense that they are supposed to confer moral standing (or, in the case of practical reason, the highest moral status) on a being independently of whether that being can benefit or harm us, and hence independently of whether it is advantageous for us to recognize or not recognize that being as worthy of moral regard. Any understanding of morality that implies that the basis of moral regard is purely strategic cannot account for the Two Great Expansions. It also can't account for why there are any Kantians or Utilitarians. The transition from a purely strategic to a subject-centered understanding of the grounding of moral standing is, in my judgment, a major instance of moral progress. You can't begin to understand it if your mind is shackled to the Cooperation Dogma.

Does Reducing Inequality Promote More Efficient Cooperation?

I don't want to give short shrift to the idea that movements toward equality or at least toward reductions of the grosser forms of inequality can *sometimes* facilitate better cooperation, in particular cooperation that is more efficient because it depends on the strong motivation of participants to do their bit voluntarily, rather than only on their being threatened with coercion if they don't. The exceptionally creative and systematic evolutionary anthropologist Peter Turchin endorses this idea: he says that equality promotes cooperation—and worries that as inequalities in wealth and power increase in contemporary societies, cooperation may break down (Turchin 2015, ch. 10).

Clearly Turchin is on to something important here; yet I think the claim that equality is required for efficient cooperation, unless it is highly qualified, is clearly false. After all, as I've already emphasized, history shows many examples where expanding cooperation brought about great gains in the efficiency of production; yet there was great inequality. These historical examples of highly successful yet deeply inegalitarian cooperative schemes didn't last forever (what does?), but it is not clear that the cause, or the main cause, of their demise was inequality.

It may be true, however, that under certain conditions— conditions that *now exist for the first time in history and only in some parts of the world*—some kinds of inequalities can reduce the efficiency of cooperation. That might be true, for example, in societies in which the ideology of equal citizenship for all compatriots has taken root. If people have internalized this ideology, and if some citizens believe they're being denied the rights that constitute equal citizenship, their motivation to cooperate might decline. If there are enough of them, and if there is enough of a decline in their motivation to cooperate voluntarily, that might adversely affect cooperation. But then we are back to Railton's squeaky-wheel theory, and we've already seen that it can't explain either of the Two Great Expansions. Nevertheless, someone like Turchin might insist that the emergence of the ideal of equal citizenship is an important step toward the First Great Expansion.

Enthusiastic Cooperation without Equality

Perhaps; but I think there are two problems with this variant of the idea that a move toward equal status for all human beings comes about because successful cooperation requires it. First of all, people can enjoy the formal status of being equal citizens—possessing on paper, as it were, the same basic rights as other members of the nation-state's community—and still not be accorded full equal basic moral status. Yet they may still cooperate.

Furthermore, I'm aware of no evidence that the ideal of equal citizenship reliably becomes transformed into or leads to the notion that all humans—not just all members of one's own polity—have the same basic moral status. After all, scholars of nationalism, including Eugen Weber in his classic *Peasants into Frenchmen* and more recently Andreas Wimmer in his outstanding *Nationalist Exclusion and Ethnic Conflict*, have argued that the modern idea of equal citizenship has historically been a force not just for inclusion but also for exclusion—exclusion from basic political rights and access to economic and cultural opportunities for members of the nation-state who are not part of the dominant ethnic group in whose image the concept of the nation is shaped (Weber 1976, 486; Wimmer 2002, 58).

For example, the extension of equal citizenship rights in France after the French Revolution didn't fully apply to some minorities (such as Bretons), or if it did, it required them to abandon their distinctive ethnic or national identity, including their language. In fact, so-called nation building, along with its nationalistic conception of equal citizenship, has historically been nation destroying—forging a modern nation-state meant obliterating all other national identities within a territory in order to privilege only one; and the understanding of what it is to be an equal citizen followed suit. Moreover, nationalism can and often does extend recognition of equal status to all who are regarded as members of the nation while at the same time relegating people of other nations to an inferior status. Nationalism is often a kind of tribalism.

Second, in modern societies, people sometimes believe that they are being accorded equal citizenship status when they aren't. For example, many Americans believe that they are all equal citizens, where this includes having equal political rights, and that they live in a democracy, understood as a society in which all have an "equal say" in how we are governed. Yet in fact they are increasingly living in something approaching an oligarchy, a polity in which the very rich exercise their "equal" political rights much more effectively than the poor and even the middle class and wield greater political power in other ways, behind the scenes of the official political processes. Where a society allows those with such great resources to use them to disproportionately influence political outcomes, it is absurd to say that we all have an equal say in how we are governed. (Do you think your "say" is anywhere near equal to that of the Koch brothers or George Soros?)

Yet this state of affairs apparently hasn't led to a reduction in cooperation, much less a breakdown of it. Ideological thinking can prevent people from seeing just how deep inequalities run and hence from being motivated to change things to achieve greater equality. I'll have a lot more to say about the obstacles ideologies pose for moral progress in chapter 8.

Perhaps even more importantly, modern consumer culture can make people believe that their material well-being is what matters most and that their lives are improving and will continue to improve in that dimension. When that happens, they may not care so much about whether their equal citizenship is substantial, not merely formal. Contemporary China may be a good example. The majority of the population seems quite willing to participate enthusiastically in social cooperation even though the society is obviously deeply hierarchical and the idea of equal citizenship is patently delusional. Apparently people can contribute enthusiastically to impressive social cooperation in extremely inegalitarian societies, so long as they believe that they, or at least their children, will continue to be better off in material terms. So successful cooperation, even in societies that feature the idea of equal citizenship, doesn't require the sort of robust equality that the First Great Expansion encompasses.

The Bottom Line: Morality Is Not (Now) All about Cooperation

All those complications, however, don't really get at my main point, which is this: even some version of the thesis that successful cooperation requires movement in the direction of equality is true, that still wouldn't account for either of the Two Great Expansions. Not the Second, because most of the animals we now think have moral standing can never be part of our cooperative arrangements; not the First, because it includes the idea that everyone is entitled to recognition of basic equal status *independently of any role they might play in cooperation and hence independently of whether they are able to make their cooperation conditional on being treated with equal regard*. Neither of the Two Great Expansions can be explained as being requirements of cooperation or of efficient cooperation. That conclusion is only surprising if you mistakenly assume that morality, including the basis of equal basic moral status and moral standing, is all about cooperation.

At this point, I want to avoid a misinterpretation of what I'm saying. I'm happy to acknowledge that certain developments in the ways human beings cooperate were a *necessary* condition for the emergence of the First Great Expansion. More specifically, humans learned to cooperate in ways that resulted in surplus reproductive success—and that success enabled the Great Uncoupling of moralities from the maximization of reproductive success. I have a lot to say about that process in chapters 5 and 6. I'm also sympathetic to the idea that features of the moral mind that evolved because they facilitated cooperation, such as sympathy that reaches beyond kin, and perspective taking, eventually—under the influence of cultural changes—came to play an important role in the First Great Expansion.

Did Moral Consistency Reasoning Cause the Two Great Expansions?

Now let's consider a different and more promising attempt to explain the Two Great Expansions: the thesis that they came about through the exercise of *moral consistency reasoning*. That explanation is quite popular; among the most prominent thinkers who subscribe to it are the provocative and influential philosopher Peter Singer (Singer 2011, 115–116, 142) and the formidable cultural evolutionary thinkers Hugo Mercier and Dan Sperber (Mercier and Sperber 2017, 314).

The basic idea is that human beings have a capacity for rationally grounded empathy—an ability to take seriously the well-being of other creatures (whether they be humans from other groups or non-human animals) because they have the ability to detect inconsistencies in their moral beliefs and then resolve those inconsistencies in a way that leads them to change their moral judgments and emotional responses.

Here's an example: you acknowledge that one ought not to inflict pain on other human beings *because pain is bad*. But if that's why one ought not to inflict pain on humans, then one shouldn't inflict it on animals, either. That a creature isn't a human is not a morally relevant difference; what matters is that it feels pain. According to what may be the most sophisticated analysis of moral consistency reasoning available so far, offered by the creative philosophical team of Campbell and Kumar, moral consistency reasoning in this case involves ironing out a conflict between one's emotionally charged judgment that inflicting pain is wrong, on the one hand, and one's belief that it is acceptable to inflict pain on animals, on the other (Campbell and Kumar 2012, 276). A broader conception of moral consistency reasoning would also cover cases where the conflict is between moral principles, that is, general moral rules. What is common to the narrower and broader conceptions of moral consistency reasoning is that they both help explain how the desire to achieve consistency in one's moral attitudes and beliefs can be an engine for moral change.

It's quite right to emphasize that moral consistency reasoning played a significant role in both of the Two Great Expansions, at least for some people who have achieved that moral reorientation. Yet it's clear that this explanation of how the circle gets expanded is seriously incomplete, because it doesn't explain why moral consistency reasoning sometimes occurs and sometimes doesn't, or why, when it does occur, it sometimes leads toward the Two Great Expansions and sometimes doesn't come anywhere near them. It's a depressing fact that moral consistency reasoning can lead either to progress or to regression. A proper explanation needs to identify the conditions under which moral consistency reasoning occurs and becomes socially and politically potent enough to reorient our conception of moral standing or equal basic moral status.

When Does the Right Kind of Moral Consistency Occur?

Presumably human beings have been capable of moral consistency reasoning for as long as there have been humans or at least as long as humans have had moralities. Or at least they've been capable of moral consistency reasoning much earlier than the beginnings of the Two Great Expansions. For example, in 2 Samuel 12, New International Version of the Bible, we find a clear instance of moral consistency reasoning. Nathan uses a parable about a rich man stealing a poor man's prized possession to trick King David into moral consistency reasoning that leads the king to conclude that he has violated his own moral principles by arranging to have Uriah the Hittite killed so that he can take the man's wife.

That episode of moral consistency reasoning supposedly took place in the late Bronze Age, almost three thousand years ago, but among a people who thought *they* (and nobody else) had an especially high moral status (being God's chosen people). And the story is told in a book that includes several instances in which God orders the utter destruction of other human groups (a.k.a. genocide), including noncombatant women and children, as if they had no moral standing at all, a book that also prescribes unnecessarily painful methods of killing food animals.

So even though some humans used moral consistency reasoning in the remote past, it didn't issue in either of the Two Great Expansions until very recently. Those two enlargements of the circle of moral regard, at least so far as they have reached a social scale and were not limited to a morally precocious minority, are much more recent. To solve our mystery, then, it isn't nearly enough to point out that humans are capable of moral consistency reasoning or that they have sometimes exercised that capacity. We need to know why it's only recently that enough of them have *exercised it in a way that leads to the Two Great Expansions*. The story turns out to be a complicated one; I tell it in chapters 5 and 6.

Here it's worth noting that though certain strains of Hindu culture have long placed significant constraints on the treatment of some animals, this practice doesn't seem to have been the result of moral consistency reasoning. Nor were these moral compunctions grounded in the belief that nonhuman animals had moral standing on their own account.

Although many people today in that tradition have made the Second Great Expansion, the idea originally wasn't that you shouldn't kill or inflict pain on nonhuman animals because they had moral standing in their own right. Rather, the reason you were supposed to avoid treating them badly was that if you did, you'd be reincarnated as one of them. It's one thing to avoid torturing a goat because you might come back as one; quite another to think it's wrong to torture goats because pain is bad and they feel it much as we do and therefore have some sort of moral standing in their own right. The results of people acting on the belief that they should avoid mistreating animals if they want to avoid a bad outcome in the next reincarnation may have been good from a moral point of view, in the sense that it led to less cruel treatment of nonhuman animals, but it doesn't imply that there was a transition to the Second Great Expansion among the people who thought in that way. This isn't a case of moral consistency reasoning, much less of moral consistency reasoning leading to the conclusion that some nonhuman animals have moral standing in their own right, independently of how our treating them affects us.

What's the point of these excursions into the history of moralities? The point of the example of Nathan's moral jujitsu in the book of Samuel is simply that even if humans not only had the capacity for moral consistency reasoning for a long time but also sometimes actually exercised it, that doesn't explain the First Great Expansion, because that enlargement of the circle of moral regard came a lot later than the first recorded uses of moral consistency reasoning. The point of the Hindu tradition example is that the fact that some cultures for a very long time have included in their moralities some constraints on how nonhuman animals are treated doesn't show that the Second Great Expansion had already come about way back then, if these constraints were not based on the idea that animals count morally in their own right, independently of how our treating them affects our well-being. My main point, however, is that although moral consistency reasoning may well have been necessary for both of the Two Great Expansions to occur, merely pointing to the fact that humans can engage in it isn't sufficient to explain why significant numbers of humans have engaged in it *only rather recently in ways that contributed to the Two Great Expansions.*

Failures of Moral Consistency Reasoning

Moral consistency reasoning has two problems. First, it often doesn't come into play when it should; second, it frequently goes awry. In some ways, the second problem may be even worse than the first. The difficulty is that moral consistency reasoning is often distorted, circumscribed in ways that are arbitrary even from the moral standpoint of those exercising it. When that happens, moral consistency reasoning can contract the circle of moral regard rather than enlarge it.

Here are a couple of examples. Wealthy folks who associate exclusively with people like themselves are likely to be quick to realize that if something is painful to them, it is also likely to be painful to other people *like them*. But they may be remarkably unaware of, or unempathetic toward, the suffering of poor people. Similarly, Serbs who have been brought up to hate Croats know that it is wrong to torture their fellow Serbs (and most other people, as well); but they may think it is perfectly acceptable to torture Croats, because they think Croats are not at all like them, at least not in ways that are relevant to whether it's permissible to torture them.

Distorted Moral Consistency Reasoning: Garbage In, Garbage Out

Here's one last example of how moral consistency reasoning can facilitate tribalistic morality rather than overcome it. The historian Claudia Koonz, in her exceptionally valuable book *The Nazi Conscience*, notes that during the Third Reich public school teachers were told by Nazi Party officials how important it was to instill in their pupils the right moral values, including the Golden Rule—but with the proviso that it only applied to "racial comrades" (Koonz 2003, 10). The Golden Rule is a marvelous mental trick for expanding the circle of moral regard and a shining example of moral consistency reasoning. Yet engaging in the role-reversal experiment it recommends only produces inclusive results if you *already* have certain beliefs about which differences and similarities are morally relevant and hence should be thought about in a consistent way. *If* "non-Aryans" lack equal moral status, then there is nothing inconsistent in treating your fellow "Aryans" as equals while treating "non-Aryans" as dangerous, unclean beasts. Simply treating like cases alike doesn't give the right answer if you are mistaken about what the morally relevant likenesses are.

So if you don't believe that the other is like you in morally relevant ways so far as basic moral status is concerned, then you can engage in moral consistency reasoning till the cows come home and still get answers that do nothing to expand your circle of moral regard. In fact, you may engage in a lot of moral consistency reasoning and act faithfully on its results and never come close to making either of the Two Great Expansions.

So what we need is an account of when and why moral consistency reasoning of a particular sort (the kind that expands the circle of moral regard) occurs and when and why it becomes widespread enough and powerful enough to cause the Two Great Expansions. We need to know why and how moral consistency reasoning is sometimes restricted in certain ways, foreclosing particular results. We also need to know what motivates people to engage in moral consistency reasoning in the first place.

Moral Consistency Reasoning by Cognitively Flawed Beings

More specifically, we need a scientifically based account of how moral consistency reasoning sometimes leads to inclusion, sometimes to exclusion—and why sometimes people don't engage in it at all, even though they hold inconsistent moral beliefs. We need to learn, from the best available research on errors of reasoning that all normal human beings are prone to and from experiments that confirm the ubiquity of implicit racial bias, how people can fail to see that, according to their own moralities, morally relevant similarities exist between themselves and other creatures, whether human or nonhuman. We also need to understand why people sometimes act on the results of their moral consistency reasoning and sometimes don't. We need to know how cultural constructions, rooted in our evolved moral nature, can lead us to conceive of the Other in ways that can restrict the scope of moral consistency reasoning.

Above all, if we care about moral progress, we need to know how cultural innovations can help remove those restrictions (for example, how someone who previously thought the Golden Rule only applied to fellow Aryans could come to think it applies more widely). In chapters 5 and 6, I explain how cultural innovations have only recently produced human-made niches in which significant numbers of people have become motivated to engage in moral consistency reasoning that leads all the way to the conclusions that all human beings have an equal basic moral status and that animals have moral standing—and to act on that conclusion, if only imperfectly.

Evolved Limitations on Who Is Seen as Being Worthy of Moral Regard

I mentioned in the introduction that some evolutionary psychologists have done fascinating work on how very young children learn to cooperate morally or, if you will, how they become good at cooperation by becoming moral. Among the most fruitful researchers of this sort are Michael Tomasello and his graduate students who have gone on to become outstanding researchers in their own right. Unfortunately, as I suggested earlier, from a moral perspective that cherishes inclusion, this research has a negative side: one of their chief findings is that children learn to cooperate morally, or to be good cooperators because they are moral, by picking and choosing with whom to cooperate on the basis of just the sort of superficial resemblances that many people now regard as morally irrelevant and that can lead moral consistency reasoning astray. These are also the same sort of resemblances that, if missing, led our early human ancestors to react with fear, distrust, or aggression toward other human beings, if the standard evolutionary moral origins story is largely correct.

Recall that, according to the standard moral origins story, in the EEA it was a matter of life or death to be able to detect whether another being of human form was one of Us or one of Them, and detection was generally based on at-a-glance similarities and differences, like clothing, hairstyle, hair texture, language, and skin tone. Well, Tomasello's team finds that young children today use the same sorts of cues.

The good news is that in Tomasello's lab, as in the EEA, those sorts of cues often provide reliable indicators of whether trying to cooperate with somebody is likely to turn out well. The bad news is that those cues have nothing to do with rightly determining whether a being has equal basic moral status. From that same evaluative perspective, the even worse news is that when people don't distinguish between what is relevant to basic moral status and what isn't, those cues can lead them to act in exclusive (tribalistic), rather than inclusive, ways.

If you think that a being with dark skin is a different kind of creature, morally speaking, from light-skinned folks like you, then your moral consistency reasoning about dark-skinned people will not lead you to conclude that you should treat them as your moral equals. And your ability to identify with their suffering, to empathize with them in the way you would with someone you regard as your moral equal, may be blocked. Your moral consistency reasoning won't lead you to expand your circle of moral regard. Garbage in, garbage out.

Tomasello and company don't claim to be providing an explanation of how human moralities could have become deeply morally inclusive. Like other evolutionary scientists, they haven't pretended to tackle that problem; it simply isn't on their research agenda so far. In fact, their work so far doesn't even fully explain how *shallowly inclusive moralities* could have come about, because it only explains inclusiveness that is restricted to coethnics broadly understood, people of the same cultural group who look and speak alike or resemble each other in various superficial ways. The psychological mechanisms that these researchers observe in small children could have been at work in the EEA, enabling limited moral recognition of strangers, if they were coethnics. Something more would be needed, however, to explain the transition to shallowly inclusive morality, which involves extending the circle of moral regard to include people of other ethnicities or, in Tomasello's terms, different cultural groups.

Progress through Failures: How Detective Stories Work

Finding out what *doesn't* solve the Big Puzzle, which is what this chapter has done, is useful. So before moving on to a more productive line of investigation, let's review what we've learned about what doesn't work. One thing that doesn't work is to proceed by relying on the Cooperation Dogma, the assumption that morality is—not just was originally—all about facilitating cooperation. Another is simply pointing to the fact that moral consistency reasoning *can* help expand the circle of moral concern. That's not enough: you also have to provide an account of the kind of the moral consistency reasoning that leads to the Two Great Expansions and an explanation of why humans sometimes engage in it and often don't.

We need an even more fundamental kind of rethinking if we are to make much headway: it's time to go back to the moral origins story that generated the Big Puzzle in the first place. What if we got that story wrong? What if the moral mind as it evolved in the EEA wasn't as hostile to inclusive moralities as a lot of people think? Some of the best detective stories feature a point in the plot where the investigator backtracks, revisiting the initial assumptions she made when she first began the investigation.

Things can go wrong in two ways if you rely on a story about the origins of morality as a guide to what morality is now like and what it can become. The first is by getting the origins story wrong. The second is by getting it right but failing to realize that things can happen later that make moralities quite different from what they were originally. My aim is to expose and to avoid both sorts of errors. In the next chapter, I show that the origins story as presented in chapter 2 is seriously inaccurate—and in ways that open up possibilities for the Two Great Expansions. In chapters 5 and 6, I step through that open door, setting out the key elements of an explanation of how some human moralities became (at a rather late date) deeply inclusive, by pointing out some powerful new developments in human culture and psychology that have only occurred in the last three hundred years or so.

4

Revisionist Prehistory: Getting the Moral Origins Story Right

In the preface, I sketched my central argument, which can be stated in the following steps: (1) what sort of moralities humans have and what sort of moral agents they are depend on the character of their social environment; (2) some individuals have much more control over the character of the social environment than others; therefore (3) some individuals have much more influence over what sort of moralities we have and what sort of moral agents we are—but those individuals are utterly unaccountable for, and usually oblivious to, those momentous effects. (4) So far, humans have unwittingly created the conditions that determine their moral fate, but they may eventually learn enough about how the moral mind interacts with different social environments to exert significant control over their moral fate rather than leaving it to chance. (5) If we care about what sort of morality is predominant in our society and what sort of moral beings we are as individuals, we should develop a scientifically informed theory of moral institutional design to ensure that the social environment we inhabit is conducive to moral progress. (6) Understanding how instances of large-scale moral progress such as the Two Great Expansions occurred can provide us with valuable information about how the moral mind interacts with specific features of the social environment and can thereby provide resources for developing a theory of moral institutional design—a theory that can help us take charge of our moral fate.

In chapter 2, I drew the outlines of one particular creation story among many: the standard evolutionary explanation of the origins of human morality. According to that story, uniquely sophisticated types of moralities, with variations among groups, emerged and spread among our remote human ancestors because they facilitated complex and powerful forms of cooperation that enhanced human reproductive fitness in the challenging conditions of the EEA. An important point to remember about that creation story is that although moralities were supposed to be a purely intragroup affair, the cooperation they facilitated within the group was important for enabling the group to compete successfully against other groups. In evolutionary terms, the natural selection pressures of that peculiar environment resulted in the moral mind being expressed in moral rules, moral motivations, and moral practices that facilitated the kind of intragroup cooperation that humans needed to engage in to survive and reproduce in that environment, including cooperation to outcompete other groups, whether through violence or other means. Given the harsh conditions of the EEA as the standard origins story characterizes them—in particular the asymmetry between the meager or nonexistent benefits a group could gain from trying to engage peacefully with strangers and the enormous risks that strangers posed—the moralities that selection produced were tribalistic, not inclusive.

Chapter 2 sharpened the distinction between tribalistic and inclusive moralities and described two large-scale moral changes—the Two Great Expansions—that not only disconfirm the thesis that humans are beings with a tribalistic moral nature but also are mysterious, given the standard evolutionary story of "moral origins." That led to the conclusion that we should question the standard evolutionary story—in particular its apparent reliance on the two un-Darwinian dogmas: the Tribalism Dogma and the Cooperation Dogma. Chapter 3 canvassed several attempts to explain how, given the standard evolutionary origin story, the circle of moral regard could have expanded. They were shown not to work: they just aren't capable of explaining the First Great Expansion and they are even worse at explaining the Second. That chapter ended with the suggestion that we need a fresh start if we are to make any headway in solving the Big Puzzle. More specifically, I said we need to go back and question the key assumptions that generated the puzzle in the first place, including the standard characterization of the EEA. Let's do that now; let's be more critical about our initial assumptions. Here's the detective story analogy: what if the famous fictional detective Hercule Poirot came to the conclusion that he hadn't figured out who committed the murder because there was no murder?

Two Assumptions That Create the Big Puzzle

Productive backtracking requires recognizing the major landmarks on the route that led us to the Big Puzzle. One of them is the inference from "this is how morality originally evolved" to "this is how morality is (and will be)." That inference *appears* cogent if (but only if) we assume that there was *one* EEA, that the environment in which human morality arose was so *uniformly* hostile to peaceful, cooperative relations among groups that it produced beings whose moral minds were tribalistic, where this means, on the strongest formulation of the Tribalism Dogma, that inclusive moralities, if they exist at all, are deeply unstable aberrations because they are contrary to our moral nature.

I've already explained why I think that the assumption that the moral mind is dualistic is more plausible. It explains the existence of both tribalistic and inclusive moralities and the evidence of the preponderance of tribalistic moralities throughout most of human history without making the unnecessarily strong assumption that the moral mind is tribalistic—and without the awkwardness of characterizing the inclusion we do see as somehow "unnatural." But let's look more closely at the assumption that there was one EEA. This amounts to believing that *throughout* the EEA, cooperation with members of other groups would have been so detrimental from the standpoint of reproductive fitness that natural selection would have produced humans whose moral nature was thoroughly tribalistic, incapable of inclusive moral responses.

One EEA or Many?

That assumption is probably wrong. In fact, there's evidence that some cooperation among groups did occur in the EEA, though it was limited and didn't spawn deeply inclusive morality in the sense of recognizing the equal basic moral status of all human beings. The archaeological record, when taken together with anthropological studies of contemporary hunter-gatherer peoples, indicates that there were at least two forms of cooperation among groups in the EEA: out-mating (mate selection of members of other groups) and long-distance trade (especially in materials like obsidian and quartz for making efficient, durable projectile points and tools). Some groups may have also formed military alliances with each other, but the archaeological evidence for this (so far) comes from the Mesolithic Era, somewhat later than the period in which, according to most evolutionary scientists, the moral mind supposedly first appeared.

Long-distance trade, military alliances, and out-mating are forms of intergroup cooperation. They require some limited trust of *some* humans who are not members of one's own immediate group, in this case the small hunter-gatherer group whose members lived with one another on a day-by-day basis. These forms of intergroup cooperation require recognizing others as beings who are somewhat like us—at least so far as their ability to engage in agreements and keep them is concerned. More specifically, all these forms of intergroup cooperation require the ability to recognize people from other groups (at least *some other groups*) as potential reciprocators in cooperation that involves following some basic moral rules, like "keep your promises" and "return the favor when others confer benefits on you." People who were hardwired or programmed solely for fear, distrust, and preemptive aggression toward members of other groups couldn't engage in these or any other forms of intergroup cooperation.

So, if early human groups engaged in long-distance trade and out-mating (if not also military alliances), we have good reason to assume that the EEA was not uniformly conducive to (purely) tribalistic morality. In other words, if these forms of intergroup cooperation occurred, then the moral mind was capable, even at this early point in our history, of producing moralities that were not purely tribalistic, that restricted cooperation and minimal moral regard to the level small bands of humans. Or, if you prefer, there wasn't just one EEA; there were several, and depending on which one you were in, there may have been greater or lesser opportunities for limited cooperation among groups *and hence selective pressures for a morality that wasn't hardwired for tribalism.*

One might be tempted to conclude that some humans in the EEA exhibited a *shallowly inclusive* morality. That would only follow, however, if the limited cooperation they engaged in was not restricted to their own ethnic or cultural group. Remember, shallowly inclusive moralities involve a kind of limited moral regard for people who are not part of one's ethnic or cultural group—the kind of regard that is needed to make market relations encompassing diverse kinds of people work. It may well be that trade and out-mating among the hunter-gatherers of the EEA was restricted to coethnics—people with whom one shared a language, as well as important customs, modes of dress, bodily adornment, and so on. Or, as we might also say: these forms of intergroup cooperation occurred only among groups who shared a culture.

Anthropologists tell us that at some point, loose associations of bands came on the scene. This may have happened through a process of fission: when moralities enabled bands to cooperate so successfully that their numbers increased to the point where they began to strain local resources, subgroups split off and moved to other areas. The "parent" and "offspring" groups would often have maintained some forms of cooperation; in particular, they could unite for defense against, or aggression toward, other groups, and they might come together periodically for mate selection and trade. As long as the groups that split off maintained a common language and similar customs with the parent group, they could sustain cooperation with each other and at the same time maintain an exclusive, "tribalistic" moral attitude toward other groups, people of other ethnicities or cultures.

Such cooperation among bands didn't require complete cultural homogeneity. It could have occurred even if, as one would expect, over time some significant cultural differences developed among the bands that split off. So once human groups reached the level of associations of bands, the distinction between in-group and out-group was no longer quite so clear and stark; and consequently, the bald claim that humans are tribalistic by nature is to that extent misleading or inaccurate.

The main point, however, is that even if humans practiced limited intergroup cooperation in the EEA, it doesn't follow that they had moved from exclusive morality all the way to shallowly inclusive morality. That transition requires cooperation between different ethnic or cultural groups.

I think it's plausible to hold that tribalistic moralities were preponderant in the EEA, though humans in some locales practiced limited cooperation with other groups of the same ethnicity or culture, and that the development of shallowly inclusive morality, which enabled cooperation among more diverse groups, came considerably later—perhaps as late as the Neolithic Revolution, when large, ethnically and culturally diverse political units were forged mainly by conquest. In chapters 5 and 6, I will offer a historical narrative that places the transition to shallowly inclusive morality largely in the world in which agriculture began replacing hunting and gathering.

Why Intergroup Cooperation in the EEA Fell Short of the First Great Expansion

Whether or not long-distance trade and out-mating in the EEA still only represented instances of exclusive morality or instead encompassed diverse ethnic or cultural groups and hence count as evidence of shallowly inclusive morality, I want to emphasize a simple but major point: those two forms of cooperation are limited in two senses. First, they are not as comprehensive as the cooperation that went on within groups that lived together on a day-to-day basis; and they were episodic rather than continuous. Second, and more importantly, those forms of cooperation could be conducted successfully without either of the participating groups having achieved a *deeply inclusive morality*.

This is most obvious in the case of trade. Recognizing that members of some other group are the kinds of beings you can engage in peaceful exchanges with doesn't mean you believe they have the same basic equal moral status that you grant to yourself and members of your own group.

You might think that out-mating practices differ from trade in that respect—that to be willing to mate with someone from another group, you have to recognize them as full moral equals. Unfortunately that isn't so. Slaveholders mated with slaves even though they professed to believe slaves were less than fully human. Indeed, sexual interaction between groups occurred even in what was perhaps the most brutal form of slavery, hereditary chattel slavery as it existed in the American South.

In fact, until very recently, and then only in certain parts of certain societies, mating between male and female humans has typically been deeply patriarchal, characterized by huge power differentials and therefore status disparities. The mere existence of the practice of mating with members of other groups, even when it is marked by various sorts of rituals, doesn't mean that either member of the mating pair regards the other as a being with full basic equal moral status.

Furthermore, we have good reason to believe that in early human societies a lot of out-mating was coercive, not cooperative—organized rape conducted by men raiding other groups to capture women. Tragically, this still goes on, both in the activities of ISIS and among some indigenous people, including the Yanomami and some other tribal societies of Amazonia. Neither population genetics studies nor the commercial genetic testing company AncestryDNA can distinguish between the products of voluntary and coercive out-mating.

Nevertheless, some forms of out-mating may have come close to according the mate from another group the same status as those born into the group. This doesn't imply, however, that people who practiced that sort of relatively egalitarian out-mating had the moral concept of a human being, that they had achieved the First Great Expansion. Why? Because it's compatible with their still believing that those other groups they didn't consider suitable for mate selection are not fully human, maybe not human at all. Being willing to mate with members of *some* other groups and to accord your mate something like equal status doesn't mean you regard people of *all* groups as having equal status.

Having said that, I want to emphasize that the basic point remains: evidence of out-mating and long-distance trade suggests that different groups in "the" EEA practiced limited cooperation, and therefore that whatever the selective pressures were like in the EEA, they didn't produce moralities that only included moral norms for interaction with those who were part of a group that lived together on a day-to-day basis.

It's not hard to see why it would have been advantageous for people in the EEA (or some local variants of it) to engage in long-distance trade and out-mating. Both of these forms of intergroup cooperation could enhance a group's reproductive fitness: trading increased your stock of survival goods, and out-mating increased your population (and hence your pool of cooperators, thus increasing the probability that your cultural innovations, as well as your genes, would be preserved and passed on).

If this characterization of limited intergroup cooperation in (some parts of) the EEA is correct, we now have the beginnings of a plausible evolutionary account of how some people in the environment in which human morality initially emerged could have had something approaching, if not fully reaching, shallowly inclusive moralities. And so we also have all the more reason to believe that the moral mind was not so inflexible as to warrant the characterization "our tribal moral nature."

A New Hypothesis: The Variable Challenges of the EEA Produced an Adaptively Plastic Capacity for Moral Responses

There are two ways to argue that the selective pressures of the EEA didn't produce a tribalistic moral mind while admitting that the moral mind, under those conditions, for the most part underwrote tribalistic moralities. The first is to do what I've just begun to do: postulate that the EEA wasn't so uniformly hostile to inclusive moral responses; that in some locales there was actually selective pressure for a flexible moral response that allowed cooperation with strangers under the right circumstances (Buchanan and Powell 2018, 80). The second is simply to appeal to the general flexibility of the moral mind.

I'll opt for the first alternative for a simple reason: the second alternative is explanatorily vacuous, because just saying that the moral mind exhibits general flexibility doesn't explain why that flexibility issues in one kind of morality in certain environments and another in different environments. The second alternative can't deliver what we're after: an explanation of moral progress (or regression) in the dimension of inclusion and of the fact that human moralities vary as to inclusion versus exclusion.

So let's develop the first alternative, *the special adaptive plasticity hypothesis*. Perhaps some locales in which the earliest humans found themselves afforded opportunities for peaceful, mutually advantageous interactions, not just with other bands of the same ethnicity or culture, but with genuine strangers. For example, in cooler, drier environments, the threat of parasites from strangers wasn't so high as it was in tropical areas, so interacting with strangers wasn't as dangerous. Or resources may have been more abundant in some areas than in others, which meant competition among groups wouldn't have been so intense. In other words, some of the threat cues that trigger tribalistic responses may not have been so strong everywhere. Here I agree with the sagacious philosopher of evolutionary biology Kim Sterelny, who observes that "relations between groups were variable and contingent throughout the Pleistocene" (Sterelny 2012, 124). In other words, some locales offered opportunities for cooperation, not just for conflict.

If there were enough of these opportunities, there would have been natural selection (selection on genes) for a moral mind that allowed flexible responses to strangers: when the conditions were right for mutually beneficial cooperation, people would be able to take advantage of them; when those conditions weren't present, they would react to strangers in a hostile, tribalistic way. According to this idea, the selective forces that produced the moral mind would have resulted in it having a special kind of flexibility, the ability to relate to strangers either in a welcoming, cooperative way or with distrust, fear, and preemptive aggression.

The standard evolutionary story of moral origins in the EEA tends to present competition among groups as violent competition—war. But groups would have competed in other ways. For example, they would have competed for members. A group that was willing to accept members of other groups—people who either left voluntarily or were kicked out or survived an epidemic or the violent destruction of the rest of their group in war—could gain strength in numbers, so long as the group was able to discern whom to let in and whom not to.

Remember, in the EEA human power was the greatest resource of all. Perhaps some groups were more welcoming than others. If they were, then, other things being equal, they would have had a reproductive advantage. Any group that was uniformly hostile toward the Other—a group whose members were "hardwired" or "programmed" for tribalism and only that—would be at a fitness disadvantage. So would any group that was promiscuously open to accepting strangers. Natural selection would favor flexibility, but discerning flexibility.

Note that a willingness to accept strangers into the group doesn't imply that groups that did so had embraced the First Great Expansion, that they regarded all humans as having an equal basic moral status, for three reasons. First, admitting strangers may have been selective: only members of certain groups, not all groups, may have been allowed in. Second, as anthropologists have documented, admission of out-group members into hunter-gatherer groups is often, perhaps always, provisional in this sense: the stranger has to demonstrate that he or she has become one of Us to be accorded full membership status. Third, admission to the group sometimes entails a permanently inferior status that cannot be overcome regardless of the stranger's efforts to assimilate. Nonetheless, admitting strangers under any of these conditions could occur only if early humans didn't have a uniformly robust exclusionary response to strangers.

That largely tribalistic moralities could develop alongside more inclusive moralities, as a result of variations in the EEA, makes it all the clearer that the moral mind is not tribalistic. One would only miss this obvious fact if one were in the grip of the two un-Darwinian dogmas, the Tribalism Dogma and the Cooperation Dogma. The whole idea of the moral mind—our moral human nature—is the idea of something that is invariant across the diversity of moralities, something that is the basis for generating different moralities under different conditions, in response to different stimuli. The special plasticity hypothesis *explains* the variation in human moralities, from more thoroughly tribalistic to deeply inclusive, by positing that the special plasticity is a part of the moral mind itself. It is the part or aspect of the moral mind that generates either tribalistic moralities or inclusive ones, depending on the environment.

Plastic Moral Responses

Let's explore the special plasticity hypothesis further. More precisely, let's take seriously the idea that the moral mind is flexible regarding responses to strangers, because in some locales of the EEA, specific features of the environment conferred a reproductive advantage on this kind of flexibility. As I noted when I first introduced our friend the water flea, evolutionary biologists have a term for a particular kind of flexibility that exists in a lineage of organisms because at some point in the past it conferred reproductive advantage: *adaptive plasticity*. After giving the example of the water flea in the introduction, I noted that adaptive plasticity is pretty common in nature, across a wide range of organisms.

The flexibility the water flea exhibits is one-way only: if predator cues disappear from the water in which the fully developed creature lives, it does not lose its spines and helmet. The kind of flexibility that human moral psychology exhibits is two-way: people who have developed inclusive moral responses can lose them if the environment comes to resemble the EEA—or if they come to believe that it does. The same facts about human moral psychology that allow inclusive moralities to develop in certain environments also make inclusion liable to regression, if the environment changes. I'll use the phrase "adaptive plasticity" to cover this kind of two-way flexible adaptation.

Adaptive plasticities have a peculiar feature: you won't notice them if you only encounter the organism that has them in one kind of environment. Remember: if you only observe water fleas in environments that include the chemical signatures of predators, it may not occur to you that other water fleas elsewhere might not have spines and helmets. You'll think that it's in the nature of water fleas to have these protective devices. Similarly, if for most of human history, our species has lived in environments in which their plastic capacity for moral responses only manifested itself in one way, in the form of exclusive moralities, you'll mistakenly believe that human beings are tribalistic by nature.

If humans tend to respond tribalistically to the Other in environments that mimic the harsher locales of the EEA, and if until recently most humans lived in such environments, then tribalism would be preponderant in human experience. But that is compatible with acknowledging that in less harsh environments humans can exhibit more inclusive responses. One good reason to believe the special plasticity hypothesis is that if it were true, it would explain a lot that can't be explained by rejecting it.

A Plea for a Richer Research Agenda in the Evolutionary Study of Morality

Let me end this chapter with a cautionary note. This book isn't really concerned mainly with exposing the errors of people who confuse the possibilities for human moralities with the actuality of human moralities in the EEA and therefore have an unduly static picture of moralities. The best evolutionary thinkers don't make that mistake (though, as I've shown, in their less careful statements, some of them certainly give the impression that they do). The most astute thinkers are aware that from the assumption that the basics of human moral psychology were fixed at some time in the Middle to Late Pleistocene, it doesn't follow that the content or character of human moralities is fixed. Nor is my main focus combating the pessimistic conclusions about the fate of morality that evoconservatives draw because they are crude biological determinists in the grips of a bogus moral origins story.

As I've said before, I have two more positive, constructive goals. My top-priority goal is to develop a theory of large-scale moral change that can illuminate the possibilities for moral progress and regression. I want to do that because it is vital to rethink our understanding of the nature of morality and the fact of unequal power in light of the realization that the moral possibilities depend on the character of the social environment, the constructed niches that humans build and that humans can reshape. We need such an understanding if we are ever able to take charge of our moral fate. In the process of explaining the Two Great Expansions, I hope to provide the elements of a more general theory of how large-scale moral change comes about—a theory that can provide resources that will enable us to exert some control over what sort of morality we have and what sort of moral agents we are, a theory that can help us engage in the vital task of moral institutional design.

To further this primary goal I hope to achieve another: to enlist science in helping us learn what we need to know in order to shape our moral fate in a progressive way. I want to demonstrate that the research agenda of even the best people who try to think about human morality in evolutionary terms is arbitrarily limited. That's because they focus only on morality as something that functions to facilitate cooperation. That may be a wise choice for the *initial* research agenda, but it's inadequate for a more comprehensive research agenda, one that attempts to see how far evolutionary thinking can take us in understanding all the important parts of human morality—and it is a fatal limitation if you want to understand how morality has changed and may change further. In brief, I hope to persuade evolutionary scientists to theorize not just the origins of morality but also moral change. Above all, I want them to help us understand large-scale moral changes that are progressive and to give us information that will help us to protect our most inclusive moralities from regression. If our goal is to combat tribalism effectively—and learn how to influence the environmental factors that shape us as moral beings—we need to get the science right. Ultimately, only genuine scientists can do that.

The needed scientific account will have to free itself from a prejudice: namely, that everything worth knowing about morality can be explained by showing how it contributes to reproductive fitness. Deeply inclusive moralities—moralities that incorporate the Two Great Expansions—don't seem to have any obvious reproductive-fitness-enhancing functions. On the contrary, it's not hard to imagine a lot of environments where inclusive moralities would be detrimental to reproductive fitness. In fact, those are just the sorts of environments that most humans lived in until very recently and in which all too many still do.

Here's the next clue for solving the Big Puzzle: if, as the standard evolutionary account says, the original character of human moralities was shaped by features of the environment in which those moralities arose, then won't the character of moralities change if the environment changes? And won't moralities and the character of human moral agents change if humans manage to construct niches in which some of our moral behavior is "fitness independent" — human-made environments in which new forms of morality can come about even if they don't contribute to reproductive fitness? That leads to another question: what is common to environments in which some important aspects of moralities are "fitness independent"? The answer is this: environments in which humans have achieved *surplus reproductive success*.

5

The First Piece of the Puzzle: Surplus Reproductive Success

In this chapter, I begin to develop a solution to the Big Puzzle; in the next, I fill in details of the solution. The solution won't be simple. It won't rely on one-liner, magic-bullet answers like the thesis that the circle of moral regard expanded because the circle of cooperation expanded or that stable or efficient cooperation requires that people be treated equally or that it was just a matter of humans somehow finally learning how to engage in moral consistency reasoning in the right way and follow through on the conclusions it yields. Those charmingly simple answers don't work, as I argued in chapter 3. Nor will I attempt to show that becoming deeply inclusive made moralities more conducive to reproductive fitness.

My proposed solution—to be honest, my protosolution—will involve evolutionary thinking, but it may not be wholly accurate to call it an evolutionary solution to the Big Puzzle. It will have significant evolutionary components, but it won't be an evolutionary explanation through and through. Given that it's going to be complicated, perhaps the best way to proceed is to simply state, in a succinct way, the main idea and then flesh it out.

The Key to Solving the Big Puzzle: A Story of Cultural Evolution

Here's the main idea: *if humans have a biologically evolved moral mind that includes an adaptive plasticity that allows them to respond either tribalistically or inclusively to strangers, and if their tendency to respond tribalistically is triggered by threat cues that mimic the harsher conditions of the EEA, then they can avoid tribalistic moralities to the extent that they use their cultural niche construction abilities to create environments in which those threat cues are absent or significantly mitigated.* In even simpler terms: *we aren't condemned to tribalistic moralities—we have the potential to develop inclusive moralities—because the character of our morality is environmentally conditioned and we can shape our environment.* With that simple idea in mind, here are some of the key elements needed to flesh it out. I'll present them in the form of a historical narrative, based on the results of my investigation in this book so far and my reading of relatively uncontroversial historical, sociological, archaeological, and anthropological primary sources.

1. Even if the EEA was often hostile toward peaceful cooperation with members of other groups—even if, consequently, moralities *in that early environment* were largely tribalistic in character—it doesn't follow that human beings are only capable of exclusive moralities. That would follow only if basic human moral psychology, the moral mind, is rigid rather than flexible, so far as the ability to respond to strangers is concerned.

2. We *know* that the moral mind is flexible regarding responses to strangers, because we observe not only tribalistic moralities but also moralities that are much more inclusive. The Two Great Expansions are a fact.

3. The best explanation of why the Two Great Expansions have occurred includes the idea that the moral mind evolved to feature a special adaptive plasticity: the potential both for tribalistic moral responses and for inclusive ones, depending on the environment. In the EEA, flexibility in responding to strangers would have enhanced reproductive fitness in locales that afforded opportunities for peaceful cooperation. For example, success in competing with other groups could be achieved by welcoming strangers rather than fending them off, responding inclusively rather than tribalistically. Or if, due to a dryer or colder local environment, the threat of foreign parasites was low and if resources were relatively abundant, the risks of trying to cooperate with another group could be acceptable.

4. For the special adaptive plasticity to "toggle" toward inclusion, it must be possible to discern that another human being is the sort of

creature with whom it is safe and beneficial to cooperate on moral terms, even though he or she doesn't resemble you in the way fellow members of your ethnic or cultural group do. This amounts to acknowledging a limited sort of moral status: in other words, you will proceed on the assumption of mutual expectations of basic forms of reciprocity—for example, you will believe that the Other is both capable of keeping promises and entitled to your keeping them. But it doesn't follow that you will only cooperate morally with beings you regard as your full moral equals or that you will recognize as equals people with whom you never expect to cooperate. Intergroup cooperation that only involves trade, out-mating, or military alliances requires only *shallowly inclusive* moralities—limited moral regard for the Other—not the deeply inclusive moralities evidenced by the Two Great Expansions. In fact, when humans in the Neolithic Revolution made the transition from small hunter-gatherer groups to large, complex, multiethnic, multicultural societies based on fixed, year-round abodes relying on agriculture and domestication of animals, they developed highly inegalitarian cooperative schemes that assigned a range of different statuses to various groups of individuals who were incorporated within that more complex kind of society. People learned how to cooperate with people quite unlike themselves, but to do so in ways that were characterized by extreme inequalities. In other words, the moral scaffolding of this form of cooperation did not include the recognition of equal basic moral status. Nor did the new, more complex, large-scale forms of morally structured cooperation require or even encourage the Second Great Expansion. On the contrary, they presented new opportunities for the unrestrained exploitation of many more nonhuman animals than ever before.

5. As human societies became larger and more complex, incorporating) more ethnically and culturally heterogeneous groups, there were selective pressures both for reducing the at-a-glance differences that earlier peoples had used to distinguish Us from Them, and for sophisticated discernment capacities that allowed people to see through the remaining superficial differences and judge that very different-looking folks were still the kinds of beings we could cooperate with. Thus, for example, the expansion of trade in the

Chinese, Egyptian, Minoan, Phoenician, and other early empires probably resulted both in the spread of some commonalities in dress, hairstyles, and so on, and also, at least in some people (merchants in particular), the ability to not be put off by the remaining differences when there were opportunities for beneficial exchanges. People got better at inferring the intentions and above all the trustworthiness (or lack of it) in a wider range of human types. Yet all of this was still compatible with inclusion not reaching all the way to the First Great Expansion. The post-Neolithic world of greatly increased intergroup cooperation was a world of deep inequalities, including the ubiquity of slavery. And the transition to it did not bring about the Second Great Expansion. This more complex world hummed along rather smoothly for millenia, even though it probably never occurred to most people either that all human beings possessed equal basic moral status or that nonhuman animals had any moral standing at all. At most, this new environment moved increasing numbers of people from exclusive moralities to shallowly inclusive moralities.

6. From the time when our ancestors first became cultural creatures, there were selective pressures to develop even greater capacities for culture, because culture was crucial for human reproductive fitness. Cumulative cultural evolution wasn't just a matter of developing new ways of operating more effectively in given environments; it included *niche construction*, the creation of new environments more favorable to the achievement of further cultural innovations, and that in turn produced selective pressures for the enhancement of abilities needed for cultural innovations. Beginning around the second half of the eighteenth century, at first mainly in western Europe but spreading rapidly elsewhere, much larger numbers of people came to live in environments that differed profoundly from the harsher conditions of the EEA. A crucial development that made these new environments possible occurred earlier: starting around 1450 CE, the modern state's monopoly on violence, as the sociologist Max Weber put it (or, as its earlier manifestation was called, the King's Peace), began dramatically reducing the threat of physical violence, a fact that Steven Pinker has convincingly documented, drawing on studies by scholars who specialize in tracking homicide

rates over time. This reduction in the risk of violence made possible the growth of markets, both because it made people more secure in their project of accumulating resources they could use to exchange with others, and because it gave them more confidence that an attempt at exchange wouldn't turn into a violent, unilateral expropriation. Markets have a remarkable feature: they allow mutually beneficial cooperation among strangers, in fact, among people who have no ties of kinship or affection or religion or culture or ethnicity. In this new environment, it paid for people to develop a suite of psychological skills sometimes given the moralizing title "the bourgeois virtues" (Elias 2000, 54–55; McCloskey 2006, 4). To take full advantage of the new opportunities provided by relatively peaceful, market-based societies, people needed to have better impulse control (especially with regard to violence), better ability to read the intentions of strangers from their behavior, better ability to think through the future consequences of their actions and how they would mesh with the consequences of the actions of others, and better ability to signal effectively to others that they were themselves reliable partners in mutually beneficial cooperative arrangements based on voluntary exchange. All of this meant that they needed to become better at reasoning, including moral reasoning, because markets only operate effectively if people generally observe some basic moral rules, and reasoning is required to know how to apply rules to new situations. It's likely that at least at the beginning of market-based societies, individuals who developed these skills had higher reproductive rates, because they did better economically, thus allowing them to live in houses with better sanitation, have healthier diets, and avoid the overcrowded living conditions that bred deadly diseases. Yet even if achieving higher standards of living *initially* conferred benefits in terms of biological reproductive fitness, we know that higher standards of living eventually *reduce* fertility—that wealth and reproductive fitness become negatively correlated at a certain point. In these new conditions, social success or, if you will, "cultural fitness" is not only compatible with low fertility but can even be enhanced by it. Having fewer children and thus being able to invest more in them can produce greater material and social rewards than having more children. Once sufficient surplus reproductive success is achieved, mating practices need no longer be driven by fitness.

7. At first, the expansion of the circle of regard that market-based, relatively physically secure societies allowed only amounted to according strangers the status of potential partners in exchange—extending shallowly inclusive moral responses to more and more people—but it paved the way for further changes in moral beliefs and attitudes that eventually resulted in the First Great Expansion. In the next chapter, I explain that new application of old capacities, assigning a pivotal role to one rather amazing human ability, what I call the capacity for critical, open-ended moral thinking. I argue that this capacity is likely to be widely exercised, in ways that can lead to the Two Great Expansions, only under certain highly unusual conditions.

8. The cultural innovations of the modern era, especially the rise of the modern state and the growth of markets, along with momentous increases in agricultural productivity beginning around 1760 CE, resulted not only in greater physical security, reductions in the frequency and severity of epidemic disease outbreaks, and increased cooperation with strangers; it also produced much greater wealth for more people than ever before. For those who reaped the material benefits of modern social arrangements, extending sympathy beyond the circle of one's close associates and acting altruistically toward strangers—not just being willing to engage in self-interested exchanges with them—became for the first time something one could do without paying a penalty in reproductive fitness or reducing one's own material prosperity to socially unacceptable levels. People who are doing much better materially than they need to in order to survive and reproduce and even live reasonably well according to the standards of their society can afford to care more about strangers, even strangers with whom they will never have any cooperative relationships whatsoever. So cultural innovations that resulted in the creation of the new niche we call modern, "developed" society gave more scope for altruism and for sympathy. For increasing numbers of people, showing moral regard for strangers—even people with whom they weren't engaged in cooperation—no longer imposed the penalties it previously did. As more and more people achieved better material circumstances, their moral horizons widened.

The cultural-innovation-driven developments summarized in items 7 and 8 in the list above amount to this: more people came to live in human-constructed environments that mitigated the harsher conditions of the EEA and therefore made them less subject to the stimuli that toggle our dualistic moral mind toward tribalistic responses. People could afford to become less tribalistic in their moralities; being more inclusive no longer carried the high reproductive fitness cost that it did in the EEA. Cumulative cultural niche construction made it less costly to be more considerate toward and even care deeply about other beings, regardless of whether or not they were seen as potential cooperators.

In other words, *the unprecedented surplus reproductive success of modern societies for the first time in human history made the escape from tribalism possible for significant numbers of people.* But something even more momentous and far-reaching occurred: *surplus reproductive success* produced *the Great Uncoupling*: the content of moralities was liberated from the demands of reproductive fitness. The surplus reproductive success that humans only recently achieved allowed us to develop moralities that would have been unviable in earlier, less bountiful circumstances, when humanity hovered closer to the edge of survival, and morality was the slave of fitness.

This doesn't mean that people who were lucky enough to inhabit this new environment automatically embraced the Two Great Expansions. But it does mean that a cultural and psychological space was created in which they could afford to do so without paying a prohibitive reproductive or economic penalty.

How Cultural Evolution Moved Us Away from the EEA

Before I speculate about what further changes had to occur for significant numbers of people to walk through the door toward greater inclusion that these new, human-constructed niches opened for them, let me make something clear: the new niches created the possibility of the Two Great Expansions *because they distanced ever increasing numbers of humans from each of the specific features of the locales of the EEA that encouraged tribalistic moral responses.* (a) Public health and sanitation measures (first pioneered in Renaissance trading centers to prevent the spread of plague from seaports and augmented in the late eighteenth century by the widespread use of vaccinations against smallpox and by scientifically based public health measures a century later) greatly decreased the threat of biological parasites transmitted by strangers. (b) The imposition first of the King's Peace and then of the more systematic and rule-of-law-governed monopoly on coercion of the modern state reduced the threat that strangers posed to physical security. It also reduced the risk that "foreigners" in our midst would free ride on our cooperative enterprises, because it created public enforcement mechanisms that worked in large-scale, anonymous urban areas where older informal social norm enforcement based on kinship and shared culture no longer sufficed. (c) There was a tremendous proliferation of new social practices and institutions for facilitating mutually beneficial cooperation among members of different groups, the growth of various kinds of markets being the most prominent, with the result that the ratio of benefits to risks in encounters with strangers changed radically from what it had been in the EEA. (d) New modes of production increased social surpluses so dramatically that violent competition for resources among groups diminished.

To summarize: if it is true that the prevalence of certain threat cues in many locales of the EEA resulted in moralities that developed *in that environment* being largely tribalistic, and if modern cultural developments have greatly reduced the strength of every one of those threat cues for increasing numbers of people, then you would expect that more people would no longer be so prone to purely tribalistic moralities. When the threat cues aren't present or at least aren't so prominent, we don't need the cultural and psychological equivalents of the water flea's spines and helmets as much as we used to.

Why the Cultural Evolution Story So Far Isn't Enough to Solve the Big Puzzle

Saying that the conditions that toggle the moral mind toward tribalistic moralities have been reduced for many people as a result of the construction of new niches characterized by surplus reproductive success is one thing. Explaining how and why some of those people actually went on to develop deeply inclusive moralities is quite another. The story of cultural niche construction I've outlined only explains why people who live in that sort of niche would at least develop shallowly inclusive moralities, a limited sort of recognition of the moral status of others, and would have had increasing *opportunities* to go farther than that, to cultivate and act on feelings for strangers and nonhuman animals independently of any prospect of cooperating with them. It doesn't yet tell us why people who could afford (from a biological or cultural fitness standpoint) to become deeply morally inclusive *would in fact become that way*.

Stepping through the Door That Cultural Evolution Opened

Prepare yourself now for a big shift in my analysis. So far, all the steps I've outlined fit under the heading of an *evolutionary* explanation of movement *toward*, but not yet reaching, the Two Great Expansions. Those speculations include hypotheses about both biological evolution and cultural evolution, because they rely on both biological and cultural selective pressures. The chief role of biological selective pressures was that they produced the moral mind; after that, cultural selection becomes the dominant mechanism for large-scale moral change—so far. In that sense, my account up to this point has been constructed within a broadly evolutionary framework.

Yet as I've just emphasized, my speculations up till now don't get us the whole distance we need to travel to solve the Big Puzzle. At most they make intelligible the possibility that humans have started on a journey that *could* bring them to the Two Great Expansions. At most my eight-stage narrative shows how evolutionary thinking can explain the transition from exclusive morality to shallowly inclusive morality and the creation of the conditions for the *possibility* of deeply inclusive morality.

The next part of my story, then, needs to bridge the gap between "some humans *became able* to become deeply morally inclusive" and "some humans *have actually become* deeply morally inclusive." The bridge that I'm about to construct won't sound sufficiently evolutionary to some people. Why? Because it will depend on a new assumption: that moral thinking and motivation can take on a life of their own, becoming relatively untethered from the sorts of evolutionary forces we are most familiar with, once the process outlined in steps 1 through 8 has occurred.

Nevertheless, I will try to convince you that this part of the story is scientific in the sense that empirical research could turn out to confirm or disconfirm my hypotheses about the power of moral thinking and moral motivation when they operate together in the right sort of environment.

I'm not going to try to provide all the necessary confirming empirical evidence. Instead I'll offer what philosophers call an "inference to the best explanation." I'll argue that the best explanation of the Two Great Expansions, in fact the only explanation available at present that has even a modicum of plausibility, requires that moral thinking and motivation have the power I attribute to them—again keeping in mind the crucial caveat: when they operate in the right environment and on the basis of the right sort of evolved moral psychology, the highly flexible moral mind that all normal humans actually have.

The story I'm going to tell doesn't make morality something supernatural or otherworldly, something that can bring about progress on its own, as it were, regardless of social context and independent of our evolved biological nature and our historically altered moral beliefs and attitudes. It isn't going to be a story that ignores the evolutionary origins of moralities or pretends that those origins have no implications for the possibilities for what moralities can be. It's also *not* going to be the sort of story that moral philosophers have often told in the past: I'm not going to assume that human morality is a purely rational affair and that rationality can expand the circle of moral regard without a lot of help from the emotions. Nor am I inviting you to accompany me on a journey through the history of ideas, presented as if it were an autonomous process. I'm taking seriously the commitment to providing a thoroughly naturalistic explanation.

Finally, it's worth recalling that my speculative explanation doesn't present moral change in the direction of greater inclusion as endogenous to moralities. That is, it doesn't characterize improvements in moralities as originating exclusively within them. Instead, as I've already said, it relies on the assumption that the use of coercion in a competition for power largely unconstrained by moral scruples played a central role in creating the conditions under which human beings could first develop shallowly inclusive moralities—a necessary condition, as it turns out, for some of them going on to develop deeply inclusive moralities. In other words, the ruthless quest for dominance that resulted in the modern state's near monopoly on violence and its support of markets, including the enforcement of property rights that solidified and even increased gross inequalities, laid the foundation for a fundamental and progressive change in human moralities.

Another Necessary Condition for the Two Great Expansions: The Capacity for Critical, Open-Ended Moral Reasoning

I believe that the Two Great Expansions would not have occurred unless human beings possessed a remarkable ability: what I referred to earlier as *the capacity for critical, open-ended moral reasoning*. In its simplest form, this is the ability to make explicit the moral rules you are following, subject them to critical scrutiny, and modify or abandon them in the light of reasoning about them. The critical light that this capacity shines on our moral life can even illuminate something as fundamental as the rules that govern how and to whom we assign moral standing and equal high basic moral status. Even more remarkably, exercising this capacity can result in a new understanding of what morality itself is about, as occurred when some people began to think that it wasn't just a matter of obeying the commands of some supposed higher authority. It was this remarkable capacity that allowed some people to embrace the Two Great Expansions.

Furthermore, I'll argue that for some people at least, this shift is not just a matter of positive feelings that we evolved to have toward those we cooperate with somehow irrationally spilling over to other beings with whom we don't and never will cooperate. So to that extent, my solution to the Big Puzzle will put me in the "rationalist" camp of moral philosophers. Yet I don't think my account is unscientific or not naturalistic. Nor is my account incompatible with a plausible sentimentalist moral psychology. My rationalism is of the moderate variety; I don't deny that emotions play a central role in moralities and in moral change. (On the contrary, as I've already said, the extension of sympathy was instrumental in the shift from shallow to inclusive moralities.) In fact, it doesn't matter much whether you characterize my position as moderately rationalistic or moderately sentimentalist or hybrid.

Let's start with moral standing, because it's the simpler of the two concepts. To say that a being has moral standing is simply to assert that it counts morally, in its own right. It is not a mere thing; to behave morally, you have to take into account that its interests matter—and not just so far as doing so benefits you or serves some other purpose. For example, to recognize that a pig has moral standing means acknowledging that morality imposes significant limits on how you are allowed to act toward it simply because of the kind of being it is, independently of any strategic purpose that might be served by observing those limits.

The extension of the concept of moral standing to nonhuman animals marks a momentous change in moral thinking, a revolution. For many people nowadays, that shift is grounded in the assumption that sentience that is the basis of moral standing: they believe that any being that can feel pain and pleasure has moral standing.

However, we shouldn't assume that our understanding of the basis of moral standing is static or that the understanding we have of it is fully consistent, much less optimal. In fact, it may be changing right now and in a way that eventually will result in recognizing that some organisms we previously thought didn't have moral standing do have it—and that some animals have a moral status approaching our own.

What I have in mind are recent revelations about the abilities of certain invertebrates (more specifically, cephalopods) and in particular octopi (Godfrey-Smith 2016, 98–106). Invertebrates don't have a spinal column with a cord running through it, and for this reason, they may not have the kind of neurology that makes it accurate to say that they feel pain and pleasure—at least not the pain and pleasure that vertebrates like sheep and dogs and humans experience.

Until now, a lot of people who think that animals have moral standing have assumed that they have it because—and only because—they are sentient, that is, because they can feel what we recognize as pain and pleasure. By implication, they denied moral standing to animals like invertebrates that they thought weren't sentient (or sentient in the "right" way, namely, the way we are). But now, in the light of recent research on invertebrates, more specifically cephalopods, which include octopi, we are learning that these creatures are much more like us than we thought and that they possess capacities that are very much like the capacities that we believe give us not only moral standing but an especially high moral status, relative to many other kinds of organisms.

Octopi turn out to be not only playful but wonderfully creative in their play, and they can quickly learn to interact playfully and intelligently with humans. One might even say they show a kind of genius in developing novel ways of interacting with items and agents in their environment. They also show great skill in niche construction: for example, they collect pieces of bivalve shells, transport them over considerable distances, and assemble them into shelters for themselves. If niche construction and the ability to act creatively are indications of intelligence, then octopi are highly intelligent.

In the light of this new appreciation of the capacities of cephalopods, some people at least are now beginning to question whether it is only sentient beings, beings that can experience pain and pleasure—at least as we understand those sensations—that have moral standing. In fact, we might even be moving toward the more radical conclusion that some creatures that aren't sentient in the way we are have a rather higher moral status than some creatures who are quite like us so far as sentience is concerned. Eventually we might even go so far as to conclude that if a being is sufficiently intelligent (and conscious and self-aware), then it has the same high moral status we humans do even if it is not sentient.

The point is that part of what we think makes it appropriate to confer a high moral status on ourselves is our intelligence, combined with consciousness and self-awareness. In fact, if we encountered an extraterrestrial being of high intelligence who was conscious and self-aware but for some reason wasn't sentient (or sentient in the way we humans are), we'd be wrong to conclude that he or she or it didn't have a moral status equal to ours. Instead we ought to conclude that sentience (or sentience as we have understood it) isn't necessary for equal high moral status, though it might be sufficient for having moral standing.

The process of rethinking our notions of moral standing or moral status involves an important kind of critical, open-ended moral thinking: moral consistency reasoning. The idea is that if we think that certain traits give *us* moral standing (or are even so valuable as to confer on us the highest moral status), then we should draw the same conclusions about *other* creatures, if they also have those same traits. We should treat like cases alike, applying our moral principles consistently, reconciling our intuitive moral responses with the values we hold most dear.

Moral consistency reasoning has a remarkable feature: it can produce radical results by proceeding in a rather conservative way. Moral consistency reasoning isn't bootstrapping. You start with values or moral principles you already have, try to identify which of them is most important, and then strive to make your beliefs, intuitive moral responses, and behavior consistent in the light of those moral priorities. Moral consistency reasoning starts at our present moral location, but it can take us to unanticipated destinations.

For that sort of reasoning to reach all the way to a reconsideration of something as morally fundamental as our understandings of equal moral status and moral standing—and for its conclusions to be sufficiently motivating to make significant changes in our behavior—a lot of factors have to be in place. For one thing, we have to know what the other creature is really like—and until recently, humans had little accurate knowledge about many creatures that, at what ultimately turns out to be a superficial level, are quite different from us.

From an evolutionary standpoint, it would hardly be surprising if our "theory of mind"—our ability to infer mental states from behavior—was rather anthropocentric; after all, that's all we needed to cooperate with other human beings. Cephalopods look so very different from us that we may have difficulty seeing just how intelligent they are—and how much their intelligence is like ours—unless we are scientifically trained to observe them. If our only interaction with them consists of killing and eating them, we aren't likely to appreciate the full range of their abilities.

To conclude that consistency in our moral responses requires reevaluating the moral standing or status of any creature, whether human or nonhuman animal, we also have to be able to see through the irrelevant differences and abandon our narcissistic prejudices, our smug confidence that we alone are so very special. In some cases, religious beliefs, especially those grounded in unscientific creation myths, may also raise a barrier to sound moral consistency reasoning about moral standing and moral status.

Believe it or not, I have encountered graduate students in an elite American university who think that no nonhuman animals feel pain, because God didn't insert souls into them. Quite apart from that bizarre theological view, the Bible contains passages asserting that God gave humans dominion over all living things and suggests that their only value is that we can use them to serve our purposes. In chapter 7, on regression to tribalism, and in chapter 8, on the evolution of moral tribalism to include intrasocietal tribalism, I will have more to say about the cultural conditions under which moral consistency reasoning is likely to function well and about the factors that can derail it. For now, I want to make clear that, given the anthropocentric or "speciesist" biases that humans are prone to, it would be surprising if current moral consistency reasoning concerning the status of nonhuman animals gets it right.

The Continuing Evolution of Understandings of the Basis for Moral Regard

The Second Great Expansion was a true moral-conceptual revolution, because it was change at the deepest levels of morality: an expanded understanding of the kinds of beings that have moral standing. Nevertheless, it may well be that the Second Great Expansion is incomplete, defective in one important way: even if sentience is a sufficient condition for having moral standing, maybe it isn't necessary. Perhaps having the sort of complex mental life that octopi have is also sufficient, even if those fascinating creatures lack sentience (or sentience as we've understood it so far, in our mammal-centric fashion).

Nowadays the moral-conceptual framework within which many humans operate includes more than just the idea of moral standing—the idea that the world divides only into two classes of things, those that matter morally on their own account and those that don't. Many people today also believe that the class of beings who have moral standing divides into two major subclasses: those that only have moral standing, and those that have an especially elevated kind of moral standing, a high moral status. People who have embraced the First Great Expansion believe not only that all human beings have moral standing, but also that all humans, and humans alone, have an especially high moral status. This amounts to believing that even if many beings count morally, human beings—all human beings—count a lot more. The idea not only that all humans count a lot more, morally speaking, but also that all of them count equally is the idea of the equal basic moral status of all humans.

It's the coming to be of that idea of basic human equality, along with serious (though admittedly imperfect and fragile) efforts to live that idea, to realize it in our personal behavior, social practices, and institutions, that I've called the First Great Expansion.

In both the First and Second Great Expansions, a change occurred in the way people think, not just in how they feel. Why? Because at least some of the people who have made both shifts, if queried, are able to give reasons for them, and in some cases it was their becoming convinced of the reasons that began the process of their feelings changing. Until recent research on octopi and other invertebrates shook us up, most of us believed that what gives nonhuman animals moral standing is the fact that they are sentient.

Before I read about that research, I relished eating octopi; now I find the very thought of doing so disgusting. For me, the moral emotion of disgust was directed toward a new target. Because of what I now believe about what octopi are like, the thought of eating them causes me to have just the same sort of *reason-based* disgust that many of us feel when we learn the horrific facts about factory farming. I've made an inference: I've moved from the proposition that high intelligence confers moral standing and the proposition that octopi are highly intelligent to the conclusion that I ought to treat octopi as beings with moral standing. Being consistent requires that. Moral integrity requires that.

I want to emphasize that I didn't change my attitude toward eating octopi automatically and nonrationally by simply imitating someone I looked up to who had stopped eating them on ethical grounds. Sadly, everyone I hang out with who isn't a vegetarian or vegan shows no evidence of worrying about the propriety of eating octopi. I also didn't change as a result of some kind of emotional contagion from others who exhibited disgust at eating octopi. (So far, I've not seen anyone else exhibiting such disgust.) My conversion was not a cognitively empty emotional reaction. Reasoning played a central role, just as it has in many people becoming vegetarians or vegans.

When I say that the growing recognition that at least some nonhuman animals have moral standing is a case of moral progress, I don't mean that this change in moral orientation has gone as far as it will go or should go. On the contrary, I think it's extremely likely that the Second Great Expansion is far from complete, even at the conceptual level, quite apart from shameful failures of implementation. It may well be that a result of further progress in recognizing the moral standing of some nonhuman animals will lead to a rejection, not of the idea that all humans have the same basic moral status, but of the idea that *only* human beings have the highest moral status. It might turn out that, according to the best understanding of the capacity that gives all human beings *equal* basic moral status, some nonhuman animals also have it.

Suppose you think that what gives all humans high moral status is that they can distinguish between what they desire and what they ought to do—that they have the concept of an "ought." Some evolutionary thinkers believe that although chimps and bonobos have a limited kind of morality in the sense that, being motivated purely by sympathy, they sometimes act altruistically toward other chimps with whom they interact closely, they don't operate with a sense of "ought." These evolutionary thinkers think that only humans do.

Suppose they're wrong. Suppose that further study of chimps (or some other animal species) reveals that they do have the capacity to distinguish between what they desire to do and what they ought to do. If we find out that some nonhuman animals have that capacity, and we think that our having it is what gives us the highest moral status, then we ought to recognize that those animals have the same high moral status that we do. That recognition wouldn't affect the other part of the conceptual shift that the First Great Expansion entails—the recognition that all humans have an *equal* high moral status—but it would require giving up the idea that humans alone have that high status.

Toward a Moderately Rationalist Understanding of Basic Moral Change

The moral psychologist Jonathan Haidt, like Steven Pinker, is a professor whose writings influence opinion far beyond the academy. Haidt has a very nonrationalistic, extremely sentimentalist understanding of human moral psychology. He emphasizes that most of the time, "the emotional dog wags the rational tail" (Haidt 2001, 830). He doesn't say whether "most of the time" means 50.01 percent of the time or 70 percent of the time or 90 percent of the time. But his rhetoric (including the dog-tail analogy) strongly suggests he doesn't mean anything as slim as a bare majority of the time. In brief, he doesn't give much credit to the role of reasoning in our moral lives.

I think he grossly underestimates the role of reasoning in the moral life generally but especially in moral change. Sometimes the rational dog wags the emotional tail and those cases are extremely important for the possibility of large-scale moral change. Reasons regarding who has moral standing are sometimes more than post hoc rationalizations of emotional changes in which reason played no role. Instead, sometimes reasoning stimulates emotional changes. That's a fair description, I think, of both the First and Second Great Expansions, at least so far as some people who have experienced them are concerned.

Nevertheless, I don't want to make the opposite error of assuming that the causal arrows only or even most of the time go from reasoning to emotions. I think the story is more complicated than either of those one-sided views. Sometimes emotions get stimulated without much in the way of inferences but nonetheless lead to changes in our moral responses and judgments. This may happen, for example, when we see a video of a starving child and instinctively say "we've got to do something about that" — without going through any process that could be aptly called moral reasoning. Yet sometimes new information (for example, about the capacities of nonhuman animals like octopi) gets us thinking and leads us to conclusions that can change our emotional responses.

There has been less consensus on what gives human beings the highest moral status than there has (until the recent revelations about cephalopods) on the idea that sentience confers moral standing. Religious folks often say that because all humans are God's children, created in his image, we all have the same high moral status. (I find that to be a disturbingly nepotistic view of basic moral status, but that's neither here nor there for present purposes.) Some moral philosophers believe that it is our practical rationality, our ability to reason about what we ought to do, that makes us so morally special among all the beings that have moral standing. Others think it is something more basic: the ability to distinguish between what is desired and what is good or between what one wants to do and what one ought to do.

A variant on the idea that practical rationality is the basis of equal basic moral status is what some of the most influential contemporary philosophers in the Kantian tradition, including Rainer Forst and Stephen Darwall, refer to as responsiveness to reasons — the ability to justify our actions to others and to be open to serious consideration of the justifications they offer. No consensus exists at present, however, even among contemporary philosophers, as to what grounds moral standing or equal basic moral status (Darwall 2009, 127, 281; Forst 2014, 23–28, 75–76).

Furthermore, what exactly high moral status amounts to and what counts as a proper acknowledgment of it is also not only subject to dispute but evolving as well. I noted in the introduction that at present the modern (post–World War II) conception of human rights is probably the most developed, substantive interpretation of the idea that all humans have a basic (high) equal moral status.

That understanding of what equal basic moral status entails began to take shape earlier, with the development of the concept of natural rights—moral rights that we are all supposed to have simply by virtue of our nature as humans. But filling out the content of the notion of equal moral status using the notion of human or natural rights is only one possibility among others; and even people who think it is the best alternative disagree about what rights are on the list.

I think it's likely that for a growing number of people an appreciation of new information about some nonhuman animals, combined with a sense that attempts to explain why human beings alone have an especially high moral status are less than fully convincing, may result in a blurring of what had previously been a basic structural feature of their moralities. They may become much less confident in the viability of the distinction between the supposedly minimal moral standing of nonhuman animals and the much higher equal standing of humans. That pretty much describes my present predicament.

Now that I've explained why I think the Two Great Expansions aren't a fait accompli but rather a work in progress, I can begin to fill out the explanation of how they began to come about. To do so, I first need to explain how human beings could come to *think* that not just members of their own tribe or cultural or ethnic or cooperative group but all human beings have an especially high moral status and that some nonhuman animals also have moral standing. What would the human mind have to be like for those two thoughts to arise in it, given the evolutionary origins of human morality? That's the first key question. In the next chapter, I try to answer it.

Before I make that attempt, another, prior question must be answered: What about the place of the capacity for critical, open-ended reasoning in the evolutionary story? Where does that capacity come from? Is there an evolutionary explanation of it? Is it an adaptation for cooperation?

Two possibilities are worth considering. The first is that this capacity is part of the moral mind, an ability that humans had from the start of their being moral in a distinctively human way. The second possibility is that even if, strictly speaking, this remarkable capacity wasn't part of the moral mind, it developed out of some

feature of the moral mind, perhaps the capacity for the most rudi-
mentary forms of moral consistency reasoning. Because the latter
capacity is required for something as basic to moralities as applying
moral rules to new situations, it seems reasonable to conclude that it
was there from the start, an element of the moral mind itself.

I don't know which option is the best. Fortunately, that doesn't
matter for most of what I want to say about large-scale moral change
in general and about the Two Great Expansions in particular. I think
it is clear that humans have the capacity for critical moral reasoning, and equally clear that it is open-ended in the sense that it has
the ability to challenge some of the most fundamental aspects of a
person's moral outlook, including her conceptions of equal moral
status and moral standing. I'm much more concerned with understanding the role of this capacity in large-scale moral change than in
establishing whether it is part of the moral mind or something that
emerged on the scaffolding of the moral mind.

Having said that, I fully acknowledge that there might turn out to
be a genuinely evolutionary explanation of why we have this capacity that makes it plausible to say that it is part of the moral mind. So
let's explore, if only briefly, the possibility that one important form
that this capacity takes, moral consistency reasoning, is susceptible
to an evolutionary explanation.

There are at least two ways that being able to engage in moral
consistency reasoning might have conferred a fitness advantage on
individuals in the early ancestral environments in which the moral
mind took shape: by making those who exhibit such reasoning more
attractive choices for partners in cooperation and by aiding the formation of coalitions. Let's consider each of these in turn, beginning
with the partner choice idea.

The outstanding philosopher of biology Kyle Stanford suggests
one way in which being able to engage in moral consistency reasoning would make one a more reliable partner in cooperation and
therefore be to one's reproductive advantage (Stanford 2018, 11, 19–
20). Suppose that you and I are in the EEA. If I do something that
you think violates our group's rules, you may refuse to partner with
me. If I'm to avoid that potentially disastrous outcome, I need some
way of reassuring you that I am in fact reliable. One way I can do

that is by trying to convince you that, in spite of appearances, I am a conscientious person, an individual with a strong moral identity and hence a reliable partner in cooperation. If I can convince you that I wasn't flouting moral rules but instead judiciously acting in a consistent way that recognized the point of the rules and which rules are most important, while discerning that there are justifiable exceptions to rules, that will be highly advantageous for me. According to this way of thinking, the capacity for moral consistency reasoning first came about because it played a strategic role, providing a defense against judgments of others that, if left intact, would result in an individual being excluded from cooperation, with the disastrous consequences for reproductive fitness this would entail.

Richmond Campbell, Jennifer Woodrow, and Victor Kumar offer a second explanation of why engaging in moral consistency reasoning would make one a more attractive partner in cooperation and thereby enhance one's fitness. They suggest that individuals who engaged in moral consistency reasoning would exhibit more predictable behavior than those who didn't, and this, too, would make them more attractive as partners in cooperation, which in turn would enhance their reproductive fitness (Campbell and Woodrow 2003, 361, 367, 371; Campbell and Kumar 2012, 303).

The pathbreaking work of Christopher Boehm provides my first example of the second type of adaptationist explanation of the capacity for moral consistency reasoning: the coalition-building account. Boehm suggests that the capacity to engage in this kind of reasoning was necessary for the formation of punishment coalitions to suppress bullies, which in turn contributed to the reproductive fitness of the suppressors (for example, by keeping control of resources that the bully would have expropriated). Boehm emphasizes that the need to control would-be dominators was a significant force in shaping human morality (he's not clear, as I noted earlier, whether "human morality" means the moral mind or the first moralities).

He emphasizes that in present-day hunter-gatherer groups that he and others have studied—and presumably in our distant ancestors whom they closely resemble—control over would-be dominators is frequently achieved by coalitions. The idea is that people talk among themselves until they reach a consensus that it is time to do something about the bully in their midst. To determine whether to act and if so when and with what degree of severity of punishment, some basic form of moral consistency reasoning would most likely be necessary. For example, it might be necessary for some members of the nascent punishment coalition to convince others that the current case was relevantly similar to a case that had occurred earlier—that the proposal to punish the current bully in this way was just like a decision that everyone approved of in another case. Moral consistency reasoning could also be valuable for convincing potential coalition members that the proposed punishment wasn't just a pretext for inflicting harm on someone that some members of the group happened to dislike. In brief, the idea is that individuals developed the capacity for moral consistency reasoning because it was useful for persuading other individuals to help curb bullies.

The exceptionally original and systematic evolutionary psychologists John Tooby and Leda Cosmides add another piece to the puzzle (Tooby and Cosmides 2010, 213–230). They, too, think that moral reasoning first developed because it enabled individuals to engage in strategic behavior vis-à-vis other individuals in ways that enhanced reproductive fitness, and they recognize that moral reasoning can be critical and open-ended rather than static. Like Boehm, they emphasize the importance of coalitions, but they focus on coalitions formed for purposes of making war against out-groups, not for suppressing bullies within the group. In their view, individuals who sought to build coalitions for violent competition with other groups needed to develop moral reasoning skills for doing so. Other things being equal, the more people a coalition builder could enlist, the more successful his coalition would be. To attract the greatest number of coalition members, leaders had to engage in reasoning that appealed to interests that were widely shared. They had to learn to identify common interests and convince people that the coalition would promote those interests. They would also have to convince potential coalition members that the goals of the coalition gave due weight to everyone's interests, that some members wouldn't be arbitrarily asked to take risks and bear costs that mainly benefited others, not themselves. So, to be effective, coalition builders would have had to develop moral reasoning skills that employed the idea of impartiality. To be persuasive, this reasoning would have to be consistent in the sense that it took the interests of each party into account, with no favoritism shown to any particular individual. Successful war-making coalition building would require moral consistency reasoning and also the development of concepts of impartiality and nonarbitrariness.

All three of these accounts might be elaborated to encompass not just moral consistency reasoning but other forms of moral reasoning as well, including reasoning that is critical of the moral status quo in rather fundamental ways. Under the right conditions, such reasoning could lead beyond the immediate strategic context to unanticipated destinations. Remember, the fact that something comes to be because it performs some function that promotes fitness doesn't mean that performing that function is all it can ever do. Even if moral consistency reasoning was originally strategic, that doesn't mean it is always like that.

Suppose that, taken together, the explanations offered by Stanford, Campbell, Woodrow, Kumar, Boehm, Tooby, and Cosmides make a convincing case that the capacity for moral consistency reasoning is an adaptation, a trait that arose because, by serving strategic purposes, it contributed to individual reproductive fitness, and that this capacity worked well because it was flexible, not limited to any particular task. If that were true, then we'd have an evolutionary explanation of the existence of the capacity for moral consistency. Yet we still wouldn't have an evolutionary explanation of how that capacity eventually came to be exercised in ways that led some people to adopt less tribalistic moralities.

Whether or not it is itself an adaptation or a by-product of an adaptation, the capacity for critical open-ended moral reasoning can greatly expand the space of possible human moralities—if it is exercised under the right conditions. In the next chapter, I offer an account of just what those conditions are.

6

Solving the Big Puzzle: How Surplus Reproductive Success Led to the Great Uncoupling of Morality from Fitness

I ended the preceding chapter with the suggestion that an attempt to explain the progressive shift from shallowly inclusive to deeply inclusive moralities should pay close attention to the capacity for critical, open-ended moral reasoning. This is the ability that cognitively normal human beings have to make the particular moral rules that they're following objects of conscious awareness and to subject those rules to critical scrutiny that sometimes results in modifying or abandoning them. It also includes the even more remarkable ability to scrutinize our most basic moral concepts and even our concept of morality. Later in this chapter, I will also argue that it can even contribute to changes in a person's moral identity.

We saw that it is one thing to show that this capacity came about because it was strategic to exercise it—so as to make oneself an attractive partner in cooperation or to build coalitions to suppress bullies or to make war on other groups—but quite another to show why it would ever come to be used in very different ways. In particular, we need an account of how anybody would ever come to use it in ways that contributed to the Two Great Expansions.

Before I say more about this peculiar capacity, I want to clarify why it's important to do so. Once human beings achieve sufficient surplus reproductive success, the character of their moralities is no longer determined by the demands of reproductive fitness. Morality becomes unshackled. The awesome flexibility of the moral mind can then produce moralities that were not viable when morality was the

slave of fitness. A key resource for exploiting this newfound freedom is the capacity for critical, open-ended moral reasoning.

A Creative and Subversive Human Capacity

I call this cognitive ability "open-ended" because its exercise *can*
go on and on. Once people start exercising this capacity, their critical reflection has no natural end point, even if in fact it has to end
somewhere, given that we are finite creatures and have a lot of other
things to do besides reflect on our moral rules and concepts. Viewed
from one angle, this capacity is incredibly subversive, because it has
the potential to pull the rug from under the status quo; from another
angle, it's a promethean creative power, because it can transform
our conception of morality and of ourselves as moral beings.

Let me quickly add a clarification: when I say this is a capacity for
open-ended critical moral reasoning, I don't mean that when people
engage in it they always follow as far as good reasoning would lead
them. The path of reasoning, whether it is moral reasoning or not,
can be blocked in many ways. One way is when you begin to see
the path's destination and simply find it too disturbing to go there.
Another is when you prematurely terminate the chain of reasoning
because you have reached the result you wanted. My hunch is that
both of these failures to go where reason leads have occurred in
our thinking about the moral standing of animals. That's one reason
why I think the Second Great Expansion is probably incomplete, not
just in terms of implementation but also in terms of changing our
confident (and almost certainly anthropocentric) beliefs about the
inferiority of nonhuman animals.

Whether or not humans have always possessed the capacity for
critical, open-ended moral reasoning, it's clear that many of them
now are capable of exercising a fairly sophisticated version of it and
that it can have large-scale social and political effects, *under certain
conditions*. What conditions are those? Once again, I can't pretend
to offer a comprehensive answer. I think I can say a bit about what
some of the *necessary* conditions are likely to be, without claiming to
be able to identify the full set of *sufficient* conditions.

When Does the Capacity for Critical, Open-Ended Moral Reasoning Contribute to the Two Great Expansions?

The necessary conditions include the kind of constructed niches that I described in the list that constituted the historical narrative in the preceding chapter (items 1–8). I won't repeat that list here. I'll only emphasize a few of its most important items, to refresh your memory so that I can then explain what further conditions are needed. Above all, humanity must have already reached the point where its knack for niche construction has lessened the harsh conditions of the EEA by providing the physical security and infrastructure for peaceful cooperation among groups that reduce the costs of being open to relating to the Other in ways that show a degree of moral regard for them. In addition, material prosperity has to have reached sufficient levels so that people can afford to act more altruistically toward strangers, even strangers they don't see as potential cooperators, and to be less ruthlessly exploitive of nonhuman animals, without paying too high a price, in terms of reproductive or cultural fitness or what they regard as success in life. Material prosperity makes it a lot easier to treat both strangers and nonhuman animals better.

In other words, I think it is probable that the exercise of the capacity for critical, open-ended moral thinking is only likely to be well developed, widespread, and socially and politically potent after humans have used their capacity for cumulative culture to construct niches that leverage them out of the harsher conditions of the EEA. In that sense, the widespread, relatively unconstrained exercise of the capacity for critical, open-ended moral thinking, like the move toward deeply inclusive morality that it can help produce, is something of a luxury good, something that requires considerable surplus reproductive success.

The commonsensical point here is that people generally have to be doing well enough in securing subsistence and security to afford to be reflective about their morality—and to put the results of their reflections into action. (I added the qualifier "generally" to acknowledge the possibility that in some cases a major social or political catastrophe can trigger deep moral reflection, if it is severe enough to make people think "we can't go on like this anymore!") Yet I think considerably more than security and material prosperity is needed to fill out the full list of conditions under which that remarkable capacity is likely to be exercised in ways that eventually lead to the two momentous moral-conceptual shifts I call the Two Great Expansions.

The Social-Epistemic Context for the Exercise of the Capacity

Here's my speculation as to what, at minimum, the list of additional conditions would have to include for it to be likely that the capacity for critical, open-ended moral reasoning would be exercised in such a way as to lead many people eventually to the idea that all human beings have the same high basic moral status and to the idea that at least some nonhuman animals have moral standing.

(i) There must be widespread literacy, along with printing presses or more advanced technologies for disseminating ideas and especially for disseminating the connections among ideas that constitute reasoning about how people ought to live or how it is permissible for them to live.

(ii) There must be considerable freedom of expression and association, so that discussion of ideas about how to live among people with diverse viewpoints can be relatively open-ended; generally speaking, the results of discussions that question some significant aspects of the moral status quo must not be prevented from arising or from spreading. This requires, among other things, that control over communication technologies must be dispersed, so that no one person or group can monopolize them and thereby constrain freedom of information and expression and curtail the exercise of critical moral reasoning.

(iii) Significant numbers of people must be exposed, either through direct experience or through reading history or works of fiction or using other media, to the fact that there are other societies with other ways of doing things, and to the fact that the moral practices and rules of their own society have changed significantly over time.

That awareness opens up the possibility of wondering whether the rules and practices people are currently following are optimal. The better understanding of people from other cultures that these new experiences and sources of information provide, when combined with the moral mind's capacity for perspective taking, enables the extension of sympathy beyond its formerly parochial limits. It also allows people to identify the common interests that all human beings, not just members of their group, have; and it contributes to the broader application of ideas of impartiality that originally operated only in the much more limited context of strategic reasoning to recruit coalition members for suppressing bullies or engaging in war or helping convince people that an individual is a reliable partner in cooperation.

(iv) There must be a developed culture of reason giving: a significant portion of the population must expect and must believe that others expect that, at least for certain areas of human behavior, justifications must be offered if they are requested. And justifications must involve the giving of genuine reasons, not brute appeals to authority or tradition. Moral consistency reasoning—reasoning that focuses on morally relevant similarities and differences in the pursuit of coherence in judgment and ultimately in action—must figure prominently among the kinds of reasoning about how to live that significant numbers of people frequently engage in.

(v) The pressures for moral conformity must not be too great, either because of a cultural practice of tolerance for moral disagreement, or because of the inadequacy of the social learning mechanisms that promote agreement on moral rules and their internalization, or because punishment practices are not sufficient to deter noncompliance, or for all three of these reasons. The social environment must allow some individuals to depart from the moral status quo.

(vi) Moral innovators, the first people who deviate from the moral status quo, must have the power to do so and must be able to afford to do so—that is, the material and social costs of their refusal to conform must not be too high. The affordability condition requires two key factors to be in place: there must be multiple cooperative schemes, and the costs of exiting one scheme and joining another must not be prohibitive. When these two conditions are in place, the greatest impediment to moral innovation is removed: the threat of exclusion from the only cooperative scheme available to the individual.

Taken together, these six conditions constitute what you might call *the social-epistemic context* in which the exercise of the capacity for critical, open-ended moral thinking is likely to reach all the way down to a reconsideration of the bases for moral regard and what consistency in conferring moral regard requires. The "social" part is obvious; the term "epistemic" is there to emphasize that these are social conditions that have a large effect on how we come to have beliefs and hence knowledge (*epistēmē* is a Greek word for "knowledge" or "understanding"). This social-epistemic context is a product of history; all the components that constitute it only came together on a large scale fairly recently, and then only in some societies, in the past three hundred years or so.

My hypothesis is that the Two Great Expansions were likely to occur only when the historical process outlined in chapter 4 (items 1–8) had transpired *and* conditions (i) to (vi) in this chapter were also present. What is more, I think that conditions (i) to (vi) are only likely to obtain on a large scale where the process outlined in items 1 to 8 has already taken place. My hypothesis is that all these environmental conditions were probably necessary for the exercise of the capacity for critical, open-ended moral reasoning to have resulted in the Two Great Expansions.

The Vital Role of Institutions

As with conditions 1 to 8, the satisfaction of conditions (i) to (vi) depends on *the character of the institutions in a society*. More specifically, none of the conditions is likely to be satisfied unless institutions promote considerable decentralization of power. This doesn't mean that society must be thoroughly nonhierarchical, that there can be no differences in power or authority among individuals or groups, no significant inequalities. Rather, if hierarchies exist, they must be multiple and relatively independent of one another: there can be no one overarching structure of power and authority. There must also be effective civil-society institutions: persisting voluntary organizations that are free to pursue their goals without undue government interference or interference by an official religious establishment and that have the resources to do so effectively. In addition, the existing array of institutions must not include severe constraints on the ability of individuals to exit one cooperative scheme and enter another, as was the case where occupations were limited by caste or other hereditary distinctions or allocated by monopolistic institutions such as guilds or gender or race-based licensure agencies.

Above all, government power must be limited and responsive to organized moral demands from sources outside it, in particular, civil-society groups. If government power is not limited, any attempted moral innovation that runs contrary to official policy or the interests of those who wield government power is liable to be suppressed. Limited government also means that some moral disagreements are regarded as not being subject to settlement by the government. For large-scale moral changes such as the First and Second Great Expansion to begin to be realized in social practice and institutions, government action will be needed (in the form of laws prohibiting discrimination, laws protecting animal welfare, etc.). If such changes are to occur without coercive imposition by a minority, moral innovators must be able to mobilize public support that government will have to heed.

In brief, *the sort of institutional order in which large-scale moral progress is likely to come about through peaceful means will be—in broadest terms—a liberal and at least minimally democratic order.* It will be liberal in the sense that it will afford considerable individual freedom, including freedom of expression, freedom to deviate from the moral status quo, and freedom of association to mobilize pressure for moral change or to engage in moral experiments. It will also be liberal in the sense that it will have no single hierarchy, but instead multiple, relatively independent hierarchies—something that can only occur if power is decentralized, which in turn requires considerable private property, so that no single entity controls all resources (and can use that control to establish a single hierarchy and wield a credible threat of exclusion from all cooperation). So far, at least, that has meant a society in which markets, operating on the basis of a system of private property rights, are a major factor in overall social organization.

Another reason to conclude that a society in which moral progress in the direction of inclusion will feature a large role for markets is that it is only that kind of society that has achieved *and sustained* the high levels of material prosperity that makes inclusion feasible and stable. State socialist societies with central planning rather than markets, like the Soviet Union, achieved high levels of productivity for short periods of time (in particular under the existential threat the Germans posed in World War II). But they didn't achieve growth and generalized material prosperity in nonemergency situations for extended periods of time. In such systems, the government's control of all the important productive resources meant that it could use the threat of exclusion from cooperation to stifle dissent—to prevent attempts at moral innovations that went against the party line.

It's worth emphasizing that a society in which large-scale moral progress is likely to occur through nonviolent means will be one in which the economic order includes multiple cooperative schemes, operating in relative independence of one another, at least so far as the conditions for individuals entering and exiting them are concerned. Without this condition, the pressures for moral conformity—and against moral innovation—will be too great. The threat of being excluded from one's current cooperative scheme will stifle moral disagreement and moral innovation, if one has no other viable options.

Finally, let me also stress that the political order must allow for agitation for moral innovation bubbling up from civil society to influence government policy, in cases where large-scale moral change requires changes in laws and social policy. In other words, government must not be able to ignore advocates for moral change if they secure widespread public support. The liberal order must be at least minimally democratic.

To avoid an all-but-inevitable misinterpretation of what I have just said, let me make clear that I am not saying that anything approaching laissez-faire capitalism is a precondition for large-scale moral progress. On the contrary, I'm convinced that laissez-faire capitalism is a moral disaster, first and foremost because it produces undeserved concentrations of wealth that violate commonsense, eminently reasonable notions of fairness and opportunity. I'm also confident that laissez-faire capitalism limits, rather than promotes, moral progress by transforming unconstrained economic inequality into stifling social and political domination. When I say that a liberal-democratic order is necessary for nonviolent moral progress, I mean an order with humanely regulated markets, not unconstrained capitalism. (I also think that for reasons of justice—and as a matter of decency as well—there must in addition be some welfare provisions—that the state's functions should not be limited to providing law and order, enforcing contracts, and protecting citizens against foreign enemies.)

Moreover, although hierarchies—structured, stable differences in power and authority—may be necessary if some individuals are to be able to buck the pressures for moral conformity and influence others to follow suit, it should be clear that inclusive moral progress will occur only if some people with greater influence are willing to listen to and advocate for those with lesser influence. In an unrestrained capitalist society, the best-off would have little or no incentive to listen to appeals for moral change that didn't serve their interests, and even less incentive to advocate for such change themselves.

In some ways, the term "open society" may be more descriptive of what I have in mind. Nonetheless, I think the term "liberal democratic society" is, all things considered, quite apt, because it emphasizes that government must be accountable to the public and institutions must allow individuals the liberty to deviate from the moral status quo and try to persuade others to follow suit.

Motivation for Exercising the Capacity: The Need for Moral Identity

I have just characterized the kind of social-epistemic environment and institutional order that creates the possibility for large-scale moral change of the magnitude of the Two Great Expansions. Good detectives know that opportunity isn't enough; one also needs a motive. So we have one more question to answer, if my protosolution is to get off the ground: we need to know why anyone would be *motivated* to exercise the capacity for critical, open-ended moral thinking and to do so in ways that could lead to their rethinking their most fundamental notions of moral standing and equal moral status. Here's the best answer to that question I can think of, for now, anyway: the deep human need for affirming moral identity supplies the motivation.

Because humans have always needed to be included in cooperation with other humans, and because we evolved to be creatures whose cooperation is structured by morality, we also evolved to care deeply about whether other people regard us as moral. If they don't, they won't cooperate with us, and that will be disastrous for us, in terms of both reproductive fitness and cultural fitness (or, if you prefer, success in life).

Furthermore, given how important cooperation is for human reproductive fitness, you would expect that in addition to evolving the capacity for morally structured cooperation, humans would also evolve a potent capacity to detect pseudo-cooperators, deceptive free riders, people who only feign being moral. If that's so, then it may well be that the most efficient way for most humans—though not all—to be regarded by others as being moral is for them actually to *be* moral, at least much of the time (Baumard et al. 2013, 66). In other words, if morality is so important for the distinctively robust and flexible cooperation that humans engage in, and if because of its importance they have developed sophisticated means of discerning whether someone really is moral, then one would expect that the ability to detect those who only feign being moral would be a strong selective pressure for the emergence of a human moral psychology that features the desire to be moral.

Whether or not trying to be moral is for most of us the best strategy for having a reputation for being moral, and therefore necessary for reaping the benefits of having that reputation, the deep desire to affirm and sustain moral identity is likely an object of selection at both the individual and group levels. Groups whose members had robust desires to affirm and sustain moral identity would outcompete groups whose members lacked that trait, other things being equal; and such groups would have greater fitness, both in successfully passing on the genes of their members and in reproducing their moral practices and other aspects of culture over time. Individuals who were seen by others to have a strong moral identity would be more desirable partners in cooperation, and greater access to cooperation with others would enhance their individual reproductive fitness; so, at the level of the individual (or his or her genes), there would also be selection for having a commitment to being moral. Finally, in "buffered" environments, under conditions of surplus reproductive success, exhibiting a strong commitment to moral identity would enhance individuals' economic prosperity, social success, and status, even if it didn't increase their reproductive fitness. For all these reasons, then, it's not surprising that most humans feel a deep and motivationally potent need to affirm and sustain their moral identity, their commitment to being moral. In fact, a good deal of empirical psychological research demonstrates that most people do care very deeply about their moral identity (Gotowiec and van Mastrigt 2018, 79; Han et al. 2018, 2–3; Hertz and Krettenauer 2016, 3; Lapsley 2015, 165; Sets 2010, 389, 393).

If humans generally have a deep-seated, socially reinforced need to think of themselves and be regarded by others as moral, then once people live in an environment that is conducive to the exercise of the capacity for critical, open-ended moral thinking—an environment in which being moral includes participating in a practice of reason giving—one would expect at least some of them to be motivated to exercise it, because they would be inclined to think that they need to do so to affirm and sustain their moral identity. In other words, if the desire to regard oneself and to be regarded by others as a moral being no longer just means the desire to "do what we do" or what God supposedly commands or tradition or the ancestors require, but becomes the desire to participate in morality as a reason-giving enterprise and to do the right thing for the right reason, then the commitment to moral identity can motivate people to exercise their capacity for critical open-ended moral reasoning.

If you care about being moral and understand that being moral means acting for good reasons and that acting for good reasons requires consistency among your moral judgments and between your moral principles and your intuitive moral responses, then you will be motivated to achieve consistency. If you become aware of a serious inconsistency in your judgments or a discrepancy between what you say you believe and how you act or feel, that awareness will stimulate you to think things through and achieve greater consistency. The social-epistemic conditions I listed earlier increase the likelihood that you will become aware of such discrepancies.

For example, if your moral identity includes a commitment to acting in ways you can justify with sound moral reasoning if called on to do so, and if you see that slaves or women are treated very badly compared to how you are treated, then you'll take seriously the need to discover a good reason for this difference in treatment and, if that can't be done, to change your evaluation of it. Because this capacity is open-ended, nothing in the moral status quo is off-limits, even our notions of moral standing and equal moral status, *if* the social environment doesn't prevent its exercise from going that far and even includes some encouragement for it to do so.

It may well be that for most individuals, the capacity for critical, open-ended moral reasoning gets activated only if the individual encounters an "irritant." (I thank Andrew Lichter for suggesting this handy term.) In other words, something has to disturb you enough to compel you to attend to an inconsistency and be motivated to try to resolve it by reasoning.

It is also likely that some people are more sensitive to inconsistencies than others, more bothered by them, for reasons having to do with the particular developmental path taken in the formation of their personalities. These more sensitive individuals can become irritated enough to engage in moral consistency reasoning and come to the conclusion that their behavior and that of others in their society is inconsistent with some shared rule. At that point, they may become irritants to others, calling their attention to the inconsistency and appealing to their moral identities, trying to get them to be disturbed by the inconsistency, too. I think I've just given a pretty accurate description of Peter Singer and other pioneers of the animal liberation movement and also of the earliest abolitionists and feminists. (When I encounter people like Singer, I feel so morally inadequate that I think about donating a kidney to a stranger — though in the end I settle instead for doing a bit more volunteer humanitarian work on the southern border of my country.)

To summarize: when a society's institutional structure is sufficiently liberal and democratic to satisfy conditions (i) to (vi), the social-epistemic environment not only doesn't prevent but in fact stimulates the exercise of the capacity for critical, open-ended moral reasoning to proceed all the way down to our notions of moral standing and equal moral status. In those conditions, it's likely that at least some people, motivated by their commitment to moral identity, will exercise the capacity for critical moral thinking in ways that can lead them to reassess their moral orientation toward the Other and their treatment of nonhuman animals, to move beyond shallowly inclusive morality to deeply inclusive morality. And if those moral pioneers enjoy social influence and prestige or are adept at mobilizing the capacity for critical, open-ended moral thinking in enough other people, the Two Great Expansions may begin to come about.

Originating versus Spreading

It's important to distinguish here between how a moral innovation first occurs and how it diffuses. I've focused on how some human beings could first undergo the transition from exclusive to shallowly inclusive to deeply inclusive morality. More specifically, I've concentrated on trying to understand how—and in what circumstances—a person of normal cognitive and moral capacities could be motivated to exercise the capacity for critical open-ended moral reasoning and do so in a way that leads her toward the Two Great Expansions.

I've not offered an account of how, once a large change in moral orientation has occurred among some people, it spreads to others. That would require a sophisticated theory of the mechanisms of social influence and learning, which I don't pretend to possess.

I want to note, however, that the processes by which moral innovations like the Two Great Expansions spread within one society and then become adopted in other societies are likely to be complex. It won't be a one-size-fits-all story.

In some cases, individuals may learn from prestigious or otherwise influential individuals in their own society who have already made these transitions through exercising their capacity for critical, open-ended moral reasoning. In other cases, people in one society may adopt the moral views and other elements of culture of the societies that have colonized them or come to dominate them in more subtle ways. Individuals may imitate the norms and practices of a culture they deem more successful or in some other way more attractive than their own. Once people become exposed to moral orientations different from their own, they may adopt them because they find that they do a better job of delivering the psychological goods and community with others that they value.

To summarize: First, if you care about being moral, and if you believe that being moral requires moral consistency, then—if you live in the right sort of social-epistemic environment and can bear the costs—you will be motivated to engage in moral consistency reasoning; and in some cases, doing so may lead to large changes in your moral outlook, including something as momentous as the Two Great Expansions. Second, even if some individuals don't travel that route themselves, they may arrive at the same destination by learning from others, in a variety of ways. With that addition to my protosolution to the Big Puzzle, I now want to take stock of what I've accomplished and what I haven't.

The Attractions of My (Proto)Solution to the Big Puzzle

It's all too obvious that I've provided at most only the basic contours of an explanation—and that I haven't offered either experimental evidence or much of anything in the way of other types of hard empirical evidence for some of the factual claims involved. But there's something to be said for my effort nonetheless. In fact, there are several things.

First, it isn't a spooky, nonnaturalistic, or overly rationalistic explanation. Especially in items (i) to (vi), it does assume that human beings can reason, and that in some cases, under certain extremely demanding environmental conditions, their reasoning can result in fundamental moral-conceptual changes, changes that can alter motivations and thereby behavior (recall my disgust at the thought of eating an octopus). Yet nothing I have said suggests that rationality is an autonomous, self-sufficient force for moral change that can be effective regardless of environmental conditions or that reason can motivate people effectively on its own, without tapping into their existing evolved emotional capacities, including the desire to see oneself as moral and the capacity to feel sympathy, guilt, disgust, and shame. Nor was my explanation overly idealistic: recall my emphasis on the role that the immoral, violent competition for dominance that resulted in the modern state played in achieving surplus reproductive success and unshackling morality from the demands of reproductive fitness. I don't assume that moral progress has an unblemished pedigree; quite the contrary.

Second, my proto-explanation fits the historical facts about *when* the Two Great Expansions occurred and *where* they first began to occur. Recall that they are both very late arrivals on the human scene, as they have become fairly widespread across a number of different societies only in the last three hundred years or so. The full set of conditions (1–8 plus [i]–[vi]) that I have listed have come to coexist (and then only in some, not all, locales) only during that time frame. That's when some modern states became increasingly liberal and democratic and in which productivity soared. That is the time frame—and those are the states—in which the Two Great Expansions began to occur.

Remember, it is only in the last three hundred years or so that the abolition of chattel slavery, the drive to extend full civil rights to people of color and other minorities, the beginning of the women's rights movement, efforts to eliminate the most egregious forms of torture of humans (including excruciating torture as punishment for various crimes), and reductions in the cruelest treatment of non-human animals have transpired. Moreover, the first states in which these changes began to occur on a large scale weren't authoritarian, centralized regimes; they were among the more liberal and democratic states at the time.

Third, my account is compatible with the plausible hypothesis that the moral mind hasn't changed since it first emerged and certainly hasn't changed in the last three hundred years, the period in which the Two Great Expansions achieved liftoff. That's because my account is an explanation of how the capacities that constitute the moral mind came to be expressed differently in response to the new niches that humans created for themselves. Nothing I've said requires a modification of the moral mind as I've described it. So my explanation of the Two Great Expansions fits well with my general point about moral change: understanding how it has occurred and can occur requires distinguishing clearly between the moral mind and the particular moralities that the moral mind underwrites in various different environments.

Yet another virtue of my proto-explanation is this: the historical narrative laid out in chapter 5 draws significantly on evolutionary thinking, in particular the ideas of natural and cultural selection, niche construction, and adaptive plasticity. That's important, given that the task I set myself at the outset was to see whether the fact of the Two Great Expansions could be squared with sound evolutionary thinking about the origins of human moralities.

One additional reason for regarding my proto-explanation as promising is worth emphasizing. My account doesn't rely in any way on an all-too-common assumption that I have demonstrated to be not only false but fatal for any prospect of providing a plausible explanation of the Two Great Expansions: the assumption that because morality originally was (perhaps) nothing more than an adaptation that enhanced reproductive fitness by facilitating cooperation, that is all it is and can be. I've given the relationship between morality and cooperation its due, without subscribing to the Cooperation Dogma.

In the next chapter, I try to enhance the plausibility of my proto-explanation by showing how its basic conceptual framework permits the construction of a powerful theory of a different kind of moral change: regression to tribalistic moralities. And in the chapter after that, I add still more plausibility to my account by showing how it can also help explain intrasocietal tribalism, the *social construction* of groups *within society* that evokes the same threat cues and accordingly the same tribalistic, exclusionary responses that encounters with members of other societies often evoked in the EEA. In that chapter, I argue that tribalism has evolved to take on new forms, forms that rely on a distinctively modern phenomenon that is itself a product of cultural evolution: ideology.

But What about Religion?

Before I do all of that, I need to address a topic that has so far been all but absent in my speculations about how the Two Great Expansions came about: religion. I haven't neglected religion entirely. I did note that sometimes religious beliefs have *impeded* the Two Great Expansions, in particular by distorting the exercise of moral consistency reasoning or even preventing people from engaging in it. One example of this is the existence of theological doctrines in the Judeo-Christian tradition that relegate nonhuman animals to the role of serving human interests. Thinking of animals in that way precludes even entertaining the idea that they have moral standing in their own right, even if one recognizes that they feel pain and experience pleasure much as we do. Another example I might have given is that, throughout most of their histories, all the major religions tolerated slavery (and in some cases, as was true of Christianity, admonished slaves to obey their masters). To that extent, religion hindered rather than facilitated movement toward the idea that all human beings have an equal high basic moral status. Also some religions divide humanity into the saved and the damned or the faithful and the infidels, a kind of thinking not particularly conducive to the recognizing fundamental moral equality of all human beings. Christian and Muslim doctrine alike have held that it's perfectly acceptable—even commendable—to behave toward heretics or infidels in ways that are otherwise be strictly forbidden, even going so far as to disregard their most fundamental human rights, including the right not to be tortured.

Nevertheless, it is clear that many people's religious beliefs have played a role in their participating in one or both of the Two Great Expansions. This is particularly true, I think, of the most recent and fully developed manifestation of the First Great Expansion, the modern human rights movement and its roots in British and American abolitionism. Before I speculate about the role that changes in the conception of Christian moral identity played in the abolition of Atlantic slavery, I want to make something clear with regard to how I am conceiving the First Great Expansion.

Recall that I use the term in a very specific way: to refer to a moral change that involves basic alterations in the understanding of equal moral status of large numbers of people *and* has begun to become socially and politically potent—that is at least beginning to transform the way individuals act and the character of social institutions, including the law. That usage is perfectly compatible with acknowledging, as I am happy to do, that various ideas of human equality emerged much earlier and that often they emerged in religious traditions. For example, we find ideas of human equality or of a common humanity in the writings of the Stoic philosophers and in other ethical and religious traditions as well, including Christianity, Islam, Judaism, Buddhism, and Confucianism.

I'm not saying, then, that no human beings had any idea of human equality until three centuries ago, and I'm certainly not denying that religions played a role in the development of these ideas from their earliest appearance. Instead I'm focusing on explaining moral changes *that combine widespread changes in moral ideas with significant implementation of those ideas in ways that transform important social practices and institutions.* That kind of change, which I call large-scale moral change, occurred much later than the first occurrences of ideas of human equality.

Similarly, the idea that humans have moral obligations regarding their treatment of animals on their own account did not first arise only three hundred years or so ago. We find discussions of such obligations in the writings of Pythagoras and Epicurus, for example, twenty-five hundred years ago. Nevertheless, it is only much more recently that a socially and politically potent and clearly articulated understanding of the moral standing of animals has emerged.

Think of it this way: for a very long time, some human beings have formed ideas of the fundamental equality of all persons, and some have recognized that at least some nonhuman animals count morally in their own right. But for these ideas to develop into a relatively coherent, articulated moral orientation shared by many people *and* to become powerful forces for change, a formidably complex set of conditions had to come together. That magic combination—that tipping point—only occurred rather recently. And it wasn't inevitable; it was an unplanned, highly unlikely occurrence.

Now let's return to the story of how moral identity can motivate the exercise of the capacity for critical, open-ended moral reasoning in ways that can contribute to large-scale moral change. I noted earlier that there are good evolutionary and social science reasons to think that moral identity is an important element in the psychology of most humans. Sometimes moral identity takes a religious form. It appears that many abolitionists were religiously motivated, as are many human rights advocates today. More specifically, their motivation to try to abolish slavery was grounded in a change in their understanding of their own moral identity—a moral identity they understood mainly in religious terms.

These remarkable people seem to have undergone a sea change in their understanding of what it is to be a Christian. They became convinced that being a Christian required one to resist and help abolish slavery. That was a momentous transformation of their moral identity, since mainstream Christian doctrine made it easy to reconcile one's conception of oneself as a Christian with complicity or even direct participation in the enslavement of other human beings. Not only did passages in the New Testament enjoin slaves to be obedient; also, one of the justifications given for slavery in mainstream Christian thinking was that it was a useful and even necessary vehicle for converting heathens to the One True Faith.

The eminent historian of slavery and emancipation Seymour Drescher suggests that Christians who rethought their moral identity in ways that led them to take up the abolitionist cause were prompted to do so in part because they had already embraced the Enlightenment's commitment to the practice of reason giving and to the recognition of natural rights, rights that all humans are supposed to have, simply by virtue of being human (Drescher 2009, 124; 1999, 23). Moreover, in American abolitionist discourse, including that of Frederick Douglass, appeals to human rights were prominent (Douglass 2005, 54). Drescher also notes that even though the term "humanity" may have occurred more frequently than the phrase "human rights" in their rhetoric, the British abolitionists' understanding of "humanity" encompassed a central component of the concept of human rights: the idea that all humans, regardless of race, have a common nature, and that properly recognizing this common nature is incompatible with according some human beings freedom and enslaving others (Drescher 2015, 182).

Note that Drescher's understanding of the connection between abolitionist motivation and Christian identity gives a prominent role to item (iv) in my earlier list: a culture of reason giving, something that was one of the main contributions of the complex cultural phenomenon we call the Enlightenment. (He also emphasizes item [i], high literacy rates and potent information technologies that were dispersed, accessible to a plurality of parties, under no one's exclusive control.)

If Drescher is correct about the connection between the spread of Enlightenment ideas about human or natural rights, often expressed in terms of a common humanity, and the Enlightenment culture of reason giving, on the one hand, and the transformation of Christian moral identity, on the other, then we needn't choose between a religious explanation of the First Great Expansion and one that features a prominent role for the exercise of the capacity for critical, open-ended moral reasoning. Religious motivation can play an important role in both of the Two Great Expansions, at least if it is connected in the right way to moral identity and if the motivation to preserve one's image of oneself as moral stimulates new critical reflection on what being moral requires.

Having said that, I want to emphasize that many people today do not understand their moral identity in religious terms. Yet their distinctively human concern about their moral identity can, under the right circumstances, motivate them to exercise the capacity for critical, open-ended moral reasoning. Moral-identity-based motivation for critical, open-ended moral thinking can play a significant role in the Two Great Expansions, whether one's moral identity is religious or secular.

We needn't assume that the process by which people's commitment to their moral identity comes to motivate them to move toward deeply inclusive morality is the same for everyone. Some people have a strong commitment to rationality, to being attentive to reasons (even though, of course, like all of us, they fall far short of being fully rational); and they have a genuine commitment to moral consistency. Such individuals, in the right social-epistemic environment, can be motivated to engage in moral reasoning that leads them to realize that their previously exclusive, tribalistic responses (to members of other human groups or to nonhuman animals) were based on morally irrelevant distinctions, and to conclude that consistency in applying the principles for determining moral status and moral standing that they already subscribe to requires enlarging the circle of moral regard.

Other people may come to more inclusive moral responses not by their own reasoning but by imitating the responses of people they view as prestigious or as moral exemplars. Still others, once more inclusive moral orientations have spread, might use what cultural evolutionary thinkers call the strategy of conformity, making their own responses congruent with those that are dominant in their social environment. A fully developed theory of the transition from shallowly inclusive to deeply inclusive morality, which I don't pretend to offer here, would need to determine how the best work on social learning could illuminate the process by which people's desire to affirm and sustain their moral identity can lead them to learn from others how to have more inclusive moral responses.

To summarize: the central role of moral identity in human moral psychology goes a considerable distance toward explaining why, under the complex set of conditions I've outlined in this and the preceding chapter, some people would be *motivated* to exercise the capacity for critical, open-ended moral thinking—sufficiently motivated to carry through to conclusions that may fundamentally reshape their moral outlooks.

If one's commitment to moral identity is strong enough and one lives in a social environment where ideas can be exchanged freely, where there is readily available knowledge about alternative ways of doing things, and where there is a culture of reason giving, one may be sufficiently motivated to exercise the capacity for critical, open-ended reasoning and to follow it to destinations that alter one's most fundamental moral orientation—one's conceptions of moral status and moral standing—*if one is fortunate enough to live in a human-created niche that makes taking that path affordable.*

The Costs of the Free Exercise of the Capacity for Critical, Open-Ended Moral Reasoning

I emphasized earlier that whether or not the capacity for critical, open-ended moral reasoning is exercised in a way that leads to a change in moral orientation as fundamental as the Two Great Expansions depends on the character of the social-epistemic environment, including the *affordability* of exercising that capacity. At this point, it is worth emphasizing that "affordability" here covers several different items. So far, I have only considered material and reproductive costs. I have argued that in certain environments, where a rare cluster of conditions come to coexist, the reproductive costs and the costs in terms of material well-being of expanding the circle of moral regard may be radically lowered. When this occurs, the capacity for critical, open-ended moral reasoning can, if it links up with the motivation to sustain moral identity in the right way, lead people to rethink their understandings of moral standing and equal moral status.

However, another kind of cost can pose an obstacle to people changing their moral outlook: the *social costs* of bucking the status quo. Those costs run from being ridiculed as eccentric to being branded a radical or a dangerous subversive, to being ostracized— excluded from forms of association and community one greatly values.

A Puzzle about the Role of Moral Pioneers

Major changes in morality, including the Two Great Expansions, don't happen all at once, with everybody participating from the start. More commonly, change begins with a small portion of the population; call them "first adopters" or, better yet, "moral pioneers." The costs of pursuing the exercise of the capacity for open-ended moral thinking wherever it leads and then trying to put the results into practice might seem prohibitively high for moral pioneers. Their costs are certainly likely to be higher, other things being equal, than the costs incurred by those who get on the bandwagon after it has already started to roll. Why do some people lead the way, given that, as moral pioneers, they're liable to incur especially high social costs?

So our Big Puzzle encompasses a subpuzzle: even if someone lives in a human-constructed niche that is quite comfortable—so that the reproductive and material costs of her revising pervasive understandings of moral standing or equal moral status are negligible for her—won't she face another formidable obstacle, namely, the social costs? Won't the anticipation of social costs override the motivation for pursuing critical moral reasoning all the way to the fundamental moral reorientation that the Two Great Expansions represent? Or even if some people persist in exercising that capacity so as to traverse the whole distance to that destination, won't they refrain from *acting* on their conclusions if the social costs of doing so are too great?

To fill out our explanation, we need to understand the conditions under which some people are willing and able to bear the social costs of being moral pioneers. The need is urgent, because evolutionary theories and anthropological research indicate that humans have developed powerful mechanisms for ensuring conformity to existing moral norms, to not challenging the moral status quo. And conformity is often achieved by imposing weighty costs on individuals who don't conform.

Once again, historical research is relevant. Historians of American abolitionism have demonstrated that early abolitionists in the Boston area—the seedbed of the movement—were in fact ostracized, cast out from social circles that had been central to their lives, and were subject to derision and even overt hostility. (For good reason, Wendell Phillips, one of the greatest abolitionist orators, habitually carried a Colt revolver in his coat pocket when he spoke publicly.) The same historians have also shown that abolitionists formed their own new associations when they became stigmatized as "radicals," often forming networks of extended abolitionist families through marriage (Friedman 1982, 226–229). They found a way to prevent the social costs of being moral pioneers from sapping their motivation to use moral consistency reasoning to work through the full implications of their commitment to basic human equality and put the results into action.

Such a strategy usually wasn't available in the earliest societies or, for that matter, for most of human history. Hunter-gatherer societies offer the clearest illustration: if you violate your group's rules, then you may be excluded from all cooperation, and exclusion might well be a death sentence. The early abolitionists in the Boston area lived in a profoundly different social environment: they could afford to follow their convictions and agitate for a new norm of equality because their society was complex enough to offer opportunities for participation in more than one cooperative scheme; and they had the economic and political freedom to take advantage of this crucial fact. So here is another illustration of a major theme of our investigation: the moral possibilities, including the opportunities for moral change, are environment sensitive. What's not possible (or at least highly unlikely) in one environment may be possible (and even likely) in another.

The point I want to emphasize now is that the social costs of being a moral pioneer in achieving fundamental moral change can vary widely for different people, depending on their wealth and power, and their possibilities for forming new associations if they are excluded for holding unpopular new views. In general, the more wealth and power you have, and the greater your "social capital" for forming new associations, the lower are the costs of your being among the first to embrace and publicly advocate new moral views.

Here, too, the painstakingly detailed documentation of the case of British abolitionism provides some important clues about the role of social costs in determining whether people will exercise the capacity for open-ended moral thinking in a way that leads them to a new understanding of moral standing or equal moral status, and try to live accordingly. Historians of British abolitionism, including Drescher, whom we met earlier, have emphasized that most of the early advocates of abolishing slavery in the British Empire came from the middle or upper-middle class. They were people who were comfortable in material terms. And they belonged to "nonconformist" Protestant churches—denominations that were Christian and Protestant but were independent of the official religious establishment, the Anglican Church, also called the Church of England (an institution that, by the way, owned many slaves in the Caribbean).

These nonconformist Protestant groups had already fought and won a prolonged battle to establish their legitimacy, and to avoid being subdued by the forces that tried to sustain the religious status quo. They had already developed resources for implementing their conception of what a community of Christians should be like in spite of powerful opposition. Their religious moral identity as nonconformists, as believers who were independent of the Church of England, had already equipped them with the ability to cope with the stigma or derision that they provoked in some quarters when they first became enthusiastic public supporters of abolition. In fact, it was part of their moral identity that they were moral pioneers, first with regard to what the proper form of Protestantism was, and later with regard to the abolition of slavery.

Had some other group tried to spearhead the abolitionist movement in Britain, a group that possessed less material wealth and less social capital and lacked a history of successfully struggling to shape what was at first a new minority religious moral identity and follow the commitment to it into new moral terrain, it might well have failed. The costs that the members of a less well-positioned group would have had to bear to try to fundamentally change the status quo might have been too high. This is another sense in which the willingness to follow critical moral thinking wherever it leads, even if the destination is an initially unpopular view, is a luxury good.

Once again, I'm not pretending to have fully solved a puzzle, in this case the puzzle of how moral pioneers become sufficiently motivated, in spite of formidable obstacles, including social costs. I'm simply emphasizing that in thinking about the full set of conditions that have to come together for it to be likely that the capacity for critical, open-ended moral reasoning will be exercised in a way that leads toward the Two Great Expansions or toward any other basic moral reorientation, we have to take into account the fact that there can be social costs of doing so even in an otherwise favorable environment in which material and reproductive costs are negligible. In other words, we have to add "acceptable social costs" to the list of necessary environmental conditions. At the same time, however, we also have to acknowledge that how high the social costs are will depend on who you are. Other things being equal, moral pioneers generally bear higher moral costs than those who get on board later. Yet some people may be successful moral pioneers because, owing to their social position and the history of the group of which they are a member, the costs they have to bear aren't unacceptably high.

So now I have one more item to add to my list of the virtues of my proto-explanation of the Two Great Expansions: it doesn't require superhuman moral motivation on the part of moral pioneers, or anyone else, for that matter. Of course, history reveals many cases of people who have been willing to bear any costs, including torture and death, to stand by their moral convictions, to preserve their moral identity. I'm not denying that. Instead, my point is that once we realize that some people can be so fortunately positioned that they can afford to be moral pioneers without being saints, we don't have to assume that saints are necessary for moral progress to occur.

Is My Solution to the Big Puzzle Evolutionary?

I've sketched several different, fairly plausible evolutionary explanations of how the capacity for critical moral reasoning, at least in the form of moral consistency reasoning, could have originated. I've also provided an admittedly speculative historical narrative that shows how some people could come to exercise that capacity in a way that changed their understanding of moral standing and moral status. But that historical explanation doesn't seem to be a fully evolutionary one. Elements of it could be presented in cultural evolutionary form, but it's not clear that all of it could be. So I'm not convinced that an adequate solution to the Big Puzzle will be an evolutionary explanation through and through. And I'm also not convinced that evolutionary science can tell us everything we need to know about how the moral mind interacts with specific social environmental factors to produce different kinds of moralities and different kinds of moral agents. Consequently, I can't confidently conclude that *evolutionary* scientific thinking will provide us with all the information we need to take charge of our moral fate. I hope that my reservations in that regard will stimulate evolutionary scientists to take up the challenge of trying to provide that information. If they do take up the challenge and succeed, they will only demonstrate what I've known all along: they are better trained for this kind of detective work than I am.

7

Turning Back the Moral Clock: Regression to Tribalistic Morality

In 1957 the world's attention focused, all too briefly, on Central High School in Little Rock, Arkansas. Still photographs and newsreel footage distributed across the globe captured a dramatic scene: soldiers of the 101st Airborne Division, armed with M1 Garand rifles, escorted a handful of African American teenagers to the entrance of the school, forcing their way through a mob of white people screaming racial epithets and spitting on the students, who stoically trudged on, eyes straight ahead.

As a nine-year-old white child living only a few blocks from this scene, I received from my parents, my teachers, my pastor, and other people I looked up to, the standard racist interpretation of the Central High School integration crisis: the trouble was caused by "outside agitators," mainly Jews and communists from the North. "Our colored people," to the extent that they were caught up in the pernicious enthusiasm for integration, had been duped, misled by these outsiders. Until they were infected with foreign ideas, they had been perfectly satisfied with their lot. It was these outside agitators who had made them discontented and uppity. The movement for public school integration, the belated attempt to implement the Supreme Court decision in *Brown v. Board of Education* (1954), was in effect a mental disorder introduced by foreigners into our otherwise healthy society. This standard racist interpretation reinforced white refusal to acknowledge the mental and moral equality of African Americans, because it represented them as gullible children, easily misled; it denied their ownership of the civil rights movement, their agency in the process of liberation.

How Contemporary Tribalism Resurrects the Threat Cues of the EEA

Does the racist take on the Central High School integration crisis sound familiar? It should. Every aspect of it faithfully tracks the EEA threat cues that prompted tribalistic moral responses in our ancestors. A group of human beings is identified as the dangerous Other. The danger they pose is portrayed as a kind of infection, in this case the spread of alien ideas that will disrupt "Our" social cooperation. (Recall that in the EEA the Other posed two distinct threats of infection: the introduction of biological parasites to which our group lacks immune resistance and the introduction of beliefs or social practices that could disrupt the specific modes of cooperation on which our group's survival depends.) Unfortunately, this kind of tribalistic rhetoric isn't a thing of the past. On January 4, 2019, a talk show host substituting for Rush Limbaugh declared that people illegally migrating to the United States were "sick"; they had the same beliefs that had made their home countries disasters, and these beliefs were just as contagious as physical diseases.

Even after six decades, I'm still ashamed that I continued to accept the racist interpretation of the Little Rock integration crisis until several years later, around age sixteen. And I still feel a deep resentment toward those to whom my moral development was entrusted for having foisted it on me. However, I didn't choose this example to reveal the sad fact of my racist upbringing or to try to assure you (or myself) of my continuing efforts to overcome it. I chose it because it's a good starting point for developing this chapter's theme: the complexity of the phenomenon of regression to tribalistic morality. Or to put the point a bit differently: I'm going to explore the evolution of tribalistic morality to include new forms of exclusion, including tribalistic responses to people within one's own society, not just members of other societies.

Intersocietal versus Intrasocietal Tribalism

Racists in Little Rock already exhibited a form of tribalistic morality before the integration crisis: as racists, they denied full equal moral status to African Americans. But their atavistic interpretation of the integration crisis also exhibited an additional kind of exclusion, another kind of othering, one that represented a regression even from a limited though significant kind of movement toward recognition of equality that had recently been reinforced by the solidarity generated among Americans by World War II—a momentous shared experience that was still a vivid memory in 1957. The War (as Americans at that time referred to it) had produced a sense of national solidarity, softening to some extent the sectional, ethnic, and religious divisions that had always been present in American society. The national collective effort to defeat the Axis powers generated the sense that "we are all Americans," and fostered the belief that this shared identity was what mattered most.

So the racist response to the integration crisis in Little Rock not only reinforced white southerners' tribalistic responses toward African Americans but also represented a deterioration of national solidarity, which is a kind of inclusiveness (even if its reverse side involved the denigration of other nations). A group of fellow Americans—thought to be chiefly Jews and communists from the North—were portrayed as if they were dangerous members of a different tribe. That may help to explain why, six years later, in 1963, when news of President Kennedy's assassination reached my middle school, some of my fellow students actually cheered. After all, he was a Yankee (northerner) and a supporter—though a rather politically cautious, if not timid, one—of the civil rights movement that threatened Our way of life.

The Little Rock integration crisis example illustrates an important point that is central to the theory of regression to tribalism I now want to develop using the explanatory framework advanced in the preceding chapters: regression can take two distinct forms, intersocietal tribalism and intrasocietal tribalism. Sometimes regression to tribalism can exhibit characteristics of both forms at once. Tribalistic tendencies not only have an evolutionary basis; they have evolved since their first appearance, and they are still evolving. New forms of intrasocietal tribalism are evolving.

Intersocietal tribalism is the primordial form, the mode of exclusion that was dominant in the EEA and has recurred all too many times since then. It consists of conceiving of other human beings who are not members of one's own society (in early times, not members of one's band or tribe) as threatening and less than fully human. In times of crisis, people who have made considerable progress toward regarding all human beings as having a basic equal moral status can regress to this primitive, original form of tribalistic morality.

For example, as the highly regarded historian John Dower documents, American propaganda cartoons during World War II portrayed the Japanese as dirty monkeys with frightfully large, sharp teeth. Japanese propaganda presented Americans as demons with revoltingly long noses (Dower 1987, 84–88). Only two decades earlier, when they were America's allies in World War I, Japanese were typically represented quite favorably, because they were helping us in the life-or-death struggle against the brutal "Huns." Apart from wartime or a surge of acts by foreign terrorists, we mostly see intersocietal tribalism in hostility toward immigrants—people who are literally foreigners, not members of our society, but wish to join it.

"Pure" versus "Impure" Intrasocietal Tribalism

Intrasocietal tribalism occurs when groups that had formerly been regarded as part of our society come to be excluded, characterized as alien and dangerous. This kind of tribalism can take two forms. In the first, impure form of intrasocietal tribalism, as in the Little Rock integration crisis case, the dangerous Other in our midst is not created out of whole cloth. Instead, some earlier division between Us and Them (in the Little Rock case, the division between northerners and southerners, Jews and Christians) is resurrected and reanimated to the point where some group that had recently been viewed as part of Us is now seen as foreign, alien, not really members of our society.

The violent ethnonational conflicts that occurred following the breakup of the Yugoslav Federation in the early 1990s supply another illustration of impure intrasocietal tribalism. Ethnic Serbs and Croats, including people who had been each other's friends and neighbors and had regarded each other as equal citizens in the Yugoslav federal state, came to see each other as members of alien, lethally dangerous tribes—different nations and in extreme cases even different races. In the Yugoslav case, the reversion to tribalism was facilitated by the fact that progress away from tribalism had been recent: memories of genocidal conflict between Serbs and Croats during the Nazi occupation of Yugoslavia four decades earlier were still vivid and provided ready fuel for regression.

Political leaders like Slobodan Milošević, who had lost legitimacy when state socialist regimes in the various units of the Yugoslav Federation collapsed, saw an opportunity to keep themselves afloat. They resurrected the division between Serbs and Croats that had been real and lethal during the Nazi occupation and recharacterized Bosniak Muslims as "Turks," thereby revitalizing fear and hatred that had been directed much earlier toward the Ottoman conquerors of the region. In Little Rock, the gradually healing wounds of the Civil War were reopened by blaming African Americans' struggle for equal rights on northerners (with an appeal to anti-Semitism and Cold War hysteria about communists in our midst thrown in for good measure). The impure variety of intrasocietal tribalism starts with preexisting divisions of Us versus Them within a society and builds on them, creating new supposed threats or resurrecting old fears, hostility, and distrust.

In contrast, pure (out of whole cloth) cases of intrasocietal tribalism are those in which a socially constructed Other is created ab initio and characterized so as to trigger EEA-like threat cue responses. In the next chapter, I continue to explore intrasocietal tribalism and argue that it tends to rely on ideologies. There I also argue for an evolutionary explanation of the existence and power of ideologies, an explanation that can, among other things, illuminate how ideologies function to elicit tribalistic moral responses toward certain constructed groups within one's own society. I make the case that intrasocietal tribalism is a distinctive feature of modern societies— societies that exhibit much more complexity, social divisions, and hierarchy than those in which morality first emerged. I also argue that so far as ideologies function to facilitate intrasocietal tribalism, they, too, are creatures of modernity.

The main topic for the present chapter is intersocietal tribalism, but it will become clear as I proceed that the basic evolved psychological dynamics are the same for intrasocietal tribalism as well. I think that intrasocietal tribalism and its especially strong reliance on ideology is worth a separate chapter, because I believe that at present it may pose an even greater threat to moral progress in the direction of the First Great Expansion than intersocietal tribalism does. That's why the next chapter is devoted to trying to understand intrasocietal tribalism.

Resurgences of anti-Semitism exhibit a toxic blend of intrasocietal and intersocietal tribalism. Jews are represented as a subgroup that has long been part of our society, but one that isn't fully assimilated and which, through the tentacles of the supposed international Jewish conspiracy, is linked to their fellow Jews in other societies. So they are portrayed both as a dangerous group within our society and also at the same time as foreign threats.

In the Middle Ages, Jews were blamed for spreading bubonic plague, the Black Death or Great Mortality that killed around a third of Europe's population. Portraying the Other as those who bring diseases to Us is the stock-in-trade of tribalism, evoking one of the primal threat cues of the EEA; and that accounts for its enduring motivational power. Unfortunately, characterizing the Other as carriers of deadly diseases didn't die with the Middle Ages. As I noted earlier, a participant in the television program *Fox and Friends* recently asserted that migrants traveling from Central America toward the US border carried smallpox (a disease that no longer exists). Similarly, it's no accident that President Trump chooses to stoke fear of immigrants and justify further militarization of the southern border by referring to migrants as an "infestation," thereby conjuring up visions of swarms of insects, rats, or other disease-bearing pests. Similarly, an infamous Nazi propaganda film, *The Eternal Jew*, opened with a shot of rats swarming out of the hold of a ship. *The contemporary tribalistic lexicon is a list of synonyms for EEA threat cues.*

The most compelling illustration of pure intrasocietal tribalism I'm familiar with is the eugenics movement, which flourished roughly from 1880 till the end of World War II. In the next chapter, I'll have a good deal more to say about this movement and its evolutionary roots, but for now I need only give a bare-bones characterization in order to clarify the idea of a type of intrasocietal tribalism that is "pure" in comparison to the cases I've already discussed.

To repeat: in pure intrasocietal tribalism, the threatening Other is the product of a radical social construction process: a new dangerous group is identified (in fact created by a feat of the imagination) rather than merely resurrecting some old supposed enemy and presenting it as a new threat.

In the case of eugenics, the newly identified threatening Other comprised all individuals who supposedly harbored defective genes. Of course, some people *do* have defective genes—in fact, we all have genetic mutations, many of which can be deleterious in some way, at least if you have two copies of the mutated gene. But the target of eugenic thinking was a fictitious group, one constructed by the human imagination: a supposedly distinct segment of the population in which virtually all "bad" genes were concentrated, whose "antisocial" behavior was strictly determined by those genes, and who passed those bad genes on at a frightening rate because of their lack of reproductive constraint.

All Tribalism Involves Social Construction of the Other

All cases of tribalistic exclusion, whether they take the form of intersocietal or intrasocietal tribalism, include some social construction of the Other, because they all involve the invention or exaggeration of characteristics attributed to the Other. Pure intrasocietal tribalism goes further: it involves imagining a new group within society that has not been identified before. Yet the new group is characterized using the same threat cue vocabulary that is employed in other forms of othering, evoking the same tribalistic moral responses.

In popular eugenic discourse, the people within our society (and in every society) who were thought to harbor bad genes were characterized as vectors of disease; they transmitted physical and mental disorders vertically, across the generations, through sexual reproduction, rather than horizontally as in ordinary epidemics. The diseases they transmitted supposedly were the cause of all major social ills, from drunkenness and crime and poverty to lax sexual mores. Because their bad genes made them lazy and morally weak, as well as mentally and physically deficient, this enemy among us posed one of the oldest threats faced by human societies from the beginning: they were free riders on our cooperation, or in the Nazi racial hygiene phrase, "useless eaters." This newly identified group, the genetically defective, posed a lethal threat to society. Unless their reproduction was checked, in the words of one prominent eugenicist of the 1920s, "in a few generations we will all be imbeciles," and civilization itself will crumble (Buchanan, Brock, Daniels, and Wikler 2001, 41–48).

Eugenic thinking therefore constructs a new internal Other in a way that triggers all the familiar EEA threat cues: they threaten our physical security (because their bad genes cause them to commit violent crimes), they spread disease (physical and mental) across the generations, and they undermine social cooperation by deliberate free riding or by unwittingly functioning as parasites, feeding on the social goods that the healthy members of society work so hard to produce. In the United States alone, this kind of pure intrasocietal tribalism was invoked to justify the forcible sterilization of around sixty-five thousand people. Mass forcible sterilizations occurred on a smaller scale in Norway, Denmark, Sweden, and Canada. In Germany, eugenic thinking culminated in the Final Solution, preceded by the medical murder of "genetically defective" Germans, Jews and "Aryans" alike, which Nazi propaganda shamelessly misdescribed as "euthanasia" (good death).

The more extreme forms of eugenic thinking constituted a regression to tribalistic morality—more specifically, pure intrasocietal tribalism—and one that is readily explainable in terms of the evolutionary framework developed in this book. That framework also explains all forms of regression to tribalistic morality, whether intersocietal tribalism or intrasocietal tribalism, pure or impure. For the remainder of the chapter, I focus on what is common to all forms of regression to tribalistic morality, but most of the examples will be drawn from the intersocietal variety, because it is the simplest, exhibiting the core features common to more complex forms.

A Framework for Explaining Regression to Tribalism

My explanation of regression to tribalism deploys six highly credible hypotheses and shows how, taken together, they account for the fact that there has been and in all likelihood will continue to be backtracking from the shift toward deeply inclusive moralities. Or to put the point differently: I'll explain why, given these hypotheses, moral change away from tribalism and toward deeply inclusive morality is extremely fragile.

H1: When people detect EEA-like threats, they tend to react in an exclusive, tribalistic way—with fear, distrust, and even preemptive aggression.

H2: If the environment changes back to EEA-like conditions, tribalistic responses will increase. A return to EEA-like conditions can occur in a number of different ways: as a result of a massive ecological collapse, violent civil strife, state failure, a severe deterioration of the economy, a lethal global pandemic, a nuclear war, and so on. (In spite of the evolutionary savvy exhibited by the writers of *The Walking Dead*, this list probably shouldn't include a zombie apocalypse.)

H3: For exclusive, tribalistic moral responses to become dominant, it is not necessary that some other group actually poses EEA-like threats; all that is necessary is that they are *believed* to do so. In other words, exclusivist responses can be provoked by misperceptions, mistaken "detection" of threat cues. So for regression to tribalism to occur, it's not necessary that there actually be a return to EEA-like conditions; all that's needed is that people *think* this has happened.

H4: False threat cues can be manufactured, socially constructed, using techniques for manipulating beliefs that have been developed through the evolution of culture and that rely on existing cultural resources.

H5: Certain people have an interest in generating tribalistic moral responses, because doing so gives them new power or sustains the power they have; and they can serve this interest either by acting in such a way as to actually re-create the threats that were predominant in the EEA (taking us back to an EEA-like environment) or by manufacturing false threat cues that mimic the risks the EEA posed.

H6: In some cases, people who have an interest in causing regression to tribalistic moralities also have a sufficient intuitive or articulated knowledge of human psychology and of the basics of what philosophers call "social epistemology" to succeed in doing so.

(Social epistemology is the study of how social practices and institutions help to foster, spread, and preserve beliefs and proceeds on the reasonable assumption that most of us get most of our beliefs from others, in ways that are strongly shaped by the particular social environment we find ourselves in.) They understand that people tend to react in a tribalistic way if they are in or think they are in EEA-like conditions. They also know how to exploit the cultural mechanisms through which beliefs are formed and spread so that they can foster false beliefs about the presence of the particular kinds of threats that were pervasive in the EEA.

In some cases, people who stoke tribalism in others may sincerely believe that the threats they proclaim are real; in others, fomenting tribalism is purely strategic. What matters is not whether the appeal to EEA-like threat cues is Machiavellian or in good faith; what matters is that the appeal works, because of our dualistic, flexible moral nature.

Let me unpack each of these six hypotheses, with special attention to those that are new to this chapter.

H1 was explained in detail in chapters 1, 3, and 4. Here I need only emphasize that, given the asymmetry of risk versus benefits of trying to act peacefully and cooperatively in the conditions that were pervasive (though not universal) in the EEA, this is just what one would expect. Humans evolved to have a tendency to respond with fear, distrust, and even preemptive aggression when the Other poses any significant threat of disease, physical attacks, free riding, or social discoordination.

H2 simply states that cultural changes that have removed many people from the harsh conditions of the EEA can be undone in a number of ways, resulting in a return to the condition in which moralities first developed among our ancestors and hence to a reinstatement or magnification of the selective pressures that tended to elicit tribalistic moral responses. Only someone who naively thinks that shifts toward inclusiveness are inevitable or that human niche construction produces indestructible results would deny this. We have considerable empirical support for H2: for example, during economic downturns, there is an upsurge of xenophobia, anti-immigrant sentiment, racism, anti-Semitism, and other forms of exclusion, an increase in the frequency and intensity of tribalistic moral responses. The loss of physical security in wartime, civil conflict, state failure, or terrorist attacks also tends to correlate with increases in tribalism.

H3 also makes sense, given a fundamental fact about human beings: we are belief-driven creatures, but we are epistemically fallible—prone to serious errors in the formation and preservation of our beliefs. What we believe makes a difference in how we act and sometimes even fully determines how we act, but we can be and often are mistaken in our beliefs. If we falsely believe that the Other poses a threat, we react just as strongly and negatively as we would if our belief were true. The beliefs, not the facts, are what matter.

H4 is well confirmed by studies of the Holocaust and other genocides, by analyses of the production of "war fever," and by research on strategies for mobilizing animosity toward immigrants. Humans have developed tried-and-true techniques for manufacturing false threat cues, *and they typically use language that refers to threats that were actually common in the EEA*. Threats can be manufactured, either out of whole cloth or by exaggerating the probability that another group has hostile intentions or is dangerous in some other way. False threat cues can be manufactured by media-spread propaganda appealing to old grievances (as in resurrecting fears in the early 1990s of a replay of World War II Croatian genocide against Serbs) or by exaggerating the propensity toward violence of members of another group, as when President Trump says that "Mexico is sending us their murderers and rapists" and inflates by orders of magnitude the proportion of illegal immigrants who are criminals.

H5 is hardly novel and fits well with what we know about the psychology of leaders and would-be leaders. Scientists who apply evolutionary thinking to understanding cooperation in early human societies, as well as anthropologists who study persisting premodern societies that resemble them, agree that in times of perceived serious threats from other groups, the members of even quite egalitarian societies are willing to confer extraordinary power on certain individuals, if only temporarily, until the crisis is over. In modern societies, stable structures of unequal power exist, and access to positions of authority in them is highly advantageous for a number of reasons. Some people are especially concerned to gain and maintain power, for a variety of reasons, prompted by a variety of motives, from raw self-interest, to the quest for greater opportunities for sexual predation, to the desire to effect what they regard as progressive change or to preserve institutions they think are valuable. One tried-and-true way to gain, sustain, or augment political power is to present yourself as the first to identify a serious threat to one's group and propose a strategy for averting it. So the interest in power can generate an interest in fomenting tribalistic moral responses and frequently does.

People who desire power have an interest in fostering tribalistic moral responses when rallying support is best achieved by identifying or creating an enemy. As I noted earlier in the chapter, the disastrous breakup of Yugoslavia illustrates this phenomenon all too well. Milošević and his Croatian counterparts quite rationally concluded that their best hope for sustaining the power they had enjoyed before the collapse of state socialism was to resurrect ethnonational conflict by stoking tribalistic moral responses and then present themselves as the saviors who would protect their people from the dangerous Other.

Both parts of H6 are not only commonsensical but supported by a wealth of historical and contemporary evidence. Promoters of tribalistic morality understand how to deliberately re-create EEA-like conditions, by acting in ways they know will elicit hostile responses from those they wish to mobilize their people against, thus creating a situation that seems to confirm the belief that the other is inherently violent and dangerous. In other words, these leaders understand that by getting people to act on the belief that the Other poses a threat, they can make the belief become true, because acting on the belief will prompt hostile reactions by the Other.

There's another well-known recipe for taking us back toward EEA-like conditions (thereby eliciting tribalistic responses). People can act in ways that systematically weaken or destroy institutions and norms that reduce the threat of violence among groups and provide ways for them to cooperate in peaceful, mutually beneficial ways. For example, the fascist German and Italian leaders and the small group of generals and admirals who controlled Japanese policy did their best to undermine confidence in, and the effectiveness of, international institutions, in particular the League of Nations, an organization that had been designed to build trust among nations and reduce the threat of war. When such efforts succeed, they create a world that seems to confirm the validity of the fears they seek to generate. The probability of violent competition among groups increases, and a strategy of preemptive violence may actually become rational, because there are no longer any institutions or norms capable of effectively restraining the resort to force.

H6 is further confirmed by studies of certain commonalities in the discourse that successful demagogues use to generate fear and distrust of the Other. Although techniques vary, certain striking similarities are readily explained using the evolutionary framework I developed in earlier chapters. People who wish to gain power by mobilizing their group against some Other show that they understand the psychology that the EEA spawned by uniformly employing a limited lexicon of terms to characterize the Other: disease ridden, filthy, violent, parasitic (free riding or downright exploitive), treacherous, animalistic (not "true human beings," like us).

In the most extreme cases, mobilizers of tribalistic morality deliberately subject the Other to harsh conditions that actually produce the traits that function as threat cues. The clearest example of this technique is the practice of creating concentration camps in which the inmates are deliberately reduced to a diseased, "animalistic" existence—lice ridden, infected with typhus and other diseases of poor sanitation and malnutrition, and set against one another in a struggle for the means of subsistence that evokes in all but the strongest a willingness to violate the most basic moral rules. When human beings are reduced to such a state, it is easier to treat them in ways that you believe no human being should ever be treated, because they no longer resemble human beings.

Fomenting Tribalism as Applied Social Epistemology

Adept promoters of tribalistic moral responses also have a basic grasp of the principles of social epistemology. They know that people form many of their beliefs under the influence of others whom they regard as reliable sources of information. That's why the leaders who deliberately foster EEA-like threat cues invariably do two things. They work hard to undermine the credibility of sources that don't present the Other as uniformly threatening and that emphasize commonality of interests across groups and opportunities for mutually beneficial cooperation. And they attempt to co-opt perceived "epistemic authorities" or opinion-makers (like teachers, popular talk show hosts and bloggers, and clergy) in order to spread their message of fear and distrust.

Whether a comprehensive explanation of regression to tribalism will be an evolutionary explanation through and through and more particularly an exclusively *adaptationist* evolutionary story is an interesting question, but one I can't pretend to answer conclusively. The next chapter, which focuses on the particular type of regression from inclusion I call intrasocietal tribalism and the role that ideology plays in it, may shed some light on the answer. Much will depend on whether the understanding of ideology I employ there is itself subject to an explanation that is evolutionary. I will suggest that it is.

An Update on the Results of the Investigation So Far

Before proceeding to the next chapter, I'll summarize the main results of this one. (1) Adaptive plasticity regarding moral responses to outgroups, the same evolved human trait that explains how morality could become more inclusive, also explains why regression to tribalism can occur. Regression to tribalism, like movement toward inclusion, is rooted in our evolved dualistic moral nature—the ability of the moral mind to express itself in both inclusive and exclusive moralities. (2) If the current environment reverts to EEA-like conditions, or if people believe this has happened, then tribalistic moral responses will be resurrected or magnified, and gains in inclusivity will be diminished or lost entirely. (3) Regression can take any of several forms: it can exhibit intersocietal or intrasocietal tribalism; and intrasocietal tribalism can be either pure or impure, depending on whether the threatening Other in our midst is wholly or only partly the product of the imagination. (4) Culture giveth, and culture taketh away: cultural innovations have lifted many people out of EEA-like environments, but cultural changes can also contribute to regression, either by causing a return to a condition that approximates the EEA or by simulating a return. (5) Whether or not gains in the movement toward deeply inclusive morality are sustained or lost will depend on who controls the environmental conditions that trigger more inclusive or more exclusive moral responses. (6) Since the contest for control is ongoing, we can never be assured that shifts toward deeply inclusive morality will continue. (7) The fact that the predominant character of our moral responses is environmentally conditioned implies that the shifts toward inclusion that have already occurred are fragile, and further moral change in the direction of inclusion is possible but in no way guaranteed.

Another Reason Why It's Wrong to Say We Are Morally Tribalistic by Nature

I conclude this chapter by exploring an implication of the analysis I've offered in it. It now turns out that there are two reasons, not one, why it is extremely misleading, if not outright false, to say that human beings are morally tribalistic by nature. The first reason was developed in the introduction and elaborated in chapter 4, where I argued that if one wants to talk of human nature at all, it would be more accurate to say that it is dualistic: the moral mind's plasticity with regard to moral responses means that we can either be tribalistic or inclusive, depending on the environment.

Now we have a second reason: this chapter has shown that tribalistic moral responses aren't natural givens, raw instincts; they are socially constructed, to a greater or lesser degree. Even in the relatively simple world of the EEA, it's likely that groups developed cultures that included specific characterizations of the Other, typically attributing to them negative characteristics that they lacked or exaggerating ones they possessed. This would have meant representing the Other as animalistic or inferior or inherently violent or treacherous and would hardly have reflected an accurate scientific understanding of what other people were really like. That kind of

cultural construction of the image of the Other was probably conducive to fitness at the group level because it helped mobilize strong
protective reactions by exaggerating the threat that out-groups
posed. Given the asymmetry of risk in encountering the Other that
was common in that early environment, exaggerating the risk that
the Other posed was probably conducive to reproductive fitness.

In the modern world—the world human beings constructed
through cumulative culture after they emerged from the EEA into
the Neolithic Revolution and beyond—tribalistic moral responses
are more heavily socially constructed. They have to be, because
reversion requires overcoming the cultural constructs that have
produced some progress in the direction of inclusion. (For example,
to convince morally normal people that they ought to butcher their
neighbors in a genocide, one has to overcome the effects of a long
history of cultural and genetic selection against violence toward
humans one closely associates with.) Tribalistic moral responses—
nowadays at least—aren't anything like instinctive reactions. They
require a lot of work to assemble; they are creations of culture, even
though they build on features of our evolved biology. That's another
reason to reject talk about our being morally tribalistic by nature, in
addition to the fact that our moral nature is not exclusively tribalistic but also includes the capacity for inclusion.

At present we face serious problems that can be put under the
heading of "tribalism," but if we want to make headway in solving them, we should avoid mischaracterizing the problem as one of
"overcoming our tribal nature." That makes it sound like the problem is how to inhibit an instinct, when in fact it is largely a matter of
how to dismantle or prevent a social construction and capitalize on
the more constructive aspect of our dual moral nature. That's why
the philosopher and psychologist Joshua Greene is dead wrong
when he says that, to overcome tribalism, we have to act "unnaturally" (Greene 2013, 147).

8

Intrasocietal Tribalism and the Evolutionary Roots of Ideology

State fairs are a long-standing cultural phenomenon in some parts of America. Blue ribbons are given for the best cows, bulls, chickens, sheep, and pigs. In some states, these popular events used to be called "livestock exhibitions," and in the 1920s and 1930s, the livestock on exhibit included human beings. I'm referring to "fitter family contests" sponsored by eugenics societies across America. Senators and governors handed out the prizes. The judges of these competitions were people who supposedly could tell which families had the best genes (Buchanan et al. 2001, 31, 43).

Case Study: Eugenics as an Example of Intrasocietal Tribalism Fueled by Ideology

The image of such "experts" carefully inspecting the teeth, measuring the heights, weighing, and administering quick, crude IQ tests to members of competing families is likely to prompt a horizontal shake of your head and bring a condescending smile to your lips. Yet despite its comical aspects, eugenics in its more extreme forms was literally lethal—and a dramatic example of the subject of this chapter: *intrasocietal tribalism and its connection to ideology*. Here's a fact I find particularly sobering—and conducive to humility: this form of tribalism won the hearts and minds of some of the most intelligent, educated, and conscientious people in some of the most democratic and human-rights-respecting countries on earth.

What Was Eugenics?

In 1883, Francis Galton defined eugenics as the "science of improving stock—not just through judicious mating, but whatever tends to give the more suitable races or strains of blood a better chance of prevailing over the less suitable than they would otherwise have." What came to be known as eugenics wasn't just a version of science; it was a major social movement that deeply penetrated politics, public policy, and education in a number of countries. As I will argue, eugenics was an ideology and as such was a system of beliefs that appealed to people's moral motivation, not an invitation to take an extended holiday from morality.

If the basic idea of eugenics is that human beings should intervene in their own reproduction if doing so is necessary to prevent serious deterioration of the human gene pool, then there seems to be nothing wrong with it. For example, if, because of some environmental change, human babies were afflicted with a high rate of genetic mutations that caused major disability and suffering, then intervention to reverse or mitigate the trend might well be not only morally permissible but morally obligatory, even if it involved changing human reproductive behavior or genetically modifying human embryos or some other biomedical intervention. Similarly, if it were possible to use biomedical technologies to greatly improve human life by changing some of the genes that are now transmitted across generations, then that, too, might be at least morally permissible, if not morally mandatory—if, and only if, it could be done in a way that did not violate individual rights or concentrate too much power in government or other social institutions or have other serious negative effects (Buchanan et al. 2001, 42–43).

Of course, some people reject the core idea of eugenics because they think it involves "interfering with nature" or "playing God"; but that position relies either on the false assumption that nature is good (or, in more modern terms, that evolution always produces morally good things or things that are optimal and hence not to be tampered with) or on a failure to understand that humans "interfere" with nature all the time, that we constantly produce outcomes that would not have occurred without our intervention. Regardless of what many Whole Foods customers seem to think, nature isn't good (or bad); it's a mixed bag.

Evolution doesn't produce perfect, harmonious, stable "master-pieces of design." Consider the human knee or the lower back, for example; or the fact that the human pharynx combines food and air intake and makes us more liable to death by choking than most other animals; or that human beings, unlike most mammals, can't produce vitamin C from what they eat and are therefore prone to scurvy, and so on. Consider also that the bioweapons experts have yet to synthesize something as toxic as botulism, a naturally occurring product of bacteria.

Evolution isn't like a master craftsman; in fact, Richard Dawkins's famous statement that evolution is "a blind watchmaker" is too charitable (Dawkins 1986, 21). Evolution, unlike a watchmaker (blind or sighted), doesn't proceed with a goal in mind, an idea of some ultimate outcome to be achieved. Rather, evolution is more like a shortsighted tinkerer who occasionally happens to make watches without trying to or even knowing what a watch is. That's why Darwin described "the works of Nature" as "clumsy, wasteful, blundering, low, and horridly cruel" (Buchanan 2011, 17, 26, 30).

As for the idea that "interfering with nature" is wrong: we alter "natural" outcomes every time we correct a baby's congenital heart defect or administer insulin to a diabetic. In fact, human progress is all about "interfering with nature." If that is "playing God," then so be it.

The relevance of the admonition to not play God is nonetheless important, if understood as shorthand for an eminently reasonable counsel of prudence: don't overestimate your wisdom in determining how to change things or which things need changing; and above all beware unintended consequences. This is sound advice, but it's a far cry from saying: don't do anything to produce outcomes that are different from what would occur "naturally" if you didn't intervene.

The problem with eugenics is not that the core idea is morally tainted. It's that the core idea became embedded in a web of false factual beliefs that led people to implement the core idea in morally abhorrent ways.

When we step back from the details of different phenomena that tend to get promiscuously lumped together under the heading "eugenics," we can see certain persistent patterns of thought. Most historians of eugenics would agree that members of the movement supported many of the following theses. Combining all these beliefs into a systematic *moral* orientation is what motivated the worst actions undertaken in the name of eugenics.

(1) *Genes determine behavior.* Genes directly produce behavior, across a wide range of environments. (This amounts to a gross failure to recognize that how or even whether genes get expressed depends on environmental conditions.)

(2) *Genes determine most or all social ills.* Bad genes produce behavior that is responsible for all the major problems facing modern societies, from drunkenness and crime and poverty to sexual immorality in all forms.

(3) *Bad genes produce lack of self-control, including failure to control sexual desires.* The same bad genes that produce other forms of bad behavior also make people less able to control their desires, including their sexual desires, and less able to understand the effects of acting on their desires.

(4) *Lack of self-control means higher reproductive rates.* As a result of the lack of self-control caused by bad genes, people with bad genes are reproducing at a higher rate than those with good genes.

(5) *The gene pool is deteriorating.* As a result of the higher reproductive rate of people with bad genes and because modern civilization, with its charitable institutions, welfare state, and advances in medicine, has prevented bad genes from being winnowed out by natural selection, the proportion of bad genes in the gene pool is rapidly increasing.

(6) *People with bad genes are social parasites.* Because their bad genes cause them to have various character defects, including lack of self-control and lack of industriousness, the genetically defective are a drain on society; they absorb large amounts of social resources without contributing to society.

(7) *Deterioration of the gene pool means the destruction of civilization.* As bad genes and the behavior they produce become predominant, all the gains of human progress will be destroyed, causing social, cultural, and political degeneration.

(8) *Supreme emergencies call for extreme measures.* The deterioration of the human gene pool is a catastrophe, and to avert it, we will have to make major changes in reproductive patterns. To avert the catastrophe, measures that in less dire circumstances would be prohibited may become not only permissible but morally obligatory.

Not everyone who is rightly labeled a eugenicist held all these tenets; the last item in particular was not universally accepted. For purposes of my argument, I need only make a more limited claim: the most tribalistic and dangerous form of eugenic thought included all eight items, including the last.

Not everyone who was concerned about the degeneration of the human gene pool reached the conclusion that large-scale coercion would be necessary to avert the catastrophe. Some believed that voluntary reproductive restraint by the genetically defective might work, if extraordinary efforts were made to educate them about the consequences of their profligate behavior and if they were given easy access to effective birth control. Yet it's clear that if you accept the "supreme emergency" frame for thinking about human reproduction, then you'll be likely to conclude that coercion is justified, if all other alternatives are insufficient to avert the catastrophe.

In chapter 6, I noted that eugenics is a clear instance of pure intrasocietal tribalism. It's intrasocietal because the dangerous Other, the explicit target of tribalistic moral responses, is not some group from outside our society; they are the enemy within. It's pure because the group that is the explicit focus of tribalistic, exclusive moral responses is imaginary, fully a social construct. There *is* no group in which all defective genes are concentrated, and there *is* no group whose behavior is rigidly determined by genes. Furthermore, no one group in society (with the possible exception of the ruling class in oppressive societies) is responsible for all major social ills. The explicit target of eugenic anxiety and hostility, then, was a set of nested fictions. In that respect, eugenics and other pure intrasocietal tribalisms differ from those that focus exclusive responses on some group that actually exists, even if that group is represented inaccurately in the tribalistic imagination.

I classify eugenics as an instance of tribalistic morality for two reasons. First, it was clearly a morality or at least included a prominent moral element. Eugenicists were not amoral. They were people who had undergone normal moral development and in most cases were committed to sustaining the moral identity they had forged in the process of that development. In fact, many prominent advocates of eugenics were deeply committed to various genuine "social justice" issues before encountering eugenic thought; they had unusually robust moral identities. When they became proponents of eugenics, they didn't jettison their moral identities; they simply redirected their moral energy toward achieving new goals.

Second, eugenic rhetoric didn't try to convince people to abandon their deepest moral commitments. Instead it instilled a web of false factual beliefs (about the genetic determinism of behavior, about the genetic sources of all social ills, etc.) that, when connected to utterly unexceptionable moral principles, yielded conclusions that many people now regard as grossly immoral. If you believe that civilized life itself is threatened by some group and that you have no other way to stop the threat than by using coercion against it, then you will likely conclude that it is morally imperative to stop them and that the permissible means for doing so are exempt from ordinary moral constraints. (That's exactly how many Brits and Americans justified Allied terror bombing of German and Japanese civilians in World War II.) Second, eugenics was exclusive: it identified a group as the dangerous Other and regarded them as not entitled to the protections that the recognition of equal basic moral status entails. So eugenics fits my characterization of tribalistic moralities. More specifically, it is a case of intrasocietal tribalism of the pure variety.

Was Eugenics an Extended Holiday from Ordinary Morality?

Some moral philosophers who have attempted an "ethical autopsy" on eugenics conclude that it was grounded in a crudely consequentialist ethics: eugenicists cared only about the good of society as a whole and didn't take seriously the idea of individual rights, conceived as constraints on what may be done to maximize the good of society. Eugenics in effect relied on a moral theory that had no place for the idea that individual rights have any value except so far as respecting them happens to promote social utility (Buchanan et al. 2001, 41–48).

That autopsy report is bogus. You needn't have been a crude consequentialist to come to the most extreme conclusions that eugenicists did. Instead you could be a firm believer in individual rights but also believe that in a supreme emergency, it's permissible to infringe them.

I borrow the term "supreme emergency" from Michael Walzer in his book *Just and Unjust Wars* (1977, ch. 16). Walzer tentatively endorses the idea that, in a genuine supreme emergency, it may be permissible to violate one of the most important principles of just warfare: the prohibition on deliberately killing innocents (usually understood as noncombatants). Walzer suggests that the Nazi regime was so evil that stopping it justified violating that basic prohibition, if there was no other way to avert the catastrophe of a victorious Nazi Germany. Walzer is no consequentialist in his moral thinking, and one need not be a consequentialist to think that individual rights (including the right not to be killed in war if one is a noncombatant) can be justifiably disregarded in the case of a supreme emergency.

I doubt that many people (apart from a thankfully small number of second-rate moral philosophers), either now or in the heyday of eugenics, are accurately described as crude consequentialists. What makes the eugenics movement so deeply disturbing is that it led morally normal people, including people who weren't crude consequentialists and ordinarily took individual rights seriously, to commit moral outrages (Buchanan 2007, 24–25).

Tribalism Doesn't Bypass Ordinary Morality; It Hijacks It

What's true of eugenics as a case of pure intrasocietal tribalism is true of all varieties of tribalism, pure and impure, intersocietal and intrasocietal: they are moralities or include a prominent moral component, and yet they typically issue in destructive, immoral behavior, not because they effect fundamental changes in people's moral outlooks, but because they hijack existing moral commitments, redirecting them toward exclusion. The problem with tribalism, then, is not that it's amoral, that it neutralizes the moral self and bypasses the commitment to moral identity. The problem, rather, is that it effectively harnesses existing moral principles and the motivational power of the commitment to moral identity to produce an immoral outcome.

I can put the same point in a different way: the rhetoric of tribalistic morality is conservative from the standpoint of moral change; to elicit tribalistic responses, it doesn't have to cause people to make fundamental moral changes, to abandon deeply internalized principles in favor of new ones, to adopt a new morality. That's what makes the rhetoric of tribalism so effective—and so dangerous. Rather than aiming to overcome peoples' basic moral commitments, it co-opts and redirects them, exploiting people's moral motivation in the service of immorality. When you think about it, that's a backhanded compliment to the power of morality over human beings and to the stability of the internalized moral principles that culture produces in us.

To make this fundamental point perfectly clear, I'll return to an example I presented earlier: Nazi propaganda didn't try to effect basic moral changes in German public school teachers, and it certainly didn't attempt to turn them into amoral beings. Had it done so, it would have abandoned a potent source of motivation, namely, people's existing moral identities. Instead it left people's most basic moral principles untouched and exploited their commitment to them. Public school teachers, remember, were exhorted to instill the Golden Rule in their students, but with the proviso that it only applied to racial comrades. Morality was exploited to further tribalistic aims. Allegiance to the Golden Rule became an accomplice in tribalistic responses to Jews and other "non-Aryans."

Because the worst large-scale atrocities are committed mainly not by sociopaths but by morally normal people, and because tribalism works by harnessing and redirecting moral commitments, it's a mistake to describe the phenomenon of genocide, as the social psychologist Albert Bandura famously does, as a case of "moral disengagement" (Bandura 2016, 2–3). That framing obscures the fact that the most extreme forms of tribalism, including the willingness to participate in or at least stand by and not resist large-scale destruction of human beings, generally require deep moral engagement.

Heinrich Himmler, head of the SS, knew this. His subordinates who were directing the mass shootings of men, women, and children in Poland told him that the soldiers doing the killing were having severe psychological problems. (What a surprise!) Himmler paid a visit to these *Einsatzgruppen* (task forces) and gave them a *moral* motivational speech. He told the soldiers that he understood their natural revulsion at shooting women and children, but that they must be strong; they must do their moral duty to help create a better world for future generations. He *didn't* tell them that there was nothing wrong with killing women and children and he didn't try to convert them into crude consequentialists, people who think that individual rights can be disregarded anytime that doing increases social utility a bit. Instead, he told them that this case of killing them was an exception to the moral rules that apply in ordinary situations, because this was in effect a supreme emergency, a situation in which civilization was supposedly threatened by a lethal Jewish-Bolshevik conspiracy.

The Power of Tribalism Is the Power of Morality

How does intrasocietal tribalism hijack ordinary morality? Usually *by invoking the threat cues of the EEA and then connecting them to the existing predominant moral framework*. Again, the case of eugenics provides a clear illustration. The "genetically defective" are presented as a distinct group (though within society, rather than as members of another society). They are characterized as fundamentally different from Us: as physically, mentally, and morally inferior. They are vectors of disease, posing a risk of biological parasitism transmitted vertically over generations. They are also portrayed as social parasites, as draining the public coffers while contributing nothing. They therefore exacerbate the competition for resources that occurs in one form or another in all human societies, depleting the surpluses that distinguish modern societies from those that existed in the EEA and through most of human history. The "genetically defective" are also said to be physically dangerous: their defective genes result in poor impulse control, which in turn breeds violent behavior. Finally, they cannot be participants in cooperation with Us, enlisted as voluntary contributors to solving the problem of gene pool deterioration, because they lack the mental and moral capacities needed for cooperation. Our relationship to the "genetically defective" is therefore zero sum—it's Them or Us—not a relationship of potentially mutually beneficial cooperation. They are, in a word, as much a threat, and the same sort of threat, as other human groups in the EEA often were.

To summarize: Once the targets of eugenic tribalism were characterized as posing all the threats that the Other often posed in the EEA, it was easy to co-opt existing moral concepts and commitments to motivate people to react tribalistically toward them. The dangerous Other was presented as the enemy in what amounts to a just war in which failure to achieve victory will be catastrophic. Consequently, if we coerce or even exterminate them (as in the German medical murder program) we are just exercising our right of self-defense. In a different framing, one that was ubiquitous in eugenic discourse, we are responding, quite reasonably, to the most serious public health threat imaginable—a threat so lethal that neutralizing it justifies infringing the individual rights that we ordinarily hold sacred.

The only difference between the tribalistic portrayal of the Other in the simpler societies of the EEA and the characterization of the "genetically defective" is that, in the latter case, the presentation of the threat cues takes the form of supposedly scientifically grounded facts and is connected to a more developed moral-conceptual framework, one that includes the notion that there are individual rights, but affirms that they may be justifiably infringed in cases of supreme emergency. Remember, morality, as I noted in chapter 1, is not just a tool for cooperation within a group; it is a potent weapon to be used against the Other. Eugenics illustrates that grim point all too well.

The Evolution of Tribalism and the Advent of Ideology

At this juncture, my argument takes a critical turn: I want to suggest that eugenics, like all other forms of intrasocietal tribalism, whether pure or impure, is *the child of modern society*. By "modern society," I don't mean contemporary society. I mean post-Neolithic Revolution society, a form of social life in which hunting and gathering have been replaced by agriculture and the domestication of animals, and in which large numbers of people composed of different cultural groups or ethnicities and different classes or castes live together year round in something resembling cities.

Stable groups didn't exist within the earliest hunter-gatherer societies. There was a sexual division of labor and there were individuals who specialized in certain skills, but nothing approached what we think of as social classes. No robust, stable division of labor separated society into large, persisting, and clearly identifiable groups. Nor were there distinct groups who were differentiated from one another because they subscribed to significantly different systems of beliefs or were members of different cultural or ethnic groups. Such differentiations only occurred with the Neolithic Revolution, the shift to agriculture and the domestication of animals, which began around ten thousand years ago. In earlier human societies, particular individuals and perhaps particular families in some cases may have been identified as free riders and accordingly subjected to various forms of exclusion. But the complex social structure required for genuine intrasocietal tribalism of the sort we see in eugenics or anti-Semitism had not yet developed.

In modern societies, tribalistic moral responses—which typically are responses to EEA-like threat cues—can be directed toward groups *within* society, because people have already become accustomed to parsing their social world into groups. Only with the emergence of group-differentiated societies, therefore, can tribalism take an intrasocietal form. In that sense, intrasocietal tribalism is a child of modernity.

Modern societies are not just more complex in their social structures; they also feature more correspondingly elaborate conceptual schemes and more sophisticated forms of discourse. That kind of complexity creates the conditions for tribalistic morality to manifest itself in correspondingly complex systems of beliefs.

What Is Ideology?

I have in mind systems of beliefs (and accompanying attitudes) that warrant the title of "ideology." I'm aware that this is a much-disputed term. I'm opting for a fairly broad conception of ideology in my attempt to provide the beginning of a cogent evolutionary explanation of ideology. That explanation will have two parts. First, I'll argue that ideology has deep evolutionary roots. In other words, ideologies are grounded in and exploit the capacity for tribalism that is one component of our dualistic moral nature. Second, I'll argue that ideology is an adaptation—a product of cultural selection—for successful intergroup competition that came on the scene rather late in the history of our species, in response to new selective pressures created by cultural changes wrought beginning with the Neolithic Revolution. In brief, I'll try to make the case that ideologies or proto-ideologies came to be because earlier ways of achieving cooperation no longer worked in that new environment. I'll argue, in other words, that *ideologies are products of cultural selection for what enables cooperation within a group under modern conditions*. Further, I'll hypothesize that in their more developed forms ideologies enable cooperation *that facilitates successful competition against other groups within society*. Finally, I'll show not only that ideologies often distinguish Us from Them in a way that relegates Them to inferiority, but also that *ideologies can erect formidable obstacles to overcoming the divisions between Us and Them*.

To clarify my broader conception of ideology, I'll first contrast it with a narrower one, the understanding of ideology that is predominant in the Marxist tradition of social thought. In this narrower conception, ideology is constituted by a single function: it serves to misrepresent social reality in ways that stabilize oppressive social orders. In the words of the philosopher Michael Rosen, the raison d'être of the concept of ideology is that it explains the phenomenon of "voluntary servitude," the fact that though the oppressed potentially have greater power than the oppressors, they often do not rise up and overthrow the system (Rosen 1996, chs. 1 and 2). According to the narrow conception, it's this explanatory function—and it alone—that makes the idea of ideology valuable.

That conception of ideology is too narrow: ideology can perform the function of stabilizing oppressive orders, but it can also do other things. For example, as Lenin in *What Is to Be Done?* and Sorel in *Reflections on Violence* argued, there is such a thing as a revolutionary (or as Lenin puts it, "proletarian") ideology: a system of beliefs that explicitly functions to motivate people to overthrow, not to acquiesce in, oppressive social orders (Lenin 2013, 81–82; Sorel 2004, 226). According to the narrow conception of ideology, the term "revolutionary ideology" is an oxymoron. The narrow conception can't be right, because the idea of a revolutionary ideology makes perfectly good sense, and more importantly, we have actual examples of that kind of ideology.

What Ideologies Are and What They Do

Here's my attempt to characterize ideology more broadly, in a way that allows, among other things, for both revolutionary and counterrevolutionary ideologies—systems of belief that motivate the slaves to throw off their shackles as well as those that promote "voluntary servitude":

An ideology is a system of beliefs and corresponding attitudes that (1) orients individuals by providing a more or less comprehensive map of the social world, offering a greatly simplified characterization of its main features; (2) includes a diagnosis of what is right or wrong or good or bad in the existing social order, while appealing to and reinforcing individuals' group-based moral identities, sometimes—but not always—in such a way as to facilitate assigning praise for what is right or good to Us and blame for what is wrong or bad to Them; and (3) supplies resources for morally justifying various cooperative actions on the part of the group to whom the ideology links the individual's identity, by referring to the diagnosis of what is right and good or wrong and bad about the social order and sometimes—but not always—by referring to who is responsible for it.

The phrase "sometimes—but not always" in this definition allows us to distinguish between *ideologies* and *extremely divisive ideologies*. The latter's moralized maps of the social world not only identify what is good and bad but also assign blame to some Other (while praising Us as the authors of all that is good or right). Not all ideologies are like that. For example, some versions of what might be called liberal cosmopolitan ideology provide a diagnosis of what ails society and the world, a prescription for improvement, and justifications for actions directed toward improvement, but may not feature in any significant way the assignment of blame for current social ills to any one group. At most that sort of ideology might characterize those who stand in the way of progress, who don't participate in the effort to bring about the ideal, in a mildly negative way (for example, as uninformed or not very clear thinking), but it needn't characterize them as morally vicious, as the enemy, and as the authors of all that is amiss.

In contrast, some ideologies are deeply divisive because they demonize the Other, condemning them morally as the perpetrators of all serious social and political ills. In what follows, I focus mainly on deeply divisive ideologies, because I think they play a central role in the most dangerous contemporary forms of intrasocietal tribalism.

Please note that the social map an ideology provides is not purely descriptive; it includes evaluations of existing social conditions and, more importantly, *moral* evaluations that have implications for the justification of action, especially collective action.

Note also the qualifier "more or less" in front of "comprehensive social map." Some ideologies, especially what we usually think of as political ideologies, are rather comprehensive: they orient the individual with respect to most of the important features of the social world. Others are less comprehensive, as is the case with the ideology of a certain profession or school of art—assuming that the term "ideology" can usefully be extended to such systems of beliefs without inflating its scope to the point of triviality.

My definition of "ideology" is quite a mouthful, but I think I can make it not only chewable but also digestible with due elaboration and some concrete illustrations. My goal in doing so will be to show how ideology, understood in this way, can explain intrasocietal tribalism, and why understanding ideologies as products of evolution can help account for their power over us.

First, notice that the broader understanding of ideology I am offering can explain how, in modern, complex societies, ideology can embody and foster both kinds of tribalism, intersocietal and intrasocietal. For example, if you are a certain type of supporter of President Trump, you may believe that what is wrong with America today is both that the Chinese and other countries are exploiting us through unfair trade practices and that the "liberals" are destroying the American dream by effecting a transition to "socialism" that will undermine individual initiative and responsibility and violate basic liberties.

Because this chapter is devoted to intrasocietal tribalism, I'll focus on how deeply divisive ideologies can sort the people of one's own society into Us and Them, attributing all that is good or right to Us and all that is bad or wrong to Them, thereby creating a division that is difficult if not impossible to overcome. And, as I will argue, even when an ideology doesn't go so far as to demonize the Other, it may present them as people we needn't listen to, and in doing so block opportunities for cooperating with them.

Some ideologies—including the most potent and destructive ones—do include the opposing-groups identity feature, defining the individual's group identity largely in contrast with the identity of another group that is represented in a harshly negative way. I will focus on ideologies that do have the opposing-groups identity feature, ideologies I label "deeply divisive." Because I think this kind of ideology is fueling the contemporary intrasocietal tribalism that many people find so alarming, I focus on it.

The Social and Psychological Functions of Ideologies

The first question we need to answer is this: what does an ideology do for those who subscribe to it? Because an ideology provides a map of the social terrain, it orients the individual, reducing the enormous complexity of modern societies to a few simple overgeneralizations (in extreme cases outright falsehoods). That's psychologically satisfying because it convinces you that the whole thing makes sense and you can reliably predict at least some outcomes. After all, some degree of simplification is necessary if the attempt to process information is ever to culminate in action. The simplified evaluative map that ideologies provide also gives you a straightforward answer to the question "whose side am I on?" across a wide range of political and moral disputes.

More importantly, the social map that an ideology provides *coordinates* the orientations of all those who subscribe to the ideology—it puts them all on the same page. The coordination is both epistemic (shared beliefs about what the facts about society are) and moral (shared diagnosis of what is good or right, bad or wrong, and who is responsible for what). This dual coordination is vital for ideologies doing one of the most important things they do: enabling collective action, a unified, coordinated response to perceived social issues and conflicts. In brief, ideologies facilitate cooperation among the members of an identity group by coordinating factual beliefs and values and by unifying factual beliefs and values in a narrative that provides a moral diagnosis of the status quo and a prescription for what is to be done. As I will argue, however, *the ways in which ideologies, especially deeply divisive ideologies, do this pose serious obstacles to cooperation with other groups—and may make full realization of the First Great Expansion impossible.*

Ideologies are evaluative social maps that make group-based moral identities salient in their evaluations. It's because ideologies connect so intimately with moral identity that people are willing to make great sacrifices, even to lay down their lives, for the sake of remaining true to their ideological beliefs. This same tight connection with moral identity also explains why ideologies can motivate people to do terrible things to other people.

The Centrality of Moralized Group-Based Identity in Ideologies

Crucial to this broader conception of ideology is the notion that ideologies reinforce and foster (and perhaps sometimes even create) group-based identities and more specifically group-based identities that have a moral dimension. I noted in chapter 5 that human beings generally have a deep desire—indeed, an irrepressible need—for moral identity. They also have a similarly powerful need for a sense of belonging, a need to recognize themselves as members of some group or groups, not just as one fact about themselves among a myriad of others, but as a fact that resides at the core of their identity. Group-based identities that have a substantial moral component satisfy both of these needs.

Recall that it's not hard to sketch a plausible evolutionary explanation for why group-based moral identity should be such a potent factor in human psychology. Humans managed to become supercooperators because they developed strong moral relations among members of cooperative groups. There was group-level selection for the sort of moral psychology that enabled human beings to cooperate, in spite of the fact that individual self-interest posed a persistent threat of free riding or of violating the norms of fairness and reciprocity that were essential for successful cooperation—including cooperation needed to compete successfully with other groups. Groups whose members strongly identified with the group would, other things being equal, outcompete those whose members didn't.

In other words, robust group-based identity, especially when it connected tightly with or encompassed moral identity, was probably an adaptation, something that came about because it enabled some groups to outcompete others and thereby achieve reproductive success. One way a moralized group-based identity does this is by helping the individual resist the siren song of self-interest and, when that fails, by motivating other members of her group to punish the offender. A moralized group identity also erects psychological barriers to defection to another group. Finally, a strong sense of identification with the group can even lead an individual to sacrifice herself for the common good. All three of these functions can be vital for successful cooperation, especially cooperation needed to outcompete other groups, including other groups within our own society.

Our Moral Identity Defined in Opposition to Theirs

Deeply divisive ideologies accentuate (or even create) group-based moral identities, and they do so by contrasting the group that is central to one's identity with another group that is characterized as not only different from us but different in threatening ways. More specifically, We are presented as being the source of what is good and right in society, because of our virtues, the shared admirable character traits that supposedly help to define us as a group. They, in contrast, are characterized as the source of what is bad or wrong owing to their defects, which the ideology typically identifies as the vices that are the mirror images of our virtues. We are hardworking, honest, and dedicated to the common good; They are shiftless, treacherous, and in relentless pursuit of their own self-interest, contemptuous of the common good. We value individual initiative and freedom; They value only enlarging the sphere of government control by making citizens dependent on "welfare." We understand the true nature of our social order; They have an inaccurate, distorted understanding of it. They emphasize individual responsibility while ignoring the structural barriers that prevent some people from bettering their situation, while We appreciate that individual initiative isn't enough for having a good life, if the structure of one's society puts one at a serious disadvantage. If We get our way, if We succeed in shaping society according to our commendable values, all will be well; if They succeed in creating or preserving a social order that realizes their values, things will be very bad.

Ideologies as Heuristics

I've said that ideologies are simplified, moralized evaluative maps of the social world. Another way to put the point is to say that they are *heuristics*, mental shortcuts that help us orient ourselves without having to rely on impossibly large amounts of information that would, even if we possessed them, require such complex calculations as to preclude timely action for finite creatures like us. The simplest kind of heuristic is a so-called rule of thumb: for example, always limit yourself to exactly two glasses of wine when you plan to drive home, rather than trying to titrate your alcohol intake precisely, on a case-by-case basis, taking into account the full range of variables, including whether the wine has an especially high alcohol content, the amount and type of food eaten, driving distance, how much sleep you had the night before, whether the route home is familiar, and so on.

Psychologists have recently discovered that cognitively normal humans employ heuristics, mental shortcuts, quite extensively. Because heuristics simplify or abstract from the complexity of the situations we face, you might say they are inherently erroneous. (On some evenings, if the conditions are just right, you could drive home safely after drinking three glasses of wine.) Yet if heuristics help us to do better than we would if we tried to take into account, on a case-by-case basis, all the data relevant to an ideal decision, that inaccuracy may be acceptable. Whether the inaccuracies that heuristics involve are acceptable or not will generally depend on the environment in which the heuristic is employed. A mental shortcut that was generally beneficial in the EEA may be a bad bargain if employed in a quite different environment, an instance of "evolutionary mismatch" or "Pleistocene hangover."

In modern societies, we face persistent competition among alternative sources of information, and the number of those sources is enormous and multiplying, as a result of the ongoing development of electronic media, especially the internet. Faced with this deluge of information, people need heuristics to determine whom to listen to and whom to ignore. Listening to all voices is not feasible. Even trying to do so would produce cognitive and moral overload.

Ideologies provide heuristics for determining whom to listen to. If we identify somebody as one of Us, then they deserve a hearing. This function is especially pronounced in deeply divisive ideologies. If Jones is one of Them, we already know that what he says will be tainted by the defects of *those people*. We know that They are either grossly misinformed or insincere or both. If they're grossly misinformed, their ideas about the way society should be will be erroneous and even dangerous. If They are insincere, what they say is purely strategic, designed to advance their perverse agenda. In either case, We have no need to listen to Them.

Here's a concrete example: Rush Limbaugh repeatedly says that "liberals" are in favor of "open borders" *because* they believe that immigrants will vote Democratic. (Needless to say, he provides no evidence whatsoever to support this flat-footed, massive psychological generalization.) The implication is that no "liberals" — none of them — really care about the welfare of immigrants. If you swallow this particular effort at character assassination, you won't be inclined to listen to the reasons that people in favor of easing immigration restrictions give for their view. You'll think the "reasons" they give are just shams.

Moreover, if you do listen to members of the group your ideology characterizes as Them, other members of your group may be suspicious of you. Refusing to listen can be a clear signal of group identity and solidarity. If you listen, you might get infected. And your very willingness to listen indicates that you may be disloyal.

Ideologies as Belief Immune Systems

If you know much about political talk radio in the United States, this will all sound depressingly familiar. Often the message one gets is that to justify not listening to someone, all you need to do is simply point out that they're a liberal (or a conservative, depending on whom you are listening to). If his audience has already bought into group-identity-based heuristics for determining whom to believe, a speaker doesn't need to engage with the *content* of what his opponent is saying or evaluate the soundness of his arguments; he just needs to identify that individual as a member of that other group. Consider, for example, the fact that the term "libtard" (short for liberal retard) is quite popular in contemporary American conservative discourse. If you think liberals are mentally deficient, you'll not feel much of an obligation to engage with them in serious conversation.

If the messenger is tainted, the listener can disregard the message. And if you know the messenger is one of Them, not one of Us, then that's all you need to know to know he's tainted. This is one example of a striking feature of ideologies that I'll elaborate on later: they structure communication in ways that facilitate intragroup solidarity and the cooperation that solidarity enables by functioning as *belief immune systems*, cognitive mechanisms that protect the distinctive beliefs of one's identity group from being challenged.

Another way an ideology's belief immune system works is by supplying inputs for cognitive dissonance mechanisms. When I was a child growing up in apartheid Arkansas, I was fed a racist ideology, as I noted in an earlier chapter. It included the belief that African Americans are naturally mentally inferior to whites. When I was about ten years old, I became aware that our African American housekeeper, Louise, was really smart. That puzzled me, so I asked my mother how it could be so, given that Louise was clearly not white. My mother had a ready reply—the racist ideology that she had already more fully imbibed than I supplied it: "Louise must have some white blood."

That racist ideology included an elaborate theory of the asymmetrical effects of having "mixed blood." One drop of "black blood" was enough to make you less than equal to whites; a substantial dose of "white blood" could do something to mitigate what would otherwise be your thoroughgoing inferiority. Racist ideology includes (erroneous) factual beliefs that provide input for cognitive dissonance resolution mechanisms that allow people to hold on to their ideological beliefs in the face of evidence that contradicts them.

Ideologies can shield people in yet another way from information that disconfirms some of the beliefs that constitute an ideology: they can foster a social experience that seems to confirm the beliefs that constitute them, the same beliefs the ideology invokes to justify the social practices that generate that social experience. Sexist ideologies typically include the belief that women are naturally inferior to men in ways that make them unfit for leadership roles in government, in religion, or in business. The most extreme sexist ideologies present women as beings whose nature makes them unfit for any role other than that of bearing and nurturing children and (perhaps) managing a household. When such ideologies are realized in social practices, they become a self-fulfilling prophecy. Women are denied the education and the opportunities to develop the skills that are required for life outside the home. That means that the pervasive social experience of what women are like seems to support the belief that they lack those abilities. Similarly, if teachers are in the thrall of a sexist ideology that includes the belief that females aren't good at math, they will spend less time developing girls' math skills, and the result will seem to confirm the belief that women aren't good at math.

Similarly, where racism thoroughly structured social practices in parts of the United States, during the Jim Crow period, African

Americans were denied the opportunities to develop "white-collar" job skills, and this created a social experience in which one only encountered African Americans doing menial jobs, which seemed to confirm the belief that they were only fit for such work. If you only see women in the domestic role or African Americans doing menial labor, you won't be confronted with examples that disconfirm ideological beliefs about the natures of women or African Americans. (You'll be like a biologist who concludes that water fleas by nature don't have spines and helmets because you've only observed water fleas in environments lacking the chemicals that trigger the development of those traits.) Ideologies justify social practices, not just by providing a system of false beliefs that present those practices as good and reasonable, but also by fostering social experiences that appear to confirm the premises of the justifications they supply.

It's because ideologies perform the belief immune system function that we say that someone is "ideological" in the pejorative sense, meaning that they are rigid in their beliefs, that no matter what information is given to them, they just won't change their minds. My theory of ideology makes it clear that the rigidity of ideological beliefs is not just a curious contingency; it's vital to ideologies performing their essential function of creating and sustaining group-based identity as an effective basis for cooperation in the competition with other groups.

As I observed earlier, ideologies simplify the social world. One way they do so is by providing a stripped-down account of what's positive and what's negative about it. They employ stereotyping, by inculcating a deterministic, essentializing social ontology of groups. We all share certain virtues. They all share certain vices. Liberals (not just some or most liberals) are such and such; conservatives (all of them) are such and such. They are all alike, essentially the same, and how They act is determined by their shared essence.

This simplification—a kind of clumping together or homogenization of all the individuals designated as the negatively characterized Other—also serves the belief immune system function of ideologies. If all of Them share values and beliefs that are opposed to ours, then there's no possibility of identifying *some* members of that group who might be amenable to reason, more open to compromise. There's no possibility of cooperating with some minority within that group to bring the rest around to the right standpoint. If They are all the same, there's no point in trying to figure out whether some of Them might be worth listening to and engaging with. If you believe They are all the same, you'll forgo opportunities to hear different views. It's the belief immune system at work once more.

By functioning as belief immune systems in all these ways, ideologies shield the distinctive beliefs that help define group identity from disconfirmation and thereby counter the threat of defection to another group. Even when defection to another group is not at issue, the belief immune system shields the individual from information that might discredit the justifications the ideology provides and thereby sap the individual's motivation to act on the basis of those justifications.

Ideologies Provide Ways of Signaling Group Identity

Ideologies can't perform their group-identity-based orienting and coordinating functions unless they include mechanisms for identifying whether an individual is one of Us or one of Them. Because group-based identity is so psychologically vital for most human beings, it's crucial to be able to signal to other members of your group that you are one of them, and for you to be able to read the signals that others give regarding their group-based identity. Ideologies create such signals and ensure that members of a group send the same signals and interpret the signals they receive in the same way. So, in addition to evaluative and epistemic coordination, ideologies provide group-membership identity signaling coordination. In fact, ideologies make signaling so important that they suck the substance out of assertions, diverting attention from their content to the supposed identity of the speaker. (If you've already discerned that she's a liberal [or a conservative], then you have no reason to listen to what she is saying.)

So far, I have mainly described what ideologies are like, and sketched the specific jobs they do: belief and value coordination, belief immunity, fostering group-based identity in part through identity signaling coordination. Now I want to suggest that ideologies have these features because they do what evolutionary theorists think morality first evolved to do: they foster cooperation—and they probably came to be *because* they do that. In other words, ideologies are an adaptation for cooperation.

In some circumstances, the cooperation that ideologies produce may confer reproductive advantages on people who subscribe to them, as is the case with certain religious or nationalist ideologies that encourage large families. More commonly, ideologies promote the cultural reproduction of a group, increasing the probability that the group will not only sustain but also increase its membership and its advantage over competing groups.

A clear advantage of the understanding of ideology I've developed here is that it counts as ideologies all the cases that most of us would agree are ideologies before our having developed a theory of ideology. It fits revolutionary ideologies, ideologies that support the political status quo, sexist ideologies, racist ideologies, and political ideologies like the tribalistic versions of American "liberalism" and "conservatism," and eugenic ideology. That's an advantage over narrower understandings (like the Marxist one) that cover only some of the cases that intuitively seem to be instances of ideologies.

Ideology, like the Intrasocietal Tribalism It Promotes, Is a Modern Phenomenon

My hypothesis is that ideologies evolved, chiefly through cultural (rather than genetic) selection to provide resources for fostering cooperation *under modern conditions*, conditions in which the old ways of fostering cooperation no longer worked. In most of the relatively homogeneous earliest hunter-gatherer societies, cooperation was most likely achieved by mechanisms that didn't require complex systems of belief. When societies became much more complex, human groups either developed new techniques for achieving cooperation or they went under, filtered out by the forces of selection. The new ways of achieving cooperation relied heavily on connecting group-based moral identity to a complex system of beliefs, one that helped people navigate the much more complicated social landscape of modern societies.

In early, comparatively simple societies, morality fostered cooperation in straightforward ways. These were small, face-to-face societies in which free riders or people who took things that didn't belong to them or appropriated more than their fair share of resources were easily detected. If someone violated the group's norms, he could swiftly and effectively be punished, for example, by being ridiculed or physically attacked by members of the group or excluded from the spoils of the hunt or by being driven out of the group.

These mechanisms for cooperation didn't require a complex system of beliefs. People didn't need an elaborate evaluative map of the social terrain because society was not very complex. Moreover, the mechanisms for detecting whether some being of human form was one of Us or one of Them used simple at-a-glance cues: differences in hairstyle, bodily adornment, language, and so on.

Modern Cooperation Is Based on Shared Systems of Beliefs

As the outstanding evolutionary philosopher of biology Kim Sterelny has argued, this simple moral psychology became inadequate for achieving successful cooperation in large-scale, ethnically heterogeneous, complex societies where cooperation could no longer be based on kinship, marriage, and shared ethnicity (Sterelny 2012, 197). A new way of achieving social cooperation, including cooperation that enabled one's society to compete successfully with other complex societies, evolved under the selective pressures of this new environment. Cooperation in complex societies was achieved, and under the circumstances could only be achieved, by reliance on shared, correspondingly *complex systems of beliefs*.

The idea, then, is that modern cooperation—cooperation based on shared systems of beliefs—is an adaptation, a "trait" of societies that came to exist because it facilitated successful cooperation in more complex societies. It was most likely a product of group-level cultural selection under new selective pressures. These new systems of beliefs, which you might characterize either as the first ideologies or as proto-ideologies, helped to facilitate cooperation in the new, complex, heterogeneous societies the Neolithic Revolution produced. They facilitated forms of cooperation that conferred advantages in competition with other societies, whether they were persisting hunter-gatherers or rival agrarian societies.

Like the earlier ways of achieving cooperation, this new way relied on the motivational potency of the evolved human need for group-based identity—more precisely, group-based identity of a moralized sort. But the source of effective group-based moral identity in more complex societies could no longer be kinship, or kinship plus marriage, or kinship plus marriage plus common ethnicity. Instead, the group-based moral identity needed for successful cooperation among diverse populations became largely a matter of shared beliefs—beliefs regarding the nature of the social order—and shared values. In other words, group-based moral identity remained crucial for cooperation, as it had been from the earliest times, but it came to be grounded in a new way. These beliefs, which included moral judgments, taken together with shared factual assumptions, created a moralized, evaluative map of the social world, structured in terms of group identity. In some, perhaps most, cases, religion formed an important component of the new system of beliefs required for sustaining successful cooperation under modern conditions.

Competition among Groups within Society as a Major Driver of Cultural Evolution

It seems likely that when modern societies achieved extended periods of physical security against attacks from rival societies, a major driver of cultural evolution became the competition for power *within society*. There was economic competition, competition for political power, and eventually competition over which group's culture would become predominant in the society as a whole. Because individuals could not hope to compete successfully as individuals, competition generally took the form of competition among groups. Whereas early or proto-ideologies were chiefly weapons deployed in competition with other societies, full-fledged ideologies are an adaptation for intragroup cooperation that facilitated successful competition with other groups within a society.

For ideologies to play this role, new ways of distinguishing Us from Them had to evolve. Today these new ways of signaling group membership run the gamut, from wearing T-shirts or hats with political messages that imply your allegiance to one political view or party, to what sort or car you drive (say, a Prius versus a big pickup truck), to the comments you make about events in the news or specific current political controversies or issues, to the sorts of items you share on Twitter or Facebook or Instagram and whom you "like" or "follow."

These signals help us determine who is an authentic member of our group. For example, in certain groups, if you favor gun control, you aren't a true American because you don't value individual freedom. If you are pro-choice, you don't value human life and are most likely an ethical relativist, if you are moral at all. You're on the side of sexual promiscuity, don't value the traditional (heterosexual, patriarchal, marriage-based) family, and probably aren't religious (which in some circles means you can't really be moral).

Perhaps competition among groups within society of some sort has existed as long as complex societies have existed, from the Neolithic Revolution onward. Be that as it may, it seems likely that for societies that did a reasonably good job of achieving security in the face of competition with other societies, group-level selection in the competition among groups within society became more potent, and more sophisticated forms of cooperation evolved to facilitate this competition. My suggestion—my speculation—is that one important way they evolved was by the development of ideologies. *Cultural selection for ideologies occurred because they helped groups compete successfully with other groups in society.*

Ideologies as an Adaptation for Competition under Modern Conditions

Ideologies emerge as an adaptation for intragroup cooperation in the competition among groups within society only when that competition takes a largely *nonviolent form*. Ideologies enable a group to compete successfully with other groups without having to overcome them by sheer force.

Of course, ideologies can, under the right circumstances, inspire violence; but by framing intergroup competition within society first and foremost as competition between systems of beliefs and values, they can be effective weapons in the intergroup struggle for economic, political, or cultural dominance without relying on naked force. When, because of the imposition of coercively backed political authority of the early city-states, or the king's peace in the Middle Ages, or the rule of law enforced by the modern state, groups within society no longer compete with spears or guns, they still compete; and a chief form of competition is competition for people's allegiance to rival ideologies. Whoever wins that competition is likely to win all the other competitions between groups, because ideologies facilitate cooperation, especially cooperation to outcompete other groups. Yet even though ideologies tend to flourish in reasonably peaceful conditions, ideological conflicts always carry the potential for violence, because ideologies rely on the same tribalistic moral responses that in early human societies motivated people to kill members of competing groups.

Ideology from an Evolutionary Point of View

So far, I've suggested that ideologies are products of evolution in two senses. First, they rely on the same basic psychology that created human moralities when they first appeared as an adaptation in the EEA: a dualistic moral mind that prompts humans to sort people into Us versus Them in an essentializing, determinist way, and to react with distrust, hostility, and even preemptive aggression *if* they perceive certain primordial threat cues to be present. So ideology is susceptible to an evolutionary explanation to the extent that the psychological basis for ideology is a product of selection in the EEA. Second, ideologies, I'm suggesting, are an adaptation to the new challenges facing human beings after the Neolithic Revolution, in particular the need to compete successfully with other groups within highly complex, multiethnic, large-scale societies in which violent competition among groups within society is usually not an option.

Ideologies Foster Intragroup Cooperation but Erect Obstacles to Intergroup Cooperation

Ideologies achieve cooperation *among members of a group* but do so at the price of severely limiting the possibilities for *intergroup* cooperation. They do this in three main ways. First, they feature belief immune systems that prevent you from listening to people from other groups, thereby foreclosing the possibility of dialogue, a sincere give-and-take of opinions that might eventually result in a narrowing of differences in judgments about what the existing social order is like and what we ought to do. The belief immune system also functions, as I noted earlier, when the social practices that the ideology supports produce an experience that seems to justify those social practices and confirm the beliefs that the ideology invokes to justify them (as when racist ideology relegates African Americans to low-skill jobs and thus produces a social experience that seems to confirm that they are only fit for low-skill jobs). Second, ideologies exaggerate the gulf between Us and Them, in part by stereotyping all of Them into a homogeneous mass. If your ideology leads you to believe that They have radically different values and beliefs than Ours, and if you believe that They are *all* that way, then you won't believe that selective engagement with the Other is possible. You will fail to see that for some members of the other group, the differences with us are not total, that there are some members of the group that you could engage productively with in mutually respectful discourse. Third, because ideologies are moralities or include a strong moral element—because they provide a moralized evaluative map of the social world—ideological disputes are by their very nature less amenable to compromise than disputes that are not framed in moral terms.

Once social issues are presented in moral terms and your opponent is characterized not just as mistaken but as morally bad or at least in serious moral error, it is harder to achieve a middle ground, more difficult to cooperate. That's because morality, as we generally conceive it, is uncompromising, absolute in its demands, once you've drawn a firm conclusion about what it requires. Preserving one's moral identity is an extremely potent commitment for most humans, and as we have seen, there are good evolutionary reasons for why this should be so. Compromising with someone you believe to be immoral or in serious moral error about things that really matter can be seen as failing to honor that commitment.

Ideologies as Resources for Moral Justifications

Ideologies are systems of belief that provide justifications for action, especially collective action, and they serve to coordinate members of the group in their responses when justifications are called for. Justifications can be called for either because they are necessary to mobilize members of the group to act or because the group's views about society or its positions on particular issues are challenged by the belief systems of other groups.

This means that ideologies can only exist in cultures that already have a practice of reason giving, in which people think it right and even necessary to marshal justifications. At a certain point in the development of modern societies, one could no longer get away with simply appealing to authority or to God's commands, and when this happened, ideologies provided resources for responding to the need for justifications.

Why Our Ideological Justifications Look So Stupid to Them and Vice Versa

In other words, in developed modern societies, intergroup competition is often conducted in significant part through a process of justification and counterjustification. Yet in many, perhaps most, cases, the primary target of justification is *not* members of the competing group; the belief immune system function of ideologies ensures that success with Them is unlikely, if they are in the grip of a rival ideology, with its own belief immune system. Instead the primary target is often oneself and other members of one's group. The justifications that our ideologies furnish foster cooperation among us and reduce the risk that any of us will defect, will repudiate our common group-based identity. They also strengthen the motivational power of our group-based moral identity. The fact that ideology-based justifications look so transparently implausible to out-group people is an indicator that they mainly function to facilitate cooperation within the group.

The justifications that ideologies provide are potent for two reasons: they are moral justifications, or have a strong moral element, which means they derive motivational power from the commitment to moral identity; and they are embedded in a system of belief that is self-reinforcing (chiefly by providing resolution mechanisms for cognitive dissonance, as in the smart Louise case, and because they drown out voices that would challenge them, by disregarding the challenge if it comes from one of Them).

Ideologies and the Culture of Reason Giving

The good news is that ideologies only exist in societies in which there is a practice of reason giving, and as we saw in chapters 4 and 5, *under the right conditions*, the practice of reason giving can empower movement toward greater inclusion. The bad news is that the practice of reason giving can be subverted by ideologies in ways that can dismantle progress toward inclusion and promote regression to tribalism, including the intrasocietal variety.

Let's return to the idea that ideologies are products of evolution in two senses: they exploit the evolved dualistic moral mind's capacity for tribalistic responses, and they are an adaptation for cooperation-cum-competition among groups within modern societies. Suppose that I'm right that strong selective pressures for ideologies exist in complex societies that feature robust, ongoing competition among groups but generally in nonviolent ways—competition for economic, political, and cultural dominance. (Note that I'm talking about cultural selection, not selection on genes—how a cultural phenomenon, in this case a particular ideology, by virtue of how its characteristics fit with the challenges of the competitive environment, has an advantage in attracting followers and replicating itself in their belief systems over time.)

Suppose also that ideologies foster intragroup cooperation and hence success in competition with other groups in ways that greatly limit cooperative solutions to intergroup conflict. If all of that is true, then there is a paradox: if ideologies achieve cooperation within the group only at the expense of throwing up formidable obstacles to cooperation among groups, then cultural evolution has produced a new form of tribalism that is endemic to modern society, even though modern society provides the material and social-epistemic conditions for movement toward inclusion.

Moreover, the very features of ideologies that enable them to foster cooperation within groups make it difficult to overcome tribalism. Ideologies unify us by dividing Us from Them. The question, then, is whether we can achieve cultural innovations that will satisfy the psychological needs that ideologies address and enable relatively nonviolent competition among groups within society but mitigate the potential for dangerous divisiveness that is inherent in ideologies.

Does Eugenics Fit This Characterization of Ideologies?

I said earlier that eugenics was an ideology that fueled a kind of intrasocietal tribalism. But later I said that ideologies are an evolved form that competition among groups within societies takes under the conditions of complex modern societies in which such competition usually proceeds by nonviolent means. With what group within society are the proponents of eugenics competing? It can't be the group of "people who by virtue of their defective genes are the root of all major social problems" because no such group exists; that's why eugenics is an example of pure or whole cloth intrasocietal tribalism.

The first answer to this question is that the group against which the ideology of eugenics was being used as a weapon in competition was the so-called dangerous class. Eugenics was largely a bourgeois (middle- and upper-class) phenomenon; all its leaders and the majority of its active adherents came from that part of society. Historians tend to agree that eugenics was in large part a reaction of the bourgeoisie against what they saw as a growing threat, the threat of "the dangerous class." The bourgeoisie, who were doing quite well in the unrestrained capitalist social order of the late nineteenth century and the early twentieth, believed that their position of power and the whole system on which it was based was under a dire threat—a threat from the great masses of poor, socially discontent, potentially revolutionary or anarchic people who were concentrated and highly visible in the slums of large cities. The bourgeoisie saw crime, drunkenness, the breakdown of traditional morality, and the threat of communist revolution or anarchy as all being concentrated in this underclass.

Instead of concluding that these phenomena were largely the result of the juggernaut of unregulated capitalism, they developed another interpretation that was congenial to their moral identity, a moral identity that, because it was already deeply infused with the ideology of capitalism, allowed them to reap the benefits of the system without having to admit that they were, if not responsible for the harms, at least complicit in their production. In other words, eugenics enhanced the cognitive dissonance resolution capacities of the bourgeoisie: it helped them reconcile the fact that the system they were benefiting from contained serious social problems with their conviction that the system was sound and that their success in it was not morally tainted. It also gave the bourgeoisie an apparently scientifically based justification for controlling the so-called dangerous class by limiting their numbers.

Capitalist ideology touted the benefits of capitalism and included an explanation of why some failed to thrive in it, blaming their lack of success on a combination of laziness and inevitable costs in a system that was beneficial overall. Eugenics strengthened the bourgeoisie's ability to reconcile their own success in the capitalist order with the inescapable fact that all was not well in society by blaming all social ills on a medical problem that afflicted other people— not something for which they were in any way responsible. To that extent, eugenics shored up the moral identity of the bourgeoisie and in turn increased their ability to engage effectively in the contest for preserving their power in the system. It helped them cooperate effectively with each other in the competition for power against those they viewed as the dangerous class.

Eugenics not only offered the bourgeoisie a way to shore up their moral identity but also supplied them with an instrument of control, a way of disciplining and containing the threat to their way of life that the dangerous class posed. That eugenics represented the dangerous class not as an enemy in class struggle but as a medical problem that threatened the whole of society—indeed, civilization itself—made it an especially morally potent instrument for competition with the dangerous class. It enabled the bourgeois supporters of eugenics to use their political power to generate laws and policies that served to contain and discipline the dangerous class while claiming—and even sincerely believing—that they were acting for the common good. As theorists of ideology from Marx onward have emphasized, ideologies, at least the most motivationally potent of them, typically represent the interest of one class as a universal interest, their good as the common good.

This first explanation offers a plausible account of why some people became eugenicists, but not all. Some prominent eugenicists were committed socialists. They thought that their being eugenicists was quite compatible with their firm belief that capitalism was rotten (and that if there was a dangerous class, it was the capitalists).

A second explanation of the appeal of eugenics can account for why it resonated with people on the left as well as the right and in the center. This explanation emphasizes that the eugenics movement increased the social power of elites, whether they were proponents or opponents of capitalism. In other words, eugenic thinking served as a weapon in the competition for power among groups within society, a competition for power that made for strange allies— ardent socialists and staunch proponents of capitalism. In an age when science was still held in high regard, the elite's endorsement of an apparently scientific response to social problems increased their power.

This second explanation has an advantage over the first, class-struggle version: it can readily accommodate the fact that the ranks of eugenicists included people across the whole political spectrum. According to the second explanation, the successful promulgation of eugenic thought served to increase the power of certain groups in society and to that extent gave them an advantage in the contest for power that occurs in all complex societies. Scientists, social reformers who signed on to the eugenic program of controlling human reproduction, educators whose social mission eugenic thinking elevated to nothing less than that of key players in a crusade to save society from ruin, and government officials and politicians who gained support by endorsing eugenics-inspired laws and policies—each of these groups were empowered by the eugenics movement and thereby reaped an advantage in the ongoing struggle for status and dominance within society.

Understood in this way, as a weapon in the struggle for power between groups within society, eugenics is not an outlier or an anomaly. It's true that if you take an ideology's rhetoric at face value, it may appear to function as a weapon in a contest with the group it explicitly targets (the supposedly genetically defective). Yet appearances can deceive: often, perhaps typically, the competitive advantage that an ideology confers is not primarily an advantage over the group it explicitly targets. That group may in fact be relatively powerless and not worthy of much of an effort to defeat it.

Instead, as I've emphasized, the chief function of ideologies is to unify Us so as to give Us a competitive advantage in the struggle for dominance within society. The competitor that our ideology allows us to compete successfully with may not be the group that the ideology explicitly targets; it may be some or even all other groups in society that are serious competitors. For example, Nazi ideology, which targeted the Jews, did empower Nazis to expropriate desirable social social positions and material wealth from them, but more importantly it strengthened the Nazis as a group vis-à-vis all other competitors for power in German society. It accomplished this by presenting the Nazis as the one party that had first recognized the full extent of the threat the Jews supposedly represented and as one whose leader knew how to deal with the supposed threat. By targeting the Jews, the Nazis gained a competitive edge over all other rivals for power. Nazi ideology allowed them to do this.

Ideologies, then, can be weapons in the competition among groups within society, even when the groups that they are used to compete against are not those they explicitly target. If that is the case, we can now understand that even though the ideological discourse of eugenics explicitly targeted a threatening group that did not exist, it performed the function of uniting a group in competition with other groups that did exist. Eugenics as an ideology empowered certain groups, giving them a competitive advantage in the struggle for social and political power, by allowing them to represent themselves as nothing less than the saviors of civilization. Thus eugenics is not only consistent with my characterization of the function of ideologies but also illustrates the full explanatory reach of that account.

Finally, ideologies can take the form of intersocietal, as well as intrasocietal, tribalism. An ideology that identifies an external threat can serve to solidify or increase the power of one group in society vis-à-vis others, especially if it presents that group as society's protector against the external threat. Even when mobilized in the service of intersocietal tribalism, ideology serves as a weapon in the competitive struggle between groups within society.

Nonviolent Competition among Groups in Society without Ideologies?

Given that ideologies impede communication between people who disagree by performing the belief immune system function and make conflicts less tractable by moralizing them, it's vital to know whether there is a less destructive alternative way for groups to achieve the unity needed for successful nonviolent competition with other groups in modern society. It seems to me there are two distinct ways in which the answer might turn out to be a hopeful "yes."

On the one hand, we might—somehow—develop new ways of achieving cooperation for the sake of successful nonviolent competition among groups within society, ways that don't rely so heavily on ideology or, better yet, make ideologies obsolete. It might turn out that mechanisms for intragroup cooperation to facilitate successful competition with other groups in society are still evolving and will evolve away from reliance on ideologies. It's important to keep this possibility in mind. To fail to do so would be to make a mistake I've warned against throughout this book: thinking that human moral evolution is a done deal.

Nevertheless, I doubt that human beings in modern societies can do without ideologies entirely. They perform a vital function: we do need a simplified evaluative map of the complex social world; and if competition among groups in society is unavoidable, then such a map can be very useful, especially if it harnesses the powerful motivational force of group-based identity.

On the other hand, we might continue to rely on ideologies to achieve cooperation for the sake of successful competition against other groups within society but somehow learn to subscribe only to those ideologies that don't make cooperation between groups so difficult, that don't erect such formidable obstacles to listening to the Other and to meeting the Other halfway in some sort of compromise. That is, we might somehow learn to reject deeply divisive ideologies. The difficulty with this second solution is that deeply divisive, extremely tribalistic ideologies might well tend to outcompete less tribalistic ones, driving them to extinction in a process of cultural evolutionary selection.

What I Don't Mean by "Ideology"

Recent fascinating and provocative research by Donald Kinder and Nathan Kalmoe purports to show that ideology is *not* what fuels political tribalism in the United States (Kinder and Kalmoe 2017, 12). Instead, they say it is "partisan affiliation" (whether a person identifies as a member of a particular party) that counts. In sharp contrast, Morgan Marietta and David Barker argue that neither ideology nor partisan affiliation is the primary driver of tribalistic divisions in America: instead, it is which of a small number of basic values that the individual prioritizes (Marietta and Barker 2019, 95).

The understanding of ideology I've developed in this chapter is compatible with recognizing that both camps are on to something important but that neither has cornered the market on the truth about ideology or contemporary intrasocietal tribalism in the United States. My conception does not require an ideology be a coherent, explicit set of organized beliefs (something Kinder and Kalmoe say few Americans have). Nor do I deny that partisan affiliation plays a role in contemporary intrasocietal tribalism. Kinder and Kalmoe may have shown that ideologies are not determinative of tribalism, but only if one defines "ideologies" in a cognitively rich way, as coherent, reasonably consistent, systems of beliefs. That's not what I mean by "ideologies." To perform the orienting function of a moralized evaluative map of the social world, beliefs needn't be that fancy.

There's another, related feature of Kinder and Kalmoe's analysis that limits its applicability to the full range of ideologies and blunts the force of its implications for my view. Like many American political scientists, they use the term "ideologies" to refer to something quite specific: systematic, organized sets of beliefs that are characterized in the United States as liberal or conservative or even as Democratic or Republican. My understanding of ideologies is not as narrow as that. This means that even if Kinder and Kalmoe are right that ideologies in their specific sense aren't major determinants of Americans' political behavior, ideologies that are less specific—and less coherent—may be doing considerable work.

Furthermore, Kinder and Kalmoe's findings are consistent with party affiliation functioning as a heuristic—a mental shortcut, a proxy for something that has some cognitive content but that falls short of their highly specific and cognitively rich notion of ideology. It might well be the case that many people use party as a proxy for a set of prioritized values they cherish. If that is so, then it's misleading to say that one has to opt for either partisan affiliation or basic values as the driver of tribalistic political divisions.

My account is even more obviously consistent with Marietta and Barker's claim that it is values that drive tribalistic divisions: after all, I say that ideologies are evaluative maps of the social world, and evaluation requires values. So my characterization of ideologies is compatible with the view that differences in which values people prioritize play an important role in dividing them into tribes within society.

At this early stage in the controversy between the partisan affiliation theorists and the values theorists, it may be too soon to say who has the stronger case. My hunch, however, is that values are likely to be a primary factor for many people and that people often affiliate with one party rather than another because they sense that it champions the values they hold most dear. In other words, they use party as a proxy or heuristic for values they may not be able to articulate in the form of a systematic, coherent set of beliefs. That's compatible with rejecting a one-size-fits-all solution—with recognizing that while for some people values are primary, for others affiliation is key and that in the latter case party affiliation may not be derivative from a clear sense that your party represents certain specific, explicitly held values. This might be true, for example, of people who vote Democratic (or Republican) because their parents always did so.

I also think it is pretty evident that political leaders and influential media figures don't just appeal to particular values or to party loyalty to mobilize their tribe and leave it at that. They don't make brute appeals to values: they supply highly rhetorical narratives to trace or at least to gesture toward supposed connections among those values; and they draw conclusions about where we ought to stand on various policy issues, given that those are our values. For example, they say that if you truly value human life, then you ought to support a ban on abortions, because "life begins at conception." The "because" signals an inference, a bit of reasoning that involves more than just a gesture toward a value.

Such people are called "thought leaders" or "opinion makers" for a reason. They don't just appeal to values: they elaborate their content and connect it with supposedly true factual beliefs that seem to vindicate them. Similarly, they don't just proclaim "I'm a Democrat" (or a Republican) and leave it at that; they have a good deal to say about what a true Democrat (or Republican) is. For example, to call someone a RINO, a "Republican in name only," makes sense only if you think being a Republican means something. Such attempts to attach some substance to the idea of being a Republican (or a Democrat) begin to sound a lot like ideology as I've characterized it.

Unless such efforts to connect values and parties to *somewhat* organized systems of beliefs play some role in the deeply divisive intrasocietal tribalism we are now seeing, it's hard to see why self-identified Republicans or conservatives would pay any attention to figures like Rush Limbaugh and Sean Hannity or would bother to read books by Bill O'Reilly, while self-identified liberals and Democrats tend to avoid them like the plague. The point is that promoters of tribalism don't just make brute appeals either to values or to party affiliation: they spin webs of belief; and there's a robust demand for their products. Even if most people never develop sophisticated, consistent systems of beliefs to support their tribalistic behavior, many people seem to hanker for *something* by way of a minimally coherent system of beliefs. If they didn't, people like Limbaugh, Hannity, and O'Reilly would be out of business.

I think it's a mistake, in other words, to think that either partisan affiliation or values stand alone as primitive, self-sufficient motivators for or determinants of intrasocietal tribalism. Many people seem to identify particular parties with particular values and they do seem to pay some attention to efforts to explain what those values entail and to defend them against opposing values. Similarly, many people apparently think that their being Republican, rather than Democratic (or vice versa), *means something*, even if they can't clearly or consistently articulate just what that is.

I'm suggesting, then, that all three concepts—partisan affiliation, values, and beliefs that link factual and moral assumptions—can be accommodated by a theory that characterizes ideologies as moralized evaluative maps of the social world that make group-based identities salient. I think that the partisan affiliation theorists make a good point when they document that the political behavior of most people in America can't be attributed to their espousing a developed, explicit, relatively coherent system of beliefs, at least not belief systems that track political scientists' conceptions of liberalism and conservatism or Democratic or Republican "philosophies." The values theorists can explain that: what matters most for many people are basic values when it comes to distinguishing Us from Them. Further, as I've suggested, some people may tacitly identify a particular party with a particular set of values rather than with a coherent political philosophy and use party as a proxy for those values: they simply associate a particular party with certain values even if they don't have a sophisticated or even explicit understanding of what the party stands for or a developed set of beliefs that explains why those values are so important and what their implications are for policies.

When I characterize ideologies as moralized evaluative social maps, I don't deny that most people who have an ideology often lack an explicit, coherent, set of beliefs that they can articulate. To perform the orienting function, ideologies needn't be like that. To orient the individual, a moralized evaluative map simply needs to link some rough understanding of the way the social world is to a set of values (and in some cases, to identify a particular party as the champion of those values). The beliefs that allow this linkage needn't be very complex or logically organized. They needn't even be consistent. That's compatible both with the value theorists' insight that at least for many people differences in basic values are an important factor in the division of society into opposing tribes *and* with the partisan affiliation theorists' negative point, namely, that ideologies *in the sense of coherent systems of belief* are not the main drivers of tribalism.

How Ideologies Undermine the First Great Expansion

Intrasocietal tribalism can occur even when many people assent to the proposition that all human beings have equal basic moral status. The denigration of the Other that deeply divisive ideologies foster can make the recognition of equal basic status a hollow gesture, not a substantial moral orientation. If you're in the grip of an ideology that fuels intrasocietal tribalism, you can convince yourself that it is enough that everyone in your society has certain basic legal rights and does not suffer clear-cut discrimination on racial or gender or ethnic grounds—that this suffices for recognizing everyone's equal basic moral status. Yet your ideology may lead you to treat some other people in ways that don't actually recognize them as having equal basic moral status.

Genuinely recognizing that everyone in your society has equal basic moral status requires more than formal equality and the absence of the grosser forms of discrimination. It requires treating everyone with equal respect. If our ideology categorizes someone as *one of those people*, as a member of the group that is treacherous or hopelessly confused about what society is like and how things should be, as someone who either unwittingly or deliberately threatens all that we regard as valuable, how *can* you respect her? If our ideology encourages Us not to listen to her because she is one of Them, to refuse to consider the content of what she says by impugning her sincerity or intelligence, that doesn't seem compatible with showing the respect that recognizing equal basic status requires.

In democratic societies, part of what it is to truly regard your fellow citizens as equals is to view them as potential coparticipants in a reason-giving process of trying to determine what the common good is and how to achieve it, as someone you can truly reason with about what is most important for all of us. In other words, democracy requires regarding all your fellow citizens literally as reason-*able* beings. Yet if we are in the grip of a deeply divisive ideology, we may be incapable of seeing the Other in these terms. Remember: the belief immune system function of ideologies doesn't just screen us from opposing beliefs; it also cuts us off from the Other by denying that she is someone with whom we can participate in a mutually respectful, sincere process of giving and taking reasons.

I'm afraid that this is precisely what has happened in the United States. I fear that ideologically driven intrasocietal tribalism is making democracy impossible by undermining the equal respect that it requires. Democracy doesn't work if you view the people you disagree with as irrational at best and evil at worst and therefore as people whom you can't cooperate with but instead as dangerous forces you must utterly defeat or be utterly defeated by.

The zero-sum, winner-take-all mentality that deeply divisive ideologies foster is incompatible with the premier virtue of political life: compromise, the willingness to proceed on the assumption that those you disagree with are entitled to receive something in return if they settle for less than their first-best option. Constitutional democracy is an attempt to institutionalize the commitment to compromise in a way that enables us to preserve our moral identity while recognizing that the moral identities of others are sometimes different.

So, if the division of Us versus Them that ideologies produce is severe enough, it can prevent the completion of the First Great Expansion while giving the appearance that the goal has been achieved. Exclusion from the community of reasonable beings is different from the denial of legal rights or racial or gender discrimination in employment, but it is exclusion nonetheless.

9

Taking Charge of Our Moral Fate

I will not apologize for the speculative character of the attempt. At this stage, either the question is answered in a vague, fragmentary and tentative way, or it must be left alone: there is not enough sound theorizing and well-regimented evidence in the domain to do otherwise.

—Dan Sperber, *Explaining Culture: A Naturalistic Approach*

Our detective story has been unusually complicated, even for the genre. I will conclude our investigation, first by outlining the central argument of the book in a few steps, then by providing a brief summary of the thinking that supports the central argument, and finally by drawing out some unexpected implications of my analysis.

Here's the central argument:

(1) Human beings evolved to have a highly flexible moral mind, a general set of competencies for having moralities that can be expressed in very different ways, depending on the social-environmental inputs that stimulate the exercise of those competencies.

(2) The environment in which the moral mind first manifested itself and the environments that have existed throughout most of human history were profoundly different from the niches that humans have only recently constructed for themselves: in the last three hundred years, some human societies have achieved high levels of surplus reproductive success, solving the problem of achieving sustainable reproduction exceptionally well.

(3) Where those favorable conditions prevailed, surplus reproductive success allowed the Great Uncoupling: morality was no

longer the slave of fitness, and the powers of the moral mind were unleashed to produce moralities that extended beyond the facilitation of cooperation and were more inclusive, less tribalistic than earlier moralities. The remarkable human capacity for critical, open-ended moral reasoning and the potent motivating force of moral identity fueled this transformation, with the result that hitherto pervasive moral assumptions were revised or abandoned as the circle of moral regard expanded.

(4) The key factor that produced surplus reproductive success and allowed the liberation of morality from the demands of fitness was the human capacity for cumulative culture; through niche construction, it forged institutions that made inclusive moral responses more affordable in reproductive and material terms and created new opportunities for the exercise of the capacity for critical, open-ended moral reasoning, which in turn facilitated changes in moral identities and helped redirect moral emotions such as sympathy and disgust to new objects.

(5) Until now, the processes by which social environments interacted with the moral mind to produce moralities and moral agents were undirected, not subject to deliberate human control; our moral fate was the plaything of morally blind forces, beyond our ken and therefore beyond our control.

(6) If humans learn enough about the moral mind and the interactions between it and specific environmental features, we can in principle take charge of our moral fate: we can exert significant influence on what sorts of moralities are predominant in our societies and what sorts of moral agents we are. Doing so would be perhaps the highest form of human autonomy. It would also be the most profound kind of creativity: the creation of the moral self in a species for whom the moral self lies at the core of our being.

Now to summarize the thinking that produced my central argument. The moral mind is highly flexible: it can generate radically different moralities, depending on the character of the stimuli that different social environments provide. Some social environments are conducive to more tribalistic moralities, some to more inclusive ones. Different inputs to the moral mind mean different outputs. Some social environments afford greater possibilities for moral progress; in others the odds are against it. So the Tribalism Dogma is wrong: humans don't have a tribalistic moral nature. Our moral nature encompasses the capacity both for tribalism and for inclusion.

Different social environments produce not only different moralities but also different kinds of persons, beings with different moral identities. Some social environments are conducive to humans being the best they can be, given human moral nature; others stunt them. The point is not that the social environment by itself determines our moral possibilities; rather, those possibilities are shaped through the *interaction* of the social environment and the highly flexible moral mind. That interaction doesn't just produce new or better solutions to cooperation problems. Even if morality first was nothing more than a bundle of solutions to cooperation problems, it has become more than that now. So the Cooperation Dogma is just as mistaken as the Tribalism Dogma. Once we abandon the intellectual straightjacket of the tribalism and cooperation dogmas, we can think clearly about morality and about the possibilities for moral change. And we can begin to prepare ourselves to embark on the project of taking charge of our moral fate.

Replacing the tribalism and cooperation dogmas with the recognition that human moral nature is highly flexible transforms the idea of moral progress. We can no longer assume that progress is inevitable or that whatever gains we have made will endure. Progress is neither more nor less natural than regression, and we mustn't take it for granted.

It is also vital to understand that the social environment that the moral mind interacts with includes whatever morality happens to be pervasive at any given time in a society. That's one important environmental factor and it must be taken into account when thinking about how to tweak or transform the social environment to maximize the probability of moral progress and reduce the risk of regression. Making moral progress in a social environment that is already saturated with tribalism is clearly more difficult than starting from one in which the pervasive morality already includes progressive elements. This gives us another reason to try to avoid regression.

Once human beings used their capacity for cumulative culture to create niches in which they achieved sufficient surplus reproductive success, the Great Uncoupling occurred: the content of moralities was no longer determined by the demands of reproductive fitness, the space of possible moralities expanded greatly, and deeply inclusive moralities became possible. Neither the Great Uncoupling nor the possibilities of moral progress it created resulted from any conscious project of improvement; they were a matter of highly improbable moral luck.

Control over the social environment, including the features that are critical for the character of morality and the moral development of individuals, is far from democratic: a small portion of the population has disproportionate control over the social environment and hence over what our moral life is like. Yet no one—neither those exercising control nor those who are affected—has paid attention to this reason for being troubled by the growth of inequality in wealth and the inequality of power it inevitably entails. We all know that there is an ongoing contest for power in society; what we have failed to see is that it's ultimately a contest for who will determine our moral fate.

We commonly think of designing institutions for economic efficiency or for well-functioning political processes, but we pay too little attention to the moral effects of different institutional designs. Once we understand that a society's morality and the moral development of individuals within it are the product of the interaction between the moral mind and the social environment, it becomes imperative to extend the idea of scientifically informed institutional design to encompass *moral* institutional design—to think hard and systematically about how the character of institutions either promotes or hinders moral progress. For the first time in our species' history, it becomes possible to liberate our moral fate from the dominion of blind chance and shape it by scientifically informed choice.

To realize this possibility, we need the best scientific minds to focus on constructing a theory of moral change grounded in an understanding of the interaction between the moral mind and the specific characteristics of human-made environments that shape its expression in particular moralities. That project will require increasing both our knowledge of what the moral mind is like and our knowledge of how its potentials are realized under specific environmental conditions.

I've marshaled support for the dependence of the character of moralities and moral agents on social environmental factors by examining one kind of large-scale morally progressive change that is extremely interesting in its own right, especially for those of us concerned the threat of tribalism: the Two Great Expansions. My investigation showed *how* the creation of new niches in which humans achieved surplus reproductive success enabled the Great Uncoupling—the liberation of moralities from the demands of reproductive fitness—which in turn created the possibility of progressive moral change in the direction of inclusion. Solving the Big Puzzle of how a type of great ape with initially largely tribalistic moralities could have come to have deeply inclusive moralities demonstrated the flexibility of the moral mind in response to different social environments.

The explanation I offered of how the Two Great Expansions came about also supplied a theory of moral regression to tribalism. That theory highlights the fact that tribalism, like inclusive morality, is still evolving. I showed how a new kind of tribalism, intrasocietal tribalism fueled by deeply divisive ideologies, threatens to hollow out the First Great Expansion. My hypothesis was that deeply divisive ideologies are an adaptation (a product of cultural selection) for competition among groups within society under modern conditions and where there is a widespread belief that democracy has failed. That hypothesis is compatible with the thesis that intrasocietal tribalism is contributing to the decline of democracy. We may be witnessing a vicious circle: disappointment in democracy may make tribalism seem like the only alternative, and tribalism may in turn make pessimism about democracy a self-fulfilling prophecy.

The complex investigation I have just summarized yields several big conclusions. First, evolutionary science doesn't tell us that large-scale moral change is impossible, or that large-scale change in the direction of greater inclusion is against our nature, or that we've reached the limit of inclusiveness. Instead, its message, properly understood, is that we have a highly flexible moral mind and a capacity to respond either tribalistically or inclusively, depending on the environment. A sound understanding of the origins of human moralities—one that rejects both the Cooperation Dogma and the Tribalism Dogma—implies that to secure further moral progress and reduce the risk of regression, we should develop a scientific, empirically grounded account of how to shape our social environment (and above all how to design institutions) to foster inclusion and, more generally, to create the conditions for achieving and sustaining moral progress. We can no longer rationalize our tribalistic failings with the comforting thought that they're "just human nature." We cannot escape the fact that we are much freer than the Tribalism Dogma portrays us as being. It's up to us whether human societies are predominantly tribalistic or something better.

Second, at this early stage in the attempt to use evolutionary science to explain large-scale moral change, it's not clear whether explanations that are thoroughly evolutionary will suffice. If we assume that the moral mind itself won't change significantly for the foreseeable future, any explanations will necessarily be largely cultural, not biological. Whether the cultural explanations will be genuinely evolutionary through and through may not be ascertainable at present, because the most robust and mathematically rigorous cultural evolutionary explanations are not applicable to the complex, messy phenomena of large-scale moral change. A practically useful understanding of the conditions that determine our moral fate must rely on evolutionary science; but other disciplines, including anthropology, history, sociology, economics, and social psychology, will most likely also play important roles.

Third, large-scale moral change can come about in two quite different ways: either because the change promotes reproductive fitness (whether biological or cultural), through selection operating independently of human intention or design; or as a result of "fitness-independent" factors—under conditions of surplus reproductive success that allow for an expansive set of options for intentional moral change. As an example of the first way, consider the development of dominance-suppression techniques and norms of fairness and reciprocity that apparently brought about moralities that differed from those of our nearest primate relatives. We have no reason to believe that this type of moral change is over; it could occur again. It all depends on what environmental pressures determine which genes and social practices are transmitted to the next generation and which aren't. The second way that moral change can come about is illustrated by the historical narrative I've provided to explain the Two Great Expansions. Moral change in this case is not driven by reproductive fitness, though of course it can only come about and persist if it doesn't disastrously undermine fitness. In this kind of moral change, "blind" processes of natural or cultural selection play a crucial role but aren't sufficient: they create opportunities for human beings to exercise their moral powers in new ways and to bring about change in part through intentional actions aimed at realizing their evolving understandings of what morality and fidelity to their own moral identities require.

Fourth, large-scale moral change of the second sort—change that doesn't come about because it promotes reproductive fitness—is much more likely to occur under conditions in which highly effective mechanisms for compliance with existing moral rules are *not* in place. This is because moral change requires, in its initial stages, noncompliance with the existing rules. In cases of profound moral change like the Two Great Expansions, it may also require the transformation of the individual's moral identity. Social conditions must permit that kind of change to occur, which in turn requires that religious or secular authorities or less formal kinds of social pressures are not able to stifle the processes that lead people to reconceive their moral identities. Social conditions must permit people to revise their conception of what it is to be a moral person.

Evolutionary scientists emphasize that in their original forms, human moralities only survived if they succeeded in curbing free riding (of both the loafer and bully varieties), reducing conflicts among group members, and coordinating their beliefs and behaviors as to how things ought to be done. In brief, the earliest moralities brought to bear potent pressures for a high degree of moral conformity, since individuals' viability as partners in cooperation and hence their reproductive success depended on it. Similarly, groups could only survive if their cultural practices successfully produced a high degree of conformity with their moral rules. Moreover, the same scientists stress that these early groups were egalitarian, at least in the sense that they had highly effective mechanisms for preventing any one individual or small subgroup of individuals from determining how things were done. That meant that no one could unilaterally change the rules.

Under these conditions, major moral innovation that was anything other than a "blind" response to selection for reproductive success (whether biological or cultural) would have been extremely difficult, if not impossible. Any would-be moral innovator would most likely be suppressed, pressured into returning to conformity with the moral status quo, and the nonhierarchical character of these earliest societies would have prevented any individual or small group of individuals from simply imposing new moral rules on their fellows.

Something had to change for large scale moral change to occur that wasn't a response to the changing requirements for reproductive success. Societies developed new modes of cooperation that worked well enough, even though the mechanisms for ensuring rule compliance no longer functioned as effectively as those that ensured moral conformity in the earliest societies. Cooperation became so productive that it could thrive even if some people violated the existing moral rules or refused to acknowledge their validity because they thought the rules were flawed or simply pointless.

Early human groups depended on virtually every able-bodied person participating in cooperation and being committed to following the moral rules that facilitated it. In contrast, modern societies can afford more free riders or people who are otherwise disaffected without ceasing to function, because productivity has increased so greatly. This too makes moral change easier: people who have not thoroughly internalized norms in the first place or who have become critical of them may be more amenable to modifying them or abandoning them in favor of new norms. Further, if it becomes apparent that society can function well even if some people violate the rules, the question of whether the rules are really necessary can arise. Here's one example among many: when homosexual behavior was first decriminalized in the UK, some people predicted a collapse of the moral structure of society. It didn't happen. There's no good evidence that compliance with the most basic moral rules diminished because of that particular change. Similarly, it turned out that moral anarchy didn't result from women taking charge of their own sexuality and abandoning traditional ideals of feminine "chastity." Either compliance with these norms didn't play as important a role in social cooperation as the doomsayers thought, or else these norms *had* previously been important, but society was resilient enough to adjust to the change in ways that avoided a breakdown of cooperation and an unraveling of the moral fabric on which cooperation depends.

It's a truism that modern societies afford more scope for individual freedom and the development of individuality than traditional societies. To a significant extent, that's a result of the *failure* of modern societies to achieve high degrees of moral conformity. That "failure" may be a necessary condition for large-scale moral change that is not simply a way of promoting reproductive fitness: moral change that begins with someone deliberately challenging the moral status quo in a context where reproductive fitness is simply not an issue.

One of the most powerful mechanisms for achieving moral conformity in earlier societies was the threat of exclusion from cooperation. As societies became much larger and more complex, it became easier to be a moral innovator because exclusion from one's present cooperative relations wasn't so costly: complex societies, so long as they are not too centralized and tightly controlled by a religious or secular authority, offer alternative opportunities for cooperation, more options for partner choice. In contrast, in the earliest societies, the costs imposed on individuals who abandoned existing norms in favor of new ones were generally prohibitively high, because exclusion from cooperation in one's group meant exclusion from cooperation—and exclusion from cooperation was disastrous.

Another surprising implication of this contrast between the earliest and much later societies is that while the egalitarianism of the former created an impediment to moral change, the inequalities of social and political power characteristic of the latter can facilitate larger, more rapid moral changes. Individuals with greater power can more easily resist the social pressure to conform to existing norms, so they can afford to initiate moral change. In addition, their greater power may enable them to influence others to follow suit. The "failure" of modern societies to avoid hierarchy—their relative lack of success compared to the avoidance of hierarchy that the earliest societies achieved—contributes to their greater possibilities for moral change, including change that we may reasonably regard as progressive.

Consider another related but much more general point. As I've already emphasized, in the earliest human groups, a high degree of agreement on moral rules was probably necessary for successful cooperation. There was strong selection pressure on all members of the group to converge on the same set of rules because successful cooperation depended on it. But in modern societies, successful cooperation often does not require thoroughgoing moral agreement. Under modern conditions, considerable moral disagreement is compatible with successful cooperation, because the rules that govern cooperation are accessible to people with widely different moral views on other matters. In other words, the moral rules that facilitate cooperation do not saturate the whole of life. For example, in most circumstances, one can participate well in running a corporation regardless of whether one is a Catholic or a Jew or a Muslim or an atheist and regardless of whether one thinks abortion is wrong or morally permissible.

The bottom line is that in modern societies, cultural innovations that produced new niches have dramatically lowered the costs, at least for some individuals, of departing from the moral status quo. Such conditions greatly expand the possibilities for moral change. This was the lesson of my discussion of moral pioneers in chapter 6.

A trade-off thus exists between moral conformity and moral change. Too little moral conformity, and cooperation breaks down. Too much moral conformity, and moral change becomes difficult, if not impossible. Where you think the balance should be struck will depend on how defective you think the moral status quo is and how confident you are that it can be improved.

The perennial debate between progressives and conservatives (and revolutionaries and reformists) is largely a disagreement about how much moral change is compatible with sufficiently stable cooperation. Since moral change requires moral disagreement, at least in the beginning, this means that conservatives and progressives disagree fundamentally about what the optimal extent of moral disagreement is. Conservatives assume that if cooperation is to be stable, there must be very little moral disagreement; progressives assume that considerable disagreement (at least in the short run, during the process of moral innovation) is compatible with stability or at least with relatively undisruptive social change. In the absence of a much more developed theory of moral change than is available today, both assumptions are little more than articles of faith. Without such a theory, the conflict between progressives and conservatives can't be resolved. That helps explain why it hasn't been resolved after all these centuries.

Without pretending to settle that debate, this book sheds new light on it. Conservatives think that successful cooperation requires that there be very little moral disagreement because they think of a society's morality as a seamless web. In other words, they believe that moral rules and practices are densely interconnected, so that if you change one item, you create an unacceptable risk that the whole thing will unravel. Progressives tend to think that you can change some things without running the risk of changing a lot more than you want to. They think that a morality is less densely interconnected than that. A metaphor more congenial to the progressive way of thinking is a loosely woven fabric with substantial seams or, in evolutionary biology terms, a modularized organism.

In this case, the progressives have evolutionary science on their side: no organism or society could long survive if it were literally like a seamless web. Adaptability through selection, whether biological or cultural, requires that some things can be changed without everything changing (Lewontin 1978, 215–216). A seamless organism or a seamless society would be too fragile, too likely to collapse in the face of random changes in its own components or external shocks. It couldn't adapt.

Nonetheless, even though the seamless-web metaphor, if taken too seriously, gives an unduly pessimistic picture of the possibilities for reconciling stability with progress, the tension remains. It may be hard to know when the thread one is snipping won't damage the rest of the fabric and when it will. The optimal trade-off between stability and change may be hard to identify. If we know little about how a society works, we will have scant hope of striking the right balance between stability and change; if we know a great deal, our prospects will be brighter. So even though the notion that society is like a seamless web is false if taken literally, we still face the question of how dense the connections are, of whether society is more like a seamless web or more like a fabric with prominent seams.

My analysis in this book suggests that there is no general, single answer to that question. In some societies, the seamless-web metaphor is somewhat apt, in others totally misleading. Modern liberal democratic societies are definitely not like seamless webs, though traditional societies or at least the earliest human societies may have been somewhat more like that. Remember, I have emphasized that liberal democratic societies have multiple, independent hierarchies and multiple, independent cooperative schemes. There is no single, overarching cooperative scheme that can only function if there is virtually unanimous agreement on, and high compliance with, one set of moral rules; and there is no sovereign moral authority with a veto on change. In that kind of society, things aren't so densely interconnected: you can change some things without changing everything. So if there is no general answer to the question "Is society like a seamless web?" then there is no general answer to the question "How much moral disagreement is compatible with stability?" It depends on the kind of society you're talking about.

Modern liberal democratic societies are much more loose-jointed, modularized, or seamed than the small, face-to-face societies in which distinctively human moralities first came on the scene. In terms of moral rules, modern liberal democratic societies are considerably less unified than most human societies that have existed before them. That's part of what we mean when we say that modern societies—at least the more liberal ones—are "pluralistic." What I'm suggesting is that to the extent that conservatives fixate on the seamless-web idea, they may be approaching the problem of the trade-off between moral conformity and moral progress in a nostalgic, backward-looking way, failing to appreciate that the institutional structures of modern liberal societies allow considerable moral disagreement—and that this is the key to their potential for achieving moral progress without unacceptable instability.

This is not to say that attempts at moral progress can't backfire—that they can't produce regression or other unintended bad consequences. My point is only that we have no general answer to the question that has divided conservatives and progressives for centuries: how much moral disagreement ought to be tolerated for the sake of moral progress depends on the institutional setting. That should be a familiar idea: I've been arguing all along that the possibilities for moral progress depend on the social environment.

If I'm right that liberal societies can afford to tolerate more disagreement than societies that are more tightly knit, and that moral disagreement is a prerequisite of moral progress, then we shouldn't bemoan the fact that our liberal society has more moral disagreement than earlier ones. Instead we should celebrate it, recognizing that it expands the possibilities for moral progress. Philosophers like Alasdair MacIntyre, who pine for the good old days when most everyone in society was (supposedly) on the same page morally speaking, are unwittingly endorsing moral stagnation (MacIntyre 1981, ch. 2).

In this book, I have tried to solve the Big Puzzle in order to confirm my thesis that the character of our morality and our moral identity as individuals depend on environmental factors that are subject to human control. I haven't offered a prescription for how to sustain the shift toward more inclusive moralities against regression to tribalism. Though I have developed a theory of the current, ideologically driven, deeply divisive intrasocietal tribalism that I and many other people find so dismaying, I haven't fleshed out a program for how to combat it. That would take another book (or two).

Yet I think it is worth emphasizing that the story I've told provides considerable resources for developing strategies to combat both intersocietal and intrasocietal tribalism. And that story opens up the possibility that further scientific investigation will show us how to curb tribalism effectively. More generally, I hope I've said enough about how moral change comes about to demonstrate the feasibility of doing something we desperately need to do if we're to take charge of our moral fate: develop a science of moral institutional design.

Most obviously, to reduce the threat of tribalistic morality, it's vitally important to maintain the hard-won distance some societies have already achieved from the harsher conditions of the EEA—the conditions that "toggle" the adaptively plastic responses in the direction of tribalism—and to help people lift themselves out of those conditions where they still exist. This means, first and foremost, continuing and amplifying efforts to reduce the risk of diseases, improving physical security, and sustaining and augmenting institutions for mutually beneficial cooperation among groups.

It's also necessary to try to prevent people from coming to *believe* that the harsh conditions of the EEA exist when in fact they don't; and that means finding ways to thwart the efforts of people who try to convince us that we are in EEA-like conditions. It's also vital to sustain and extend the social-epistemic conditions for moral progress, including freedom of expression and association, civil-society organizations that can effectively influence government, a robust culture of reason giving, and communication technologies that provide opportunities for enhancing the human capacity for perspective taking and for extending sympathy to strangers. And it's extremely important to ensure that communication technologies are not under any central or unified control, whether it be public or private.

Doing all of that is a tall order indeed, but it still may not be sufficient to combat ideologically driven intrasocietal tribalism. If I'm right in thinking that this kind of tribalism is an adaptation, in modern societies, for competition among groups, then the only way to eliminate or contain it may be to provide a less destructive form of competition that adequately serves the needs and interests that animate competition among groups.

My hunch is that the ideologically driven intrasocietal tribalism we are seeing today in the United States and a number of other countries is a response to the perceived failure of democracy. In other words, a metacompetition is occurring, a competition between intrasocietal tribalism and democracy as adaptations for competition among groups within society, and democracy may be losing. (When I use the term "adaptation" here, I'm using the language of cultural selection, not biological [genetic] selection.)

When democracy works the way it's supposed to, it provides a mechanism for nonviolent competition among groups in society that doesn't have the destructive consequences of ideologically driven intrasocietal tribalism. It may well be that ideologies of the deeply divisive type flourish when people have lost faith in democracy. If that is so, then an important element in an effective strategy for preventing intrasocietal tribalism from thwarting the full realization of the First Great Expansion will be the revitalization of democracy. The hope is that genuine democracy will outperform intrasocietal tribalism in the competition among adaptations for competition among groups within society.

Democracy both presupposes and reinforces the commitment to settling disagreements through reasonable compromise, and that in turn requires the kind of mutual respect that deeply divisive ideologies destroy. The question is whether deeply divisive tribalism has already so badly undermined mutual respect and the willingness to compromise that an insufficient number of people with the know-how and resources to do so will be willing to take on the hard task of trying to revitalize democracy. I don't know the answer to that question.

As I said earlier, I suspect that humans living in complex societies can't do without ideologies. They need a simplifying, evaluative map of the social world that locates them in it and ascribes a group-based identity to them. If I'm right about that, the goal is not to abolish ideologies but to tame them. We need to think long and hard about what sorts of institutions can help shape ideologies in ways that make them less toxic and enable them to be more productive of valuable social change.

The problem, then, may be not ideologies per se but rather deeply divisive ideologies, because they undermine democracy—the best adaptation for intergroup competition within society that humans have devised so far. In addition to being toxic to democracy, deeply divisive ideologies erode the gains of the First Great Expansion by relegating the Other to an inferior status, destroying the mutual respect that is essential to regarding another person as one's moral equal. More precisely, they undermine democracy by backtracking on the First Great Expansion.

One often hears that to combat tribalism, we have to learn to listen to each other. That's good advice, but incomplete and taken by itself not very helpful. What's needed are institutions that provide incentives for listening and for compromise, institutions that encourage people who disagree with each other not to operate in the zero-sum, winner-take-all mode.

That almost certainly means, among other things, changing existing political institutions so that they provide powerful incentives for coalition building across ideological boundaries. A system of proportional representation and more extensive use of supermajority requirements for votes on important issues might help. Both of these mechanisms provide incentives for coalition building, and coalition building requires compromise and therefore a commitment to appealing to reasons that can sway those you disagree with. In an environment in which coalition building is necessary for political success, people who show mutual respect and a willingness to compromise should have a cultural fitness advantage; their political culture should reproduce itself over time more effectively; they should come out on top when they compete with groups that remain deeply tribalistic.

Another way in which the right sort of institutions could curb the most divisive ideologies would be to provide incentives for people to "unbundle" the various issues that ideologies clump together. That would lower the stakes: our side could lose on one issue without fearing that we will lose across the board. We would no longer have to regard every minor skirmish as Armageddon.

In evolutionary terms, what we need is an adaptation for competition among groups in society that breaks up the monolithic culture wars into a plurality of independent contests. It's hard to see how we might achieve this sort of unbundling, and more generally do away with the zero-sum, winner-take-all mentality that characterizes deeply divisive ideologies, without abandoning a two-party-only system that forces voters to choose between fundamentally different bundles.

Yet another proposal for moral institutional design warrants discussion—though I'm afraid some people, especially Americans, may be too quick to dismiss it out of hand. Perhaps we should rethink our understanding of freedom of expression and its limits in the light of what we know about evolved human moral psychology, and then consider how the institutionalization of that vital freedom should take this knowledge into account.

I have argued that certain forms of discourse and certain images evoke tribalistic moral responses by mimicking the threat cues of the EEA. This means that not all "hate speech" is equally dangerous: forms that mimic EEA threat cues carry a special risk. In complex modern societies, where intrasocietal tribalism is fueled by deeply divisive ideologies and made all the more potent by information technologies such as the internet, bombarding the evolved moral mind with words and images that evoke the lethal threats our ancestors faced in the EEA can have disastrous consequences.

If we come to know enough about how those sorts of words and images interact with the moral mind to produce behavior that is physically violent or undermines the minimal mutual respect that democracy requires, shouldn't we take steps to prevent this from happening? If certain exercises of freedom of expression are especially dangerous, as a result of the evolved moral mind's potential for tribalism, shouldn't that fact influence how we understand and institutionalize freedom of expression?

There are several different approaches to limiting exercises of freedom of expression that use EEA-like threat cues to stimulate violence or to destroy the mutually respectful disagreement and compromise that democracy requires. Some are more problematic than others. Government censorship might be unacceptable—too subject to abuse and error. Other approaches, such as voluntary agreements among social media platforms to exclude discourse and images that evoke tribalistic responses, might be not only less dangerous but also more effective. The central point is that these strategies would be more targeted and scientifically informed than attempts to limit freedom of expression in the name of something so vague as the grab-bag category of "hate speech."

At present, I'm not willing to take a stand on whether any such effort would be permissible, all things considered, much less to advocate one approach as superior to others. I simply want to stimulate a conversation about the implications for freedom of expression of the analysis of the evolutionary roots of tribalism I've offered in this book. This is a conversation we desperately need to have.

My aim in this book hasn't been to provide a prescription for how to design institutions to combat tribalism. I simply want to stress that *for the same reasons that the right sort of institutions were critical for achieving gains in inclusion, an effective response to tribalism must be institutional, too*. In both cases, it's a matter of using our formidable powers of niche construction wisely; and in a world in which human life is thoroughly shaped by institutions, that means paying close attention to moral institutional design. Simply exhorting people to be more civil or more tolerant of different points of view won't be enough without structural changes in the heavily institutional niche in which we live. If I'm right that intrasocietal tribalism is flourishing because of the perception that democracy is failing, then the most important focus of institutional design should be to improve existing democratic institutions.

Any effort to design institutions—or for that matter any attempt to change anything—carries the risk of unintended bad consequences. For the foreseeable future, the safest way to design institutions for better moral results might be to proceed defensively: to concentrate on structuring them so as to minimize the risk of the worst sorts of regression or at least to curb the more dangerous regressive tendencies that are already at work.

Yet opportunities may arise for responsible design with a more positive goal. The better we understand the general conditions for progressive moral change, the better our prospects become for getting good results through moral institutional design. Some possible moral improvements may be hard to predict, simply because the human genius for constructing new niches seems to know no bounds. Nevertheless, as our knowledge of the human moral mind and its interaction with different environmental factors increases, it may eventually become feasible—and morally mandatory—to undertake more ambitious institutional design, to use what we've learned about recent progress in the direction of inclusion to extend that dimension of progress still further.

I've made the case that humanity can for the first time take charge of its moral fate if we learn enough about the moral mind and how it interacts with specific environmental features to be able to engage in scientifically informed moral institutional design. I want to make clear, however, that I'm not advocating that something so profoundly important as what sort of moralities we have and what sort of moral beings we are should be determined by some elite, scientific or otherwise. To be morally and prudentially acceptable, any attempt to maximize human moral potential through scientifically informed moral institutional design would have to take place within the political processes of a liberal democratic order—if those resources are still intact. Or if democracy has already broken down under the onslaught of tribalism, some other kind of bottom-up, not top-down, process would have to be used. Getting the science right is necessary, but very far from sufficient, for a responsible effort take charge of our moral fate. The citizens of a democratic society ought to show proper deference to scientific expertise when it comes to the facts, but scientific expertise is not an entitlement to social control.

My worst fear, however, is not that scientists will dominate us with knowledge about how the moral mind works; it is that contemporary intrasocietal tribalism is undermining the credibility of genuine science. The ability of the scientific community to produce knowledge of great potential value—whether in the case of climate change or moral institutional design—will be of no avail if a substantial portion of the population is so blinded by ideology that they are unable to distinguish between genuine experts and mere pretenders or if they think that genuine expertise has been disabled by ideological bias (as when Rush Limbaugh proclaims that we can't believe climate experts' predictions about global warming, because they are liberals).

As I close this detective story, I hope you will share my feelings: a sense of hopefulness liberated from the pessimistic thought that we are morally tribalistic by nature, tempered with the sober recognition that the moral progress we have achieved is fragile and may collapse if we don't stop the regression we are now witnessing. On balance, I'm guardedly optimistic. We've gotten beyond tribalism before; perhaps we can learn to escape the new forms it's now taking.

References

Bandura, A. 2016. *Moral Disengagement: How People Do Harm and Live with Themselves*. New York: Worth Publishers.

Baumard, N., J. B. Andre, and D. Sperber. 2013. "A Mutualistic Approach to Morality." *Behavioral and Brain Science* 36 (1): 59–122.

Boehm, C. 2000. *Hierarchy in the Forest: The Evolution of Egalitarian Behavior*. Cambridge, MA: Harvard University Press.

Boehm, C. 2012. *Moral Origins: The Evolution of Virtue, Altruism, and Shame*. New York: Basic Books.

Bowles, S. 2008a. "Conflict: Altruism's Midwife?" *Nature* 456 (7220): 326–327.

Bowles, S. 2008b. "Policies Designed for Self-Interested Citizens May Undermine 'The Moral Sentiments': Evidence from Economic Experiments." *Science* 320 (5883): 1605–1609.

Bowles, S. 2009. "Did Warfare among Ancestral Hunter-Gatherers Affect the Evolution of Human Behaviors?" *Science* 324 (5932): 1293–1298.

Bowles, S., and H. Gintis. 2013. *A Cooperative Species*. Princeton: Princeton University Press.

Brandon, R. 1990. *Environment and Adaptation*. Cambridge, MA: MIT Press.

Buchanan, A. 2007. "Institutions, Beliefs and Ethics: Eugenics as a Case Study." *Journal of Political Philosophy* 15 (1): 22–45.

Buchanan, A. 2011. *Better than Human: The Promise and Perils of Enhancing Ourselves*. Oxford: Oxford University Press.

Buchanan, A., D. Brock, N. Daniels, and D. Wikler. 2001. *From Chance to Choice: Genetics and Justice*. Cambridge: Cambridge University Press.

Buchanan, A., and R. Powell. 2018. *The Evolution of Moral Progress: A Biocultural Theory*. Oxford: Oxford University Press.

Campbell, R., and V. Kumar. 2012. "Moral Reasoning on the Ground." *Ethics* 122 (2): 273–312.

Campbell, R., and J. Woodrow. 2003. "Why Moore's Open Question Is Open: The Evolution of Moral Supervenience." *Journal of Value Inquiry* 37 (3): 353–372.

Choi, J.-K., and S. Bowles. 2007. "The Coevolution of Parochial Altruism and War." *Science* 318 (5850): 636–640.

Curry, O. S., D. A. Mullins, and H. Whitehouse. 2019. "Is It Good to Cooperate? Testing the Theory of Morality-as-Cooperation in 60 Societies." *Current Anthropology* 60 (1): 47–69.

Darwall, S. 2009. *The Second-Person Standpoint: Morality, Respect, Accountability.* Cambridge, MA: Harvard University Press.

Darwin, C. 2003. *The Origin of Species: 150th Anniversary Edition.* New York: Signet. Reprinted from the first edition (London: John Murray, 1859).

Davies, N. 1996. *Europe: A History.* Oxford: Oxford University Press.

Dawkins, R. 1986. *The Blind Watchmaker.* New York: Norton.

Douglass, F. 2005. *Narrative of the Life of Frederick Douglass, an American Slave.* New York: Signet Classics. (Originally published in 1895.)

Dower, J. 1987. *War without Mercy: Race and Power in the Pacific War.* New York: Pantheon Press.

Drescher, S. 1999. *From Slavery to Freedom: Comparative Studies in the Rise and Fall of Atlantic Slavery.* New York: New York University Press.

Drescher, S. 2009. *Abolition: A History of Slavery and Antislavery.* Cambridge: Cambridge University Press.

Drescher, S. 2015. "Liberty, Equality, Humanity: Antislavery and Civil Society in Britain and France." In *The Rise and Demise of the Slave Trade in the Atlantic World,* ed. Philip Misevich and Kristen Mann. Rochester: University of Rochester Press.

Edgerton, R. 1992. *Sick Societies: Challenging the Myth of Primitive Harmony.* New York: Free Press.

Elias, N. 2000. *The Civilizing Process: Sociogenetic and Psychogenetic Investigations.* Oxford: Blackwell.

Forst, R. 2014. *The Right to Justification: Elements of a Constructivist Theory of Justice.* New York: Columbia University Press.

Friedman, L. 1982. *Gregarious Saints: Self and Community in American Abolitionism, 1830–1870.* Cambridge: Cambridge University Press.

Godfrey-Smith, P. 2016. *Other Minds: The Octopus, the Sea, and the Deep Origins of Consciousness.* New York: Farrar, Straus and Giroux.

Goldsmith, J., and E. Posner. 2005. *The Limits of International Law.* New York: Oxford University Press.

Gotowiec, S., and S. van Mastrigt. 2018. "Having versus Doing: The Roles of Moral Identity Internalization and Symbolization for Prosocial Behaviors." *Journal of Social Psychology* 158: 1–17.

Greene, J. 2013. *Moral Tribes: Emotion, Reason, and the Gap between Us and Them.* New York: Penguin Books.

Haidt, J. 2001. "The Emotional Dog and Its Rational Tail: A Social Intuitionist Approach to Moral Judgment." *Psychological Review* 184 (1): 814–834.

Han, H., I. Liauw, and A. Floyd Kuntz. 2018. "Moral Identity Predicts the Development of Presence of Meaning during Emerging Adulthood." *Emerging Adulthood* 6 (6): 1–8.

Hardy, S., and G. Carlo. 2011. "Moral Identity: What Is It, How Does It Develop, and Is It Linked to Moral Action?" *Child Development Perspectives* 5 (3): 212–218.

Haselton, M. G., and D. Nettle. 2006. "The Paranoid Optimist: An Integrative Evolutionary Model of Cognitive Biases." *Personality and Social Psychology* 10 (1): 47–66.

Henrich, J. 2015. *The Secret of Our Success: How Culture Is Driving Human Evolution, Domesticating Our Species, and Making Us Smarter.* Princeton: Princeton University Press.

Hertz, S., and T. Krettenauer. 2016. "Does Moral Identity Effectively Predict Moral Behavior? A Meta-Analysis." *Review of General Psychology* 20 (2): 129–140.

Hobbes, T. 1982. *Leviathan.* New York: Penguin. (Originally published in 1651.)

Joyce, R. 2006. *The Evolution of Morality.* Cambridge, MA: MIT Press.

Keeley, L. 1996. *War before Civilization.* Oxford: Oxford University Press.

Kinder, D., and N. Kalmoe. 2017. *Neither Liberal nor Conservative: The Ideological Innocence of the American Public.* Chicago: University of Chicago Press.

Kitcher, P. 2011. *The Ethical Project.* Cambridge, MA: Harvard University Press.

Koonz, C. 2003. *The Nazi Conscience.* Cambridge, MA: Belknap Press.

Lambert, P. 1997. "Patterns of Violence in Prehistoric Hunter-Gather Societies of Coastal California." In *Troubled Times: Violence and Warfare in the Past*, ed. D. Martin and D. Frayer. Amsterdam: Gordon and Breach.

Lapsley, D. 2015. "Moral Identity and Developmental Theory: Commentary on Krettenauer and Hertz." *Human Development* 58 (3): 164–171.

Lenin, V. I. 2013. *What Is to Be Done?* Mansfield, CT: Martino.

Lewontin, R. 1978. "Adaptation." *Scientific American* 239 (3): 213–229.

MacIntyre, A. 1981. *After Virtue.* Notre Dame, IN: University of Notre Dame Press.

Marietta, M., and D. Barker. 2019. *One Nation, Two Realities: Dueling Facts in American Democracy.* New York: Oxford University Press.

McCloskey, D. N. 2006. *The Bourgeois Virtues: Ethics for an Age of Commerce.* Chicago: University of Chicago Press.

Mercier, H., and D. Sperber. 2017. *The Enigma of Reason.* Cambridge, MA: Harvard University Press.

Nisbett, R. E., and D. Cohen. 1996. *Culture of Honor: The Psychology of Violence in the South.* Boulder, CO: Westview Press.

Pinker, S. 2012. *The Better Angels of Our Nature: Why Violence Has Declined.* New York: Penguin.

Pinker, S. 2018. *Enlightenment Now: The Case for Reason, Science, Humanism, and Progress.* New York: Viking.

Railton, P. 1986. "Moral Realism." *Philosophical Review* 95 (2): 163–207.

Richerson, P., and R. Boyd. 2005. *Not by Genes Alone: How Culture Transformed Human Evolution.* Chicago: University of Chicago Press.

Rosen, M. 1996. *On Voluntary Servitude: False Consciousness and the Theory of Ideology.* Cambridge: Routledge.

Sets, J. 2010. "The Social Psychology of Moral Identity." In *Handbook of the Sociology of Morality,* ed. S. Hitlin and S. Vaisey. New York: Springer.

Sikkink, C. 2012. *The Justice Cascade.* New York: W. W. Norton.

Simmons, B. 2009. *Mobilizing for Human Rights.* New York: Cambridge University Press.

Singer, P. 2011. *The Expanding Circle: Ethics, Evolution, and Moral Progress.* Princeton: Princeton University Press.

Sober, E., and D. S. Wilson. 1999. *Unto Others: The Evolution and Psychology of Unselfish Behavior.* Cambridge, MA: Harvard University Press.

Sorel, G. 2004. *Reflections on Violence.* Ed. J. Jennings. Cambridge: Cambridge University Press.

Sperber, D. 1996. *Explaining Culture: A Naturalistic Approach.* Oxford: Blackwell.

Stanford, K. 2019. "The Difference between Ice Cream and Nazis: Moral Externalization and the Evolution of Human Cooperation." *Behavioral and Brain Sciences* 41:1–49.

Sterelny, K. 2012. *The Evolved Apprentice: How Evolution Made Humans Unique.* Cambridge, MA: MIT Press.

Street, S. 2006. "A Darwinian Dilemma for Realist Theories of Value." *Philosophical Studies* 127 (1): 109–166.

Tomasello, M. 2016. *A Natural History of Human Morality.* Cambridge, MA: Harvard University Press.

Tooby, J., and L. Cosmides. 2010. "Groups in Mind: Coalitional Psychology and the Roots of War and Morality." In *Human Morality and Sociability: Evolutionary and Comparative Perspectives*, ed. H. Høgh-Olesen. New York: Palgrave Macmillan.

Turchin, P. 2015. *Ultrasociety: How 10,000 Years of War Made Humans the Greatest Cooperators on Earth*. Chaplin, CT: Beresta Books.

Walzer, M. 1977. *Just and Unjust Wars: A Moral Argument with Historical Illustrations*. New York: Basic Books.

Weber, E. 1976. *Peasants into Frenchmen: The Modernization of Rural France, 1870–1914*. Stanford: Stanford University Press.

Wimmer, A. 2002. *Nationalist Exclusion and Ethnic Conflict: Shadow of Modernity*. Cambridge: Cambridge University Press.

Index